GUIDE TO SELECTIONS FROM THE

# MONTGOMERY COUNTY SENTINEL

Maryland

January 1, 1913
–
December 31, 1916

*John D. Bowman*

HERITAGE BOOKS
2012

# HERITAGE BOOKS
*AN IMPRINT OF HERITAGE BOOKS, INC.*

### Books, CDs, and more—Worldwide

For our listing of thousands of titles see our website at
www.HeritageBooks.com

Published 2012 by
HERITAGE BOOKS, INC.
Publishing Division
100 Railroad Ave. #104
Westminster, Maryland 21157

Copyright © 2012 John D. Bowman

Other Heritage Books by the author:
*Guide to Selections from the* Montgomery County Sentinel, *Maryland:*
January 1, 1856–December 31, 1875
January 1, 1876–December 31, 1881
January 1, 1882–December 31, 1887
January 1, 1888–December 30, 1892
January 1, 1893–December 31, 1896
January 1, 1897–December 31, 1901
January 1, 1902–December 31, 1904
January 1, 1905–December 31, 1908
January 1, 1909–December 27, 1912
January 1, 1913–December 31, 1916

All rights reserved. No part of this book may be reproduced or transmitted in any form or by any means, electronic or mechanical, including photocopying, recording or by any information storage and retrieval system without written permission from the author, except for the inclusion of brief quotations in a review.

International Standard Book Numbers
Paperbound: 978-0-7884-5387-8
Clothbound: 978-0-7884-3446-4

# FOREWORD

The *Montgomery County Sentinel* was first published as a weekly newspaper on Aug. 11, 1855, by Matthew Fields. It has thereafter been continuously published on a weekly basis until the present.

There were brief interruptions while Mr. Fields [a Southern sympathizer] was twice held by Union military forces before and during the Civil War. Following the war, publication was continued by Mr. Fields or his family until 1932, when, following the death of Mr. Fields' widow in 1930, the paper was sold outside of the Fields family.

The early focus of the Sentinel was on advertising and politics. Relatively little space was devoted to the reporting of local news; and such news reports were usually brief and to the point without elaboration. Editorial comment could be – and frequently was – to the point and without euphemism.

This compilation of selected Montgomery County Sentinel extracts is taken from available microfilm records. Many weekly issues are missing – some existing copies are torn or otherwise partly mutilated or illegible; - two thirds of the issues for the years 1860 through 1865 are missing – there are no issues for the entire years of 1867, 1869, 1870 - only one issue in the year 1868, and three in 1871.

Microfilm reels of the Montgomery County Sentinel are held at Enoch Pratt Free Library, Baltimore; Montgomery County Historical Society, Rockville; Montgomery County Public Library, Rockville; and Maryland Hall of Records, Annapolis.

References to events which happened 'at this place' are to be understood as happening in Rockville; 'ult' or 'ultimo' refers to the month prior to the month of publication; 'inst' refers to the month of the publication. A name mentioned only once in the index may appear more than once on the page referred to.

Compiled by:
John D. Bowman
April 2011

Jan. 3, 1913:
Mr. Leonidas Ricketts and Mrs. Ella F. Monday were married on Wednesday of last week, in Rockville.

Miss Margaret Inez Thomas, daughter of Mr. & Mrs. Ashley Thomas of McLean, Va., and Mr. Edward Lewis Burdette of Clarksburg, were married last Saturday in Rockville.

Mrs. Anna Jane Cornelison, daughter of the late James W. Graff, died last Sunday.

Miss Rosa B. Embrey and Mr. Frank Counselman were married last week, in Bethesda.

The Rockville Lodge of Masons has elected officers for the coming year as follows: Worshipful master, Walter A. Williams; Senior warden, W. Russell Brewer; Junior warden, George W. Henderson; secretary, Jas. F. Allen; treasurer, Richard H. Stokes.

Mr. & Mrs. J. W. Gardner announce the marriage on December 27th, of their daughter, Essie Lillian, to Mr. Edgar R. Stephens.

Mr. Herman C. Briggs, of Gaithersburg, and Miss Lottye Belle Ward, of Washington, were married on Saturday the 28th, in Washington.

Eugene A. Poole, of Poolesville, and a resident of Rockville for a number of years, a prominent artist, died last Friday, in Pittsburg.

A number of men have organized to bring a Chautauqua to Rockville. Those mentioned are Messrs. W. W. Welsh, Dr. O. M. Linthicum, Judge E. C. Peter, Col. Spencer C. Jones, H. Stokes, W. Hicks, Harry G. Poss, Wallace E. Ricketts, Hatton S. Waters, Dr. C. H. Mannar, Thomas Vinson, W. R. Pumphrey, John F. Collins, John H. Heagy., J. F. Kelchner, Robert G. Hilton, Roland Wootton, Frank Higgins, Berry E. Clark, C. J. Maddox, Robert B. Peter, Henry Viett, W. B. Burdette, R. W. Vinson, G. Minor Anderson, Stephen H. Quigley, Major John McDonald, Dr. R. C. Warfield, Henry C. Allnutt, C. L. Howard, Dr. F. N. Henderson, and G. H. Lamar.

The first annual banquet of the alumni of the Montgomery County High School at Rockville was held last Monday. Names mentioned are Supt. E. B. Jones, George H. Lamar, Charles L. Warfield, Mary Brewer, Clifton Norris, H. S. Beall, C. G. Warfield,
Cont'd. on next page.

Jan 3, 1913, cont'd:
G. P. Warfield, M. S. Ward, Mrs. C. W. Beck, Mrs. O. M. Linthicum, Mrs. Geo. H. Lamar, Mrs. R. E. L. Smith, Mrs. W. S. Ward, Mrs. R. C. Warfield, Mrs. Howard Larcombe, Gaither Warfield, Paul Anderson, Vivian Robey, Alice Spates, Olive Gilliss, Maude England, Amy Robertson, Robert L. Warfield, Margaret Higgins, William C. Beck, Jr., Louise Larcombe In addition, guests as follows were present: Esther Tyner, Elizabeth Rhodes, Margaret Higgins, Rebecca Lamar, Helen Brunett, Mary Davis, Edith Prettyman, Ruby Robertson, Lucille Gardiner, Virginia Brewer, Katherine Hughes, Lucy Brewer, Miss Heenan, Amy Pumphrey, Mary Brewer, Estelle E. Ricketts, Lena Ricketts, Nannie England, Elsie England, Lillian England, Lillian Morgan, Lee Athey, Lucy Garrett, Helen Pumphrey, Lucile Welsh, Mr. & Mrs. George H. Lamar, Mr. & Mrs. Howard Larcombe, Mr. & Mrs. Wilson S. Ward, Dr. & Mrs. R. C. Warfield, Mrs. Wm. C. Beck, Mrs. O. M. Linthicum, Messrs. C. G. Myers, R. Leroy Warfield, Wm. C. Beck, Jr., Frank Higgins, Byron White, Elgar Smith, Edward Green, C. G. Warfield, Harry Beall, Earle Anderson, Edwin Broome, Adrian Brunett, Lucius Lamar, Jesse Higgins, Roger Whiteford, S. M. Hamilton, Clifton Norris, Madison Cutts, George Brewer, Theodore Ricketts, Brownell Riggs, J. G. England, and Wm. F. Prettyman.

Jan. 10, 1913:
Dr. James S. Carlin, a native of Montgomery County, died last Saturday at his home near Boyds.
The members of the Agriculturat Society of Montgomery County met last Wednesday in Rockville. The following named were elected directors to serve during the coming year: Josiah W. Jones, Lee Offutt, Charles F. Kirk, John C. Bentley, John E. Muncaster, William Dorsey, Z. M. Waters, Jr., Charles Veirs, Chas. E. Allnutt, Joseph H. Bradley, H. H. Griffith, and F. Hazel Cashell. Others mentioned are Charles F. Kirk, John C. Bentley, Charles E. Allnutt, Wm. Dorsey, Charles F. Brooke, Frank M. Hallowell, and Washington B. Chichester.
The County Commissioners have appointed W. Irving Rabbitt and Frank A. Weiner to be constables for the Rockville and Bethesda districts respectively.

Jan. 17, 1913:

Miss Clara E. Demuth, daughter of Mr. R. J. Demuth of Norbeck, died last Friday.

Miss Daisy Lowe and Mr. Jesse Thompson were married last week in Rockville.

Miss Ruth B. Dowden and Mr. Cleveland Schwartz were married on Wednesday of last week.

Mrs. Alice Gott, a life-long resident of Montgomery County, widow of the late Dr. Richard T. Gott, died last Friday. She was the daughter of the late Dr. Thomas Poole.

At the annual stockholder's meeting of the Montgomery County National Bank, the following were elected directors: Spencer C. Jones, Jas. B. Henderson, Wm. B. Mobley, Jas. E. Williams, Lawrence Allnutt, Wilson B. Tschiffely, Jos. T. Moore, Richard H. Stokes, Frederick P. Hays, Wm. T. Griffith, Perrie E. Waters, and Lee Offutt. Spencer C. Jones was named President, Jas. B. Henderson, vice President, Richard H. Stokes, cashier, and Geo. M. Henderson, assistant cashier.

Miss Alice Douglass Wallach and Mr. Wm. B. McGregor were married last Saturday.

Bernard Monday, a native of Germany and a resident of Rockville for many years, died last Tuesday.

Jan. 24, 1913:

The large flour and grist mill belonging to Jos. H. Mullinix burned completely recently.

The County Commissioners have appointed Edward V. Caywood constable for the Bethesda district, replacing Walter Shaw, resigned. Also, they have appointed Maurice T. Cissel and William T. Hobbs constables for the Olney and Colesville districts respectively.

The County Commissioners have appointed the following dog tax collectors: Perry Ensey, Laytonsville district; Randolph Luhn, Poolesville district; W. Irving Rabbitt, Rockville district; Ira Hall, Darnestown; H. H. Dailey, Olney; Thomas Small, Gaithersburg; Richard Gray, Barnesville; John O. King, Damascus.

Mrs. Dorothy Wykoff Kinney and her sister Mrs. Marie Kinney Martin died Jan. 18$^{th}$, at their home, 'Sunny Slope Farm', Clopper.

Cont'd. on next page.

Jan 24, 1913, cont'd:

Mrs. Bertie Parsley and Mr. Richard T. Ward were married Wednesday of last week by Rev. Willis Mosedale; and at the same time and place, Miss Elsie May Nicholson and Mr. James Roger Parsley were also married.

At the annual meeting of the stockholders of the First National Bank of Gaithersburg, the following directors were elected: John B. Diamond, James Anderson, H. Maurice Talbott, Nathan Cooke, John W. Walker, Albert F. Meem, Samuel R. Plummer, Elisha C. Etchison, Zadoc M. Cooke, James S. Windsor, Clarence H. Hoskinson, Joshua T. Higgins, and Ignatius T. Fulks. John B. Diamond was elected President, James Anderson vice president, Robert B. Moore, cashier, and Frank B. Severance, teller.

Mr. Brice W. Howard, of Brookeville, died last Friday at his home.

Annie A. Burriss, who died December 13, 1912, was remembered.

Jan 31, 1913:

The body of John Paul Jones, first Admiral of the U. S. Navy, was laid to rest last Sunday in the new crypt under the Naval Academy chapel.

Miss Mary Easton has been appointed assistant teacher at Poolesville.

James Wyckoff Kinney died Jan. 24$^{th}$, at his home in Clopper.

Oliver H. P. Clark and Miss Irma Boykin were married - no date stated.

Dr. Eugene Jones, and Messrs. Gist Blair, Arthur Peter, John L. Weaver have been appointed members of the reception committee for the inauguration of President-elect Woodrow Wilson.

The early records of the County Commissioners office, beginning in 1793, have been bound into 20 volumes and are now in the Commissioners office.

Mrs. Sarah L. Beckwith, wife of John Beckwith, died Tuesday.

Mr. Edward K. Watkins, a life-long resident of this County, died on the 21$^{st}$.

Mrs. Hannah S. Muncaster, wife of Wm. E. Muncaster, died last Thursday.

Cont'd. on next page.

Jan. 31, 1913, cont'd:

Mr. Frank L. Bell, who died on Thursday of last week, was buried last Saturday.

George H. Barnesly committed suicide last Friday. He was unmarried.

Mr. J. Dawson Williams announced his candidacy for the Democratic nomination for the State Senate seat now held by Blair Lee.

The Travilah Gun Club met Saturday. The names mentioned are Owen Grimes, Clyde Harriss, H. W. Fawcett, Aubrey McCrossin, and Geo. R. Rice, Jr.

Mrs. Sarah L. Beckwith, wife of Jos. Beckwith, died Tuesday.

Mr. Edward K. Watkins, a life-long resident of this County, died on the 21$^{st}$. [two items]

Feb. 7, 1913.

Mrs. Eleanor J. Watkins, widow of Oliver Watkins, died Wednesday.

Miss Ella J. Milstead and Mr. Willard S. Hearn were married – no date - at the home of the father of the bride.

George Peter has been elected cashier of the Farmer's Banking & Trust Company, Kensington branch, replacing W. J. Kelley, resigned.

Dr. Eugene Jones has resigned as chairman and member of the executive committee of the Kensington Bank. J. Phillip Herrmann has been chosen as his replacement on the committee. Alfred C. Warthen is the new chairman.

Elden B. Hartshorne, of Kensington, has been appointed instructor in chemistry at Dartmouth College. He has resigned as a clerk at the U. S. Pension office

Walter L. Collier, formerly of Seneca, and Miss Lula C. Ballenger were married Jan. 22$^{nd.}$, in Charlestown, W. Va.

Walter H. Belt, well known in the Laytonsville area, shot and killed Jesse J. Evely on Thursday afternoon, following an argument between the two men at the home of Stephen B. Dorsey, near Unity. The matter was not reported to the authorities until late Thursday night. Sheriff Howard has brought Belt to the jail.

Feb. 14, 1913:

Mrs. Elizabeth Myers, wife of George W. Myers, died on Wednesday of last week.

The stockholders of the Washington & Rockville Electric Railway Co. met and elected the following directors for 1 year: Milton E. Ailes, Woodbury Blair, Clarence P. King, Clarence F. Norment, W. F. Ham, Wm. B. Hibbs, L. W. Glazebrook, Geo. Truesdell, and Charles J. Bell.

James Daymude, son of Wm. Daymude, died last Saturday.

Benjamin Rush White, aged 84 years, died Monday at his home near Glen Echo.

Mrs. Maria Tallard Brewer died suddenly on Wednesday of last week. She was formerly a Miss Hays, of Montgomery County.

James W. Bean died last Friday at his home at Derwood.

Mrs. Emma J. Day, wife of James E. Day, died last Sunday.

The barn and stable on the farm of William H. Fawcett, at Travilah, burned last Saturday.

Mrs. Georgia Fell, wife of Randolph M. Fell, died last Sunday. She was the daughter of the late Richard T. Ray.

Mrs. Emma E. Biggs, wife of A. Edgar Biggs, died last Friday, at her home in Germantown.

Harrison Lackland England, son of John G. England, and Miss Dorothy Putman Smith, daughter of Mr. Willard P. Smith of New York city, were married on last Friday in Washington.

At a meeting of the Montgomery County Pomona Grange, in Olney, on Jan. 30$^{th}$, the following officers were elected for the coming year: Master, R. Bentley Thomas; Overseer, Alexander Gude; Lecturer, Mrs. Elizabeth H. Patterson; Steward, Howard Marlow; Assistant Steward, Calvin Bready; Chaplain, Samuel T. Harding; Treasurer, S. W. Beall; Secretary, Mrs. E. L. Hartshorne; Gate Keeper, Earl M. Stewart; Ceres, Mrs. Ethel F. Thomas; Pomona, Miss Pearl Marlowe; Flora, Mrs. Eleanor Neitzey; L. A. S., Miss Mary E. Thomas

. The School Commissioners held their regular monthly meeting on Tuesday the 11$^{th}$, and accepted the resignation of Miss M. A. E. Phillips as principal of the Burtonsville school, and appointed Mr. Marion F. Manion to fill the vacancy. Miss Mary F. Tracey was appointed principal of the school at Cropley, to succeed Miss Charlotte Saunders, resigned. George Gloyd was appointed teacher of

Cont'd. on next page.

Feb. 14, 1913, cont'd:
manual training at the Gaithersburg high school, and Edgar Thompson in the grammar schools at Kensington and Chevy Chase.

Feb. 21, 1913:
Information has been received that Mrs. Geo. C. Dawson has died suddenly at her home in S. Dakota. Burial will be in the Rockville cemetery. See also item in issue of March $7^{th}$.

Mr. John Jacob Baker and Mrs. Annie M. Rollison, both of Germantown, were married in Rockville on last Saturday.

It has been announced that Miss Lula Beall Gott and Mr. Oliver Belt White will be married on Feb. 26, in Christ Episcopal Church, Barnesville.

Mrs. Evelyn Wailes Glascott, daughter of H. Maurice Talbott, and J. Darby Bowman were married in Washington last Saturday.

Mrs. Mary G. Shorts, widow of Thomas Shorts, died on Thursday of last week.

Mr. Lysander Etchison died suddenly several days ago, in Baltimore. He was a native of this County, but had been living in Baltimore. See also March $7^{th}$.

John C. Power, a resident of Derwood for many years, died last Friday.

Miss Mary L. Hege, daughter of Mr. S. B. Hege, died on Thursday of last week.

There will be a memorial service on Thursday, in Christ Church, Rockville, for the late rector of the parish, Dr. Thomas J. Packard. Mrs. G. Minor Anderson, Mrs. P. R. Stansbury, and Mrs. W. C. Beck are in charge of the arrangements.

Brice Worthington Howard died January 20, 1913.

Feb. 28, 1913:
Robert L. Warfield has resigned as principal of the commercial department of the Rockville High School.

Mr. Nathan W. Saunders and Mrs. Sarah Andrews were married on Wednesday of last week, in Rockville.

Miss Willie Mills and Mr. Walter Connelly were married on Wednesday of last week, in Rockville.

Mr. & Mrs. C. F. Willard announce the engagement of their daughter, Martha Lauretta, to Mr. Thomas Opie Green.

Cont'd. on next page.

Feb 28, 1913, cont'd:

The large straw-baling and machinery establishment of Charles Johnson, at Germantown, burned to the ground last Tuesday morning, with considerable loss.

Miss Bertha Lawson and Mr. A. Somers Darby were married on Wednesday of last week.

Jurors as follows have been drawn to serve in the coming March term of the Circuit Court:   Wm. H. Wachter, Wm. A. Bogley, Jr., Edgar Gartrell, Ewell R. Plummer, John Gardner, Charles B. Murphy, Edward R. Allnutt, Samuel R. Jarboe, Thornton B. Titus, J. Furr White, Washington Hicks, John H. O'Neale, Robert H. Hoskinson, Frank Wilson, George W. Mullican, Ulysses M. Ricketts, Henry C. Chaney, Newton Stabler, Thomas E. Shaw, Douglas M. Blandford, Wm. L. Schaeffer, John T. Higdon, Reverdy B. Beall, Richard C. Drum-Hunt, Benjamin Perry, Robert L. Garrett, James L. Townsend, J. Hillis Robertson, Maurice J. Stabler, James E. Howes, Jas. E. Rabbitt, Maurice Phoebus, Albert T. Rabbitt, James M. Elder, Wm. H. Embrey, James M. Harrison, James L. Magruder, Frederick P. Hays, George H. Johnson, James O. Cubitt, Franklin E. Burdette, Nathan E. Sheckells, W. J. Purdum, Victor E. Brunett, Edward P. Rabbitt, Arthur W. Stonestreet, Nicholas M. Howes, Enos C. Keys.

Mr. Henry H. Helmsen, age 94, died on Thursday at the home of his daughter, Mrs. A. C. Robertson, near Bethesda. He was a native of Germany, and had lived in this county for many years.

Mr. S. Thomas Brown, a native of Clarksburg but a resident of Washington, D. C. for many years, died last Saturday.

March 7, 1913:

Miss Mary Gertrude Plummer and Mr. George Hill, both of Woodmont, were married on Thursday of last week, in Rockville.

The barn on the farm of Zadoc Magruder burned on Monday. Horses, and some hay etc. belonging to Samuel Leizear, were lost.

Joseph W. Cashell, son of County Commissioner Hazel W. Cashell, died last Friday.

Mrs. Laura Ellison Ellis and Mr. Gist Blair were married last Monday, in New York.

Mrs. Margaret E. Barnes, wife of J. William Barnes, died last Friday at the home of her son-in-law, Mr. Albert L. Hall, in Rockville. She was a Miss Coupard before her marriage

Cont'd. on next page.

March 7, 1913 cont'd:

Miss Lula Beall Gott and Mr. Oliver Belt White were married on Wednesday of last week.

John G. England, of Rockville, died suddenly last Friday, in Washington following a visit there with his son, J. Arthur England. In a separate item, the classmates of his daughter Maude expressed their condolences.

March 14, 1913:

Rev. Forrest J. Prettyman has been chosen Chaplain of the U. S. Senate.

The dwelling house and barn of the farm of George Edwards, near Fairland, burned last Friday.

Mr. Bowie F. Waters, former State's Attorney for Montgomery County, has been appointed to assist in the prosecution of the case against Walter A. Belt, charged with the murder of Jesse J. Evely.

The following, recently drawn as jurors, have been excused: James E. Rabbitt, James O. Cubitt, Victor E. Brunett, Enos C. Keys. Their places will be taken by Geo. F. Leapley, Herbert L. Diamond, Richard H. Offutt, Elmer E. Hoyle, Jas. E. Schrider, and Dorsey W. Nicholson.

Frederick Johnson, colored, is in critical condition after having been shot last Saturday. Alphonso Jackson has been arrested and jailed for the shooting.

The barn on the farm of Howard Griffith was destroyed by fire Monday morning. Six horses were killed.

Miss Virginia Bready, of the Rockville area, and Mr. Warren Stankey, of Des Moines, were married last week in Indianapolis.

State Senator Blair Lee has asked President Wilson to appoint George H. Lamar to the position of Assistant Attorney General of the U. S. The request is under advisement.

Miss Nellie Irene Boyer and Mr. Henry T. Zimmerman of Frederick, were married last Friday.

Mr. Merritt O. Chance has been chosen to be chief clerk of the Postoffice Department.

Tax assessors as follows have been appointed by the County Commissioners:

Laytonsville district: Aden D. Allnutt.

Cont'd. on next page.

March 14, 1913, cont'd:
>Clarksburg, Dorsey Warfield.
>Poolesville, Walter W. Pyles.
>Rockville, Alfred Ray.
>Darnestown, Newton C. Rice.
>Bethesda, Jos. F. Whalen.
>Olney, Leonard Weer.
>Gaithersburg, Jas. Clagett.
>Potomac, Willard C. Fisher
>Barnesville, Wm. Lynch.
>Damascus, Noah Watkins.

Ben G. Davis, town clerk of Takoma Park, has been promoted to the position of confidential secretary to Secretary of State Bryan.

The house on the Samuel D. Waters property, Silver Spring, burned completely on last Monday night. Thirteen people were evacuated safely. The house was being used by John C. Cissel as a rooming house.

The following deaths were reported:
>Virginia Eaden, infant daughter of Mr. & Mrs. Robert Eaden, died on Thursday of last week.
>
>Miss Ida C. Atwood, daughter of the late Wm. Atwood, died last Monday.
>
>Mrs. Susannah Trail Ricketts died last Saturday. She was the wife of Wm. W. Ricketts, of near Montrose.
>
>Mrs. L. V. Warner died March 8th.
>
>Mrs. Emily M. C. Beall, wife of John W. Beall, died last Sunday.
>
>Mr. Henry H. Miller, of Sandy Spring, died last Saturday.

Mr. James Elder was struck and killed by the east-bound express train, at Derwood, on March 7th. The train was nearly 3 hours late, and Mr. Elder's view was obstructed by some cars standing on a siding. The automatic gate at the crossing was out of order, and the man who had formerly stood guard there had been removed the day before the accident. Mr. Elder had recently been drawn for jury service in the Circuit Court. See also resolution of condolences in issue of May 2nd. 1913, and remembrance in May 9th.

Mrs. Mary G. Willsey, formerly Miss Mary G. Braddock, of Rockville, died February 23, 1913, in Napa, California. She was the daughter of George R. Braddock.

March 21, 1913: &&&

Charles Mills, of Travillah, will furnish the lumber with which the stables at the Fair Grounds will be rebuilt.

Mr. Wm. L. Birgfeld has been appointed official stenographer to the committee which will visit Europe this summer to study farming problems. Jas. B. Morman is the delegate from Maryland.

Dr. Bruce Thomas, formerly of Rockville, died last Friday.

Mrs. Margaret A. Collins, daughter of the late Albert King, of Rockville, was struck and killed by an automobile last Monday.

The death of the following was reported:

Mrs. William M. Mathis, died on Thursday of last week at the home of her son-in-law William Hill, in Washington Grove.

Mrs. Alice Virginia Graham, widow of John E. Graham died last Monday at the home of her daughter, Mrs. G. Wm. Riggs, Rockville.

Mrs. Martha Johnson Hobbs died at her home near Colesville – no date.

Dr. Robert H. Campbell, formerly of Rockville, died last Monday at his home in New Orleans.

Mach 28, 1913:

Rev. Chas. H. Lafferty, of Rockville, has accepted a call to the Episcopal churches of Poolesville and Barnesville, and will move to that parish on April 1$^{st}$.

Miss Cora Burdette and Mr. George W. Howard were married on Monday.

Mr. Simon D. Best died last Friday at the home of his daughter, Mrs. Samuel Haines.

Miss Margaret B. Law and Mr. Newton R. Cass were married on Monday.

The County Commissioners have appointed George T. Windham and Frank D. Stubbs tax collectors for the Colesville and Wheaton districts respectvely; and have appointed William Magruder assessor for the Laytonsville district in the place of Aden D. Allnutt, declined. Aubrey D. Allnutt and Walter T. Magruder have been appointed constables for the Potomac and Wheaton districts respectively.

A jury in the Circuit Court, Rockville, has awarded $950 in

Cont'd. on next page.

March 28, 1913, cont'd:
damages to Miss Agnes Gallagher, of Washington, against William H. Bobinger, proprietor of Cabin John Hotel, for injuries suffered on Labor Day, 1910.

Dollie E. Rabbitt, who died March 26, 1912, was remembered. Also see item in April 4th. 1913.

April 4, 1913:
    John Pierpont Morgan died on last Monday, in Rome. The article examines his career.
    Mrs. Gertrude W. Stonestreet and Dr. Thomas Reed Gough, both of Barnesville, were married March 25th, in Washington.
    Fire of unknown origin destroyed the store at Barnesville owned by Oscar K. Poole and occupied by Linwood Hays.
    Mrs. Fannie B. Curtis, wife of George V. Curtis, died on Wednesday of last week.
    The lodge of Independent Order of Good Templars, at Damascus, has installed officers as follows: Chief Templar, Mrs. Emory E. Mullinix; vice Templar, Mrs. Vernon Watkins; Secretary, Miss Mabel Carr; assistant secretary, Mehrle Warfield; financial secretary, Thurman Warfield; Treasurer, Jas. Hilton; Chaplain, Emory R. Mullinix; Marshall, Bradley Day; past chief templar, C. J. Warfield; deputy marshall, Edwina Mullinix; Guard, Robert Etchison; Sentinel, Russell Moore; Lodge Deputy, Vernon D. Watkins; Organist, Miss Maude Mullinix.
    Mrs. Ellen Umstead died last Saturday at the home of her daughter and son-in-law, Mr. & Mrs. James T. Bean, near Bethesda.
    Mr. George H. Lamar addressed the Waverly Literary Society at the Gaithersburg High School on March 25. Others mentioned are Laura Frizzell, Guy Neel, Donald Snyder, Grace Buxton, Marjorie Waters, Harry McCabe, and Miss Henderson.
    Rev. Paris B. Stauffer, former rector of Christ Episcopal Church, Kensington, has accepted a call to Shrewsbury parish, Kent County, and will move there shortly.

April 11, 1913:
    Mr. George W. B. Bartlett has returned to his home near Gaithersburg, after spending the winter in Florida.
    Mr. Z. McC. Waters has been appointed tax assessor for the
                                                  Cont'd. on next page.

April 11, 1913, cont'd:
Laytonsville district.

The speed limit for automobiles in Rockville has been increased to 10 miles per hour.

Wm. A. Pumphrey, son of Mr. & Mrs. W. Reuben Pumphrey, of Rockville, died Monday, of cancer. See also issue of May $2^{nd}$.

Dr. Robert H. Campbell, who died recently in New Orleans, was buried in Rockville cemetery on last Monday.

Mrs. Mary J. Brunett, widow of Louis L. Brunett, died on Wednesday of last week. She is the mother of John L. Brunett, Clerk of the Circuit Court.

Rev. Frank B. Cowell, pastor of the Baptist churches at Germantown, Travilah, Barnesville, and Cedar Grove, has accepted a call to serve in Rhode Island. He will leave here June $1^{st}$.

An entertainment was presented on Friday for the benefit of the library of the Dawsonville school. The names mentioned are Margaret Waters, Bertha Stang, Emily Allnutt, Rebekah Nourse, Peter Stang, Ann Decker, Natalie Allnutt, Russell Allnutt, Ellen Allnutt, Margaret Darby, Elizabeth Darby, Valeria Darby, Mariel Gott, Alice Allnutt, Josephine Stang, and Louise Gott.

W. Frank Ricketts and W. V. Magruder have been appointed road commissioners for the Rockville and Bethesda districts respectively, by George G. Bradley, Jr., Commissioner.

Clarence Daymude, who died February $8^{th}$, 1913, was remembered.

Louisa Page, who died April $12^{th}$, 1913, was remembered.

April 18, 1913:

Mr. Eli Tucker and Mrs. Mary Lucretia Tucker, both of the vicinity of Ednor, were married last Saturday.

Miss Margaret K. Windham, of Montgomery County, and Mr. Luther Boblets, of N. Carolina, were married – no date stated.

The construction of an ice plant at Rockville has begun. Names mentioned are Milton Dorcas and Clarence Anders.

Walter Smallwood, who pitched last season for the Brookeville High School baseball team, has been signed by the Richmond team of the Virginia League.

Miss Mary Olive Simpson, of Kensington, and Archibald M. Jamieson were married on Monday.

Cont'd. on next page.

April 18, 1913, cont'd:

Mr. T. Paret Hicks, son of Mr. & Mrs. Washington Hicks, of Rockville, and Miss Gladys Alice Crowl of Baltimore, were married of Thursday of last week.

The Confederate Monument committee met last Friday to arrange for the unveiling of the monument which is to be erected in Rockville next June. The names mentioned are Col. Spencer C. Jones, Judge Edward C. Peter, Mayor Lee Offutt, Rev. E. C. Rich, Anna Hoyle, Mr. John W. Holland, Hunton Sellman, F. A. Tschiffely, and George R. Rice.

Prof. Willis L. Moore has been dismissed by President Wilson as chief of the weather bureau.

April 25, 1913:

W. E. Atwood has been appointed postmaster at Spencerville, replacing Wm. H. Phair, resigned.

Miss Margaret Valentin, of Rockville, and Mr. Harry Simons, of Manitoba, Canada, were married last Friday, in Rockville.

Mr. John William Brown, a well known farmer, died on Thursday of last week at his home near Barnesville.

A meeting of the teachers of the primary grades of the County's public schools was held last Saturday, with about 25 in attendance. Names mentioned are Edwin W. Broome, and Misses Mary M. Brewer, Maude V. Broome, Marie Boardman, Ella V. Kreig, Frances L. V. Horner, and Helen Schwartz.

The Rockville Musical Club presented 'Pinafore' on Thursday evening of last week. Names mentioned are Mrs. Berry E. Clark, director, and cast members Murray Hamilton, Berry E. Clark, Jos. Whitemore, Paul Lehman, Bache Abert, John Dawson, Mrs. Somervell Dawson, Lillian Morgan, Priscilla Dawson, Lillian Keochling, and Mary Almoney.

The Social Service League thanked the following for their financial support received during the past year: W. A. Brooke, A. G. Thomas, Oscar L. Johnson, Sarah Farquhar, Eugene A. Stevens. Rose Henderson, John Joy Edson, Missionary Society of the Presbyterian Church of Rockville, Womans Guild of Grace Church at Silver Spring, Mrs. Elmer Wright, Mrs. Sarah T. Miller, Judge E. C. Peter, Albert Almoney, R. B. Farquhar, Eulalie Bouic, Edward Horner, Mrs. G. H. McGrew, M. T. Russell, Wm. B. Jackson, Elizabeth

Cont'd. on next page.

April 25, 1913, cont'd:
T. Noyes, Gist Blair, C. M. Grubb, Mrs. W. C. Beck, Mrs. Emily Massey, L. T. Brooke, R. E. L. Smith, Jos. T. Moore, Mrs. W. W. Bishop, Rockville Cemetery Association, Mrs. Violet Blair Janin, Mrs. Katherine Sargeant Olds.

The Waverly Literary Society of Gaithersburg School met on Friday the 16$^{th}$, with the following names mentioned: Marguerite Welti, H. Holland, Blanche Golden, Ravenwell Monrad, Iva Fulks, Laura Ward, Agnes Frizzell, Alice Trundle, Minnie Dorsey, Mable King, Laura Frizzell, Marjorie Grimes, Bell Watkins, Evelyn Walker.

In other Gaithersburg High School news, it was reported that the senior class had elected Minnie Carlisle as President, Nettie Phoebus vice President, Mabel King, Secretary, and Iva Fulks as Treasurer. The freshman class also elected officers, as follows: Marjorie Waters, President; Emma King, vice President; Marguerite Welti, Secretary; Donald Snyder, Treasurer.

May 2, 1913:
Robert L. Hickerson and Upton B. Mackall have been appointed and qualified as Justices of the Peace.

Mrs. Eleanor Magruder, wife of Winfield S Magruder, died suddenly last Tuesday.

Mrs. Sarah Eleanor Childs, widow of Jos. S. Childs, died Friday.

Miss Lillian Aldah Magaha, daughter of Mr. & Mrs. Thomas Magaha of Rockville, and Mr. William F. Gittings were married last Saturday.

Miss Ruth A. Sheckels, adopted daughter of Mr. & Mrs. George Warfield, of Damascus, and Harry F. Pearce, were married – no date stated.

Henry H. Hough died suddenly last Friday at his home near Forest Glen.

Henry R. Gingell, a resident of the Bethesda district, died last Friday.

Miss Adelaide Hoffman, daughter of Mr. & Mrs. John Hoffman, of Catonsville, and Dr. Clifton M. Devilbiss, of Laytonsville, were married last Saturday.

The spring meeting of the teachers of the intermediate grades of the County public schools was held last Saturday, with about 40
Cont'd. on next page.

May 2, 1913, cont'd:
in attendance. Names mentioned are Miss Lucile Welsh, W. K. Burgee, Miss Mary C. Davis, Mrs. Florence E. M. Barksdale, and Prof. Wood.

In the news from the Gaithersburg High School, note was taken of a meeting of the Waverly Literary Society, with the following persons mentioned: Dorothy Hoyle, Minnie Carlisle, Eleanor Darby, Iantha Monred, Agnes Frizzell, Guy Neel, Anna M. McCollough, Emma King, Floyd Hyatt, Margaretta Henry, Donald Snyder, Guy Meem, Harry McCabe, John Ward, Mary E. Waeche, Olive Selby, Marjorie Plummer, Annie Trundle, Miss Welsh.

Arrangements continue for the unveiling of the Confederate monument in Rockville. The names mentioned are George R. Rice, Spencer C. Jones, Elgar L. Tschiffely, Francis S. Kilgour, Mrs. John Jones, Mrs. William. H. Talbott, Miss F. May Sellman, Mrs. T. R. Hall, Miss Margaret Fields, Frank Horner, Misses Elizabeth White, Eloise Chiswell, Masters F. S. Tschiffely, Hunton Sellman, and Miss Nana Hays.

At a meeting of citizens of the $5^{th}$. election district. held at Burtonsville on April $26^{th}$, Odorion W. Robey was endorsed for the office of County Commissioner; and Alfred M. Earp was endorsed for the office of member of the House of Delegates.

May 9, 1913:
Miss Margaret E. Barnes, of Washington, and Mr. Mason Miller, of Silver Spring, were married on April $24^{th}$.

William H. Lamar, of Rockville, has been appointed Assistant Attorney-General of the U. S. Postoffice Department.

Edmund Jones, of Rockville, representing Western High School, Washington, won 3 first prizes in a recent athletic event at Md. Agricultural College.

Mrs. Elizabeth A. Fields, widow of the late Jetson G. Fields, died last Wednesday.

The annual stockholder's meeting of the Farmers' Banking & Trust Company was held last Monday. Directors elected are Samuel L. Phillips, John Joy Edson, Edward C. Peter, Harry Griffith, Arthur Williams, John W. Walker, Horace D. Waters, James E. Deets, Wm. W. Welsh, Wm. W. Darby, Albert M. Bouic, Robert G. Hilton, Arthur Peter. Mr. Hilton was then elected President; Mr. Edward Peter was
Cont'd. on next page.

May 9, 1913, cont'd:
elected first vice-president ; Wm. W. Welsh was elected second vice-president and treasurer; John J. Higgins assistant treasurer; Roland Wootton, assistant secretary; Bache Abert, clerk.

Nathan J. Walker died last Sunday at the home of his daughter, Mrs. Mirrian Carlisle.

In Takoma Park, E. E. Blodgett, F. L. Lewton, and H. E. Royer were chosen members of the Town Council for the next 2 years.

In Kensington, A. N. Dobson and Geo. W. Hyatt were elected members of the Town Council.

In Glen Echo, Wm. H. Roach and O. F. James were elected members of the Town Council for the next 2 years.

The Waverly Literary Society at the Gaithersburg High School met on last Friday. The names mentioned are Marjorie Waters, Nora Grimes, Grace Eury, Mary White, Olive Selby, Ralph Etchison, Amy White, Minnie Davis, Laura Ward, and Laura Frizzell.

In other news from the Gaithersburg High School, it was reported that the junior class has elected Mary White, President; Ralph Etchison, vice President; Marjorie Plummer, secretary; and Dorothy Hoyle, treasurer.

The following have announced their candidacies for the offices noted, subject to the results of the Democratic primaries:

J. Dawson Williams, for State Senate

Eugene H. Waters, Alfred M. Earp, for House of Delegates.

Jas. P. Gott, B. Peyton Whalen, Wm. T. Warfield, W. Frank Gaither, Thomas L. Lechlider, William Bradley Carr, for Sheriff.

Eugene A. McAtee, Odorion W. Robey, Jas. D. Young, John R. Lewis, Wm. H. Griffith, Crittenden H. Walker, R. E. Kanode, for County Commissioner from districts noted.

W. Ernest Offutt, for County Surveyor.

May 16, 1913:

The Governor has appointed Columbus Brashears, of the Colesville district, to be a forest warden for the County.

In Barnesville, Arthur L. Jones, Clagett C. Hines, and Linwood J. Hays were elected members of the Town Council.

Cont'd. on next page.

May 16, 1913, cont'd:

On last Tuesday fire destroyed the house on the farm of Capt. James Anderson, near Martinsburg.

In Garrett Park, Johnson Hellen was re-elected councilman; and a run-off election must be held to break a tie between J. F. Defandorf and A. S. Worthington for councilman.

It is announced that Miss Mary White, daughter of Mr. & Mrs. Thomas O. White, of Barnesville, and Mr. William Fleming Lankford of Pocomoke City, will be married June $4^{th}$.

The graduates of Sandy Spring High School this year will be Misses Virginia L. Childs, Lydia Chichester, Doris Lea, Elizabeth P. Gilpin, Deborah A. Iddings, Annie Miller, Alice H. Waters, Katherine Moore, and Lydia H. Tatum; and Wm. M. E. Hess, Henry R. Shoemaker, John T. Bancroft, John J. Downey, John L. Purvis, and Francis A. Thomas.

The name of Phillips Key Goldsborough has been changed to Phillips Lee Goldsborough, upon the petition of his mother, Mrs. Lila Dodge Goldsborough

James A. Miles, who has been sought after a long absence from his home in Poolesville, has been located in a hospital in Ledore, Colo.

The following named will graduate from the Rockville High School this year: Misses Amy V. Robertson, Mary R. England, Elizabeth O. Knight, Alice L. Spates, Bessie C. Brake, Edith E. O. Gilliss, Valeria Robertson, Mary Kelley, Vivian C. K. Robey, and Charles R. Garrett, Gaither P. Warfield, Paul S. Anderson, and Nathan S. White.

John H. Peters, well known farmer of the Rockville area, died on Thursday of last week, at his home.

Mrs. Roberta Linthicum, wife of Joseph H. Linthicum, died on Thursday of last week at her home near Monrovia.

Mrs. Mary S. Howes, wife of George R. Howes, died last Friday at her home near Unity.

James Carstairs Christopher died last Tuesday at his home at Laytonsville.

Mrs. Jennie E. Clagett, widow of John H. Clagett of Damascus, died last Friday in Baltimore.

Mrs. Margaret Webb Warfield, wife of Dr. Robert C. Warfield, died last Monday at her home in Rockville.

Cont'd. on next page.

May 16, 1913, cont'd:

The guarantors of the Rockville Chautaqua met last week. Among the names mentioned are Clinton Allnutt, Mrs. John R. Henderson, Mrs. Berry E. Clark, Miss Sophie Higgins, Mrs. Winfred Berry, Willis B. Burdette, George H. Lamar, Mrs. W. H. Talbott, Mrs. W. W. Welsh, Judge Edward C. Peter, Mrs. Ella Linthicum, Col. Spencer C. Jones, Robert G. Hilton, Thos. Vinson, Mrs. George E. Lewis, Mrs. Stansbury, Miss Marie Talbott, Prof. Wilson Ward, Miss Mary Brewer, Prof. Louis Watson, Norman Bouic, Berry E. Clark, Roland Wootton, Stephen Quigley, C. H. Mannar, F. N. Henderson, Hatton Waters, J. F. Kelchner, O. M. Linthicum, Darby Bowman, C. L. Howard, Geo. E. Lewis, Rev. John R. Henderson, Rev. O. W. Henderson, Rev. Thomas Haughton-Burke, Rev. John Coolahan, Rev. F. M. Richardson, Frank Higgins, and W. W. Welsh.

Church elections have been held at several churches, with the results as follows: At Cropley Presbyterian Church, the following names are mentioned: L. Hill, W. H. Bolton, P. E. Redden, O. Lynch. C. F. Bodine, A. F. Hill, G. E. Ricketts, Mrs. C. F. Bodine, Mrs. C. S. Pennifill, Mrs. J. R. Redden, Mrs. W. H. Redden, Mrs. A. F. Hill, Mrs. T. Bissett, A. D. Brooke, F. Gray, Beulah Bissett. At Hermon Presbyterian Church the following names are mentioned: F. P. Stone, J. M. Harrison, J. P. Vaughn, W. E. Hamilton, W. B. Myers, L. W. Moore, Mrs. J. P. Stone, Mrs. A. Myers, Mrs. S. Harper, Mrs. E. Stearn, Mrs. F. C. Lewis, Mrs. F. Embrey, Mrs. A. Kinney, Mrs. F. P. Stone, Mrs. M. J. Embrey, Miss M. Harrison, Mrs. R. W. Stone.

The Social Service League thanked the following named for their contributions: Thomas E. Robertson, Mr. & Mrs. C. R. Hartshorne, Miss Lena Barwick, M. M. Haviland, Haviland Mills, W. S. Corby, Dr. Charles Farquhar, Walter C. Clephane, Mrs. Lee Offutt, Mrs. Clarence Hickerson, Miss Mamie Hogg, Miss Mary Janet Miller, Miss Annie Wilson, Mrs. Geo. Ashworth, Miss Helen E. Robinson, Mrs. E. W. Moore, J. P. Hermann, Mrs. Chas. Holland, Miss Eliza Miller, Dr. J. W. Bird, Francis Thomas, Mrs. J. H. Cunningham, Mrs. J. W. Buck, Mrs. F. B. Chapman, Miss A. F. Gayley, Dr. Jas. Nelson, Miss Mary E. Thomas, Miss Eliza Miller, Mrs. Paul Cook, Mrs. Archibald Small, Mrs. Martha Keys, Mrs. Helen Thompson, Mrs. Wm. L. Lewis, Miss Mary B. Brooke, Wm. E. Muncaster, E. W. Brown, Mrs. John J. Higgins, Miss Edith Ford, Mrs. O. H. Tibbott,

Cont'd. on next page.

May 16, 1913, cont'd:
Mrs. R. J. Service, Presbyterian Missionary Society Bethesda, Mrs. Albert Osborne, Mrs. Amelia H. Huntley, Woman's Club Washington Grove, Mrs. Wm. H. Lewis, Home Interest Club Forest Glen, Eugene E. Stevens.
Mrs. Robert C. Warfield was remembered .by the Inquiry Club.

May 23, 1913.
Prof. G. W. Walker, of Browningsville, announced the engagement of his daughter, Miss Parepa Wesley Walker, to Mr. T. H. Day, of Philadelphia. See issue of June 27, 1913.
Graduates from Germantown High School this year will be Lyndall L. Boyer, Minnie N. Dorsey, Mildred M. Iglehart, Helen M. Simpers, Mary A. Waters, Isabel P. Watkins, and Chas. Johnson.
Graduates of the Gaithersburg High School this year are Misses Ada Duvall, Emma F. Hyatt, Pearl I. Hyatt, Mabel P. King, Grace M. Buxton, Iva C. Fulks, Minnie F. Carlisle, Annie M. McCullough, Laura Frizzell, Amy R. White, Ellen T. Wilson, Agnes M. Frizzell, Nettie E. Phoebus, and Evelyn B. Walker.
Ernest Phoebus, son of Joseph Phoebus, and Miss Carrie V. Andrews were married on Thursday of last week.
Mrs. Annie L. Bready, wife of Samuel K. Bready, died last Friday at the home of her daughter, Mrs. John G. Stone, in Potomac.
Mrs. Melissa J. Higgins, wife of Charles H. Higgins, died last Monday, at her home in Gaithersburg.
The graduates of the Brookeville High School this year are Helen Mae Brown, Annie Lucille Higgins, Frances Alma Louthan, Anna Brewer Musgrove, Lulu Belle White, Charles Frederick Jones, Mary Lee Gaither, Louise Mobley Gaither, Elizabeth Bowie Nicholson, Leta Wood Riggs, Margaret Howard Riggs, Lillian Olivia Johnson, Mary Elizabeth Peddicord, Marian Norman Howard, and Dowell Jennings Howard.
The monument in memory of the Confederate soldiers of Montgomery County will be unveiled in Rockville on June $3^{rd}$. The names mentioned are Col. Spencer C. Jones, John R. Lewis, Judge Edward C. Peter, Rev. James Taylor, Hon. J. Thomas Heflin, Miss Anna Lee Hoyle, Masters Frederick Adolphus Tschiffely, and Hunton Dade Sellman, Misses Bessie Jones, Eloise Chiswell, Hon.
Cont'd. on next page.

May 23, 1913, cont'd:
Frank Clark, Rev. Lewis Watson, Mayor Lee Offutt, Edgar Tschiffely, Benjamin Canby, Joseph T. White, Francis S. Kilgour, John Holland, George R. Rice, Miss May Sellman, Mr. R. P. Hays, Mrs. John Jones, Miss Anna R. Canby, Mrs. William H. Talbott, Miss F. May Sellman.

The oratorical contest, sponsored by Mr. B. H. Warner, will be held May $24^{th}$. The names mentioned are Clyde Allnutt, Arthur Cromwell, Charles Allnutt, R. Percy Soper, Frank Severance, Malvin Myerly, E. L. Prescott, William Chitty, William Allnutt, Walter Neel, Harold L. Baker, E. D. Adams, and Edward Janney.

The Social Service League expressed thanks for contributions from the following named: Miss Mary Brewer, Thos. E. Robertson, John L. Weaver, E. E. Stevens, M. M. Haviland, Miss Agnes Matlack, Mrs. Hattersly W. Talbott, Mrs. L. L. Nicholson, Mrs. C. W. Prettyman, Mrs. H. T. Newcombe, Mrs. J. C. Welliver, Miss L. F. Prettyman, Henry C. Allnutt, Mrs. E. L. Bullard, Mrs. H. J. Finley, Mrs. Wm. Law, Mrs. J. L. Dynes, Mrs. William Chitty, Mrs. A. E. Shoemaker, R. L. Corby, Bentley Thomas, A. B. Farquhar, R. M. Hallowell.

The following have been named trustees of public schools: Washington Hicks, Mrs. George H. Lamar, Thomas Hoskinson, Jacob Bodmer, Arthur P. Fletchall, Alexander G. Carlisle, T. I. Fulks, Dr. R. B. Haddox, Millard Rice, Charles H. Nourse, James S. Windsor, John C. Bentley, Francis W. Downey, Mrs. Emily Coulter, Henry Howard, Josiah J. Hutton, J. Clinton Dorsey, Perrie E. Waters, Charles T. Johnson, Upton Bowman, J. W. Burdette, James D. Young, and Phillip B. Souder.

The Union Bible class published a resolution of remembrance of Mrs. Margaret Warfield. In another item, the Woman's Club of Rockville published a similar resolution.

Mrs. Eleanor Magruder was remembered by the Win One Bible Class of Rockville.

May 30, 1913:
Harry Spurgeon Beall, son of Vernon Beall of this County, will graduate on June 11 from Western Maryland College

Mrs. Amanda Donaldson died last Monday at the home of her daughter, Mrs. Armstrong, in Kensington. She was 89 years old.

Cont'd. on next page.

May 30, 1913, cont'd:
    The engagement of Miss Sophie Brown to Mr. George R. Rice, Jr. was announced.
    Miss Edith Stanley Prescott and Mr. E. Cecil Allnutt were married last Saturday in Alexandria, Va.
    Robert L. Garrett has been appointed a special constable for the Bethesda district. He will be mounted on a motorcycle, and will patrol the principal roads of the district. His salary will be $600 per year.
    Dorsey R. Bean, of Rockville, and Miss Julia A. Gaskins, of Washington, D. C., were married last Tuesday.
    The annual oratorical contest of the public schools was held last Saturday. The names mentioned are Berry E. Clark, who provided two solos, Brainard H. Warner, Jr., who presented the awards, and Miss Virgie A. Brewer, Rev. Frank M. Richardson, and Clifford H. Robertson, judges. Frank Severance, of Gaithersburg was the winner in the division of one and two room schools, with second prize to Edgar Hildebrand, of the Barnesville district, and third prize to John Ryan Devereaux, of Bethesda. In the grammar and high school division, the first prize was awarded to Walter Neel, of Germantown, the second prize went to Edwin L. Prescott of Rockville High School, and third prize went to Malvin Myerly of Poolesville High School.
    The E. V. White chapter of United Daughters of the Confederacy met on May 21$^{st}$ at 'Blenheim', the home of Mrs. John Jones. The names mentioned are Mrs. Jones Hoyle, Nannie D. Jones, Eloise Wootton Chiswell, Bettie Williams Jones, and Edward Chiswell Wootton. The Chapter expressed unanimous disapproval of the inscription on the Confederate monument in Rockville.
    Mrs. Lucretia Poole, who died May 17$^{th}$, wife of R. K. Poole, was remembered

June 6, 1913:
    David S. Edwards, of Boyds, and Miss Bertie Stewart, of Dickerson, were married last Monday, in Rockville.
    Among the graduates this year at the State Normal School are Estelle Ricketts, Lillian Sage, Elsie M. Soper, and May M. Williams.
    Michael Peters, of Colesville, died last week at his home.
    Having been authorized to form a new parish, the Christ
                          Cont'd. on next page.

June 6, 1913, cont'd:
Episcopal Church of Kensington met for the election of officers. The following names are mentioned: Merritt O. Chance, Warren Price, George Peter, Arthur Williams, Frank A. Birgfield, John M. S. Bowie, A. F. McKeever, C. W. Clum, H. O. Trowbridge, J. Dawson Williams, James H. Adams, and Rev. Geo. W. Atkinson, Jr.

Reginald Hays, of Barnesville, died at his home - no date of death stated. He was unmarried.

The Executive Board of the Montgomery County Federation of Women's Clubs remembered Mrs. Margaret Webb Warfield.

June 13, 1913:
Reuben Keys has left Rockville, and accepted a position in Washington.

Mr. E. Barrett Prettyman has resigned as principal of the Kensington grammar school.

Norman Peter, of Kensington, has accepted a position in the plant bureau of the U. S. Agricultural department, and has gone to Akron, Col.

George Peter, son of Judge Peter, has gone to Virginia where he will work with the corps of government engineers in making a survey.

Anna Thomas, colored, was killed by a train, at Randolph.

The school commissioners have received resignations from the following teachers: Mary E. Green, M. Landella Etchison, Lillian Chaney, and Sallie Fontaine.

Irving Lewis Towers will graduate from Maryland Agricultural College on the 18th of this month, and will be awarded a bachelors degree. Henry Whitmore White and Lea Gilpin Wilson will be awarded certificates.

The following from Montgomery County have been awarded Bachelor of Law degrees at the recent annual graduation exercises at Georgetown Law school: George H. Braddock, Wm. T. Miller, Paul H. Moreland, Alexander F. Prescott, Jr., Havey L. Rabbitt, Donald H. Stewart, Robert Leroy Warfield; and, in addition, the degree of Master of Patent Law was awarded to George H. Braddock.

In Washington Grove, Mrs. Amelia H. Huntley has become the first woman to be elected a trustee. John T. Meany, B. H. Brockway, J.W. Duvall, S. H. Walker, and R. H. Walker are also

Cont'd. on next page.

June 13, 1913, cont'd:
named.

Maynard Sellman recently employed in Albert Wootton's store in Poolesville, has left there to enter business with his uncle in Texas. His place will be taken by Merle Cissell.

Miss Margaret Williams, a recent graduate of the State Normal School, is at home in Poolesville.

Closing exercises of the Poolesville High School were held on May 30$^{th}$. The names mentioned are D. J. Willard, Edwin R. Broome, R. W. Stout, Catherine Fisher, Lottie Mainhart, Blanche Griffith, Carolyn Williams, Marie Chiswell, Florence Allnutt, Elizabeth Jones, Maude Young, Virginia Gott, Rebecca Griffith, Beulah Brooks, Grace Wise, Mary Fyffe, Thelma Pyles, Alice Haller, Lingan Soper, Malvin Work, Lester Haller, Charles Kohlhoss, James Work, Calvin Jones, Willie Roberts, Karl Fisher, Nathan Norris, Willie Price, Carroll Pyles, Linda Watts, Genevieve Mossburg, Elsie Fink, Lillie Bosley, Mary Shumaker, Minnie Bodmer, Edna Soper, Kathleen Gott, Lulu Chiswell, and Elizabeth Horine.

June 20, 1913:

It is announced that Miss Sallie Travers Fontaine will marry Mr. Walter E. Perry on June 25$^{th}$. See issue of June 27$^{th}$.

Miss Mary Elizabeth Bean and Joseph M. Howes were married last Saturday.

The School Commissioners have announced the resignation of the following named teachers: Florence Conroy, Viola Gilliss, Henrietta Rich, Mrs. M. S. Penn, and Mary Roller.

As a result of examinations, free scholarships have been awarded as follows: to Gaither Warfield, a scholarship to either Johns Hopkins or the Univ. of Virginia; Ralph Etchison, to Washington College; Paul Anderson, to Blue Ridge College.

The annual closing exercises of the Rockville Academy were held last Friday. The only graduate was Helen Brunett. Certificates of proficiency were awarded to Lydia Almoney, Zelda Fisher, Mary Frye, Anna Mobley, Gertrude Ward, Josephine Watson, Russell Houser, Claiborne Mannar, and Lewis R. Watson Jr.

The executive committee of the Social Service League met for the election of directors, and for appointment of committee chairmen. The following are mentioned: Mrs. John B. Brewer, Dr. Jas. E.

Cont'd. on next page.

June 20, 1913, cont'd:
Deets, Dr. H. B. Haddox, Joseph T. Janney, Mrs. T. Randolph Hall, Mrs. Jos. M. White, Mrs. Archibald Small, Mrs. Wm. B. Mobley, Carter Clagett, George W. Rice, Wm. Law, Asa M. Stabler, Alban G. Thomas, Mrs. J. Frank Wilson, Rev. T. A. Houghton-Burke, Rev. Frank M. Richardson, Rev. Oscar W. Henderson, Mrs. Benjamin H. Miller, Mrs. Morris L. Croxall, P. K. Thurston, Mrs. William L. Lewis, Mrs. Joseph W. Buck, Mrs. Mary A. Green, Miss Isabel Kingdon, Mrs. Robert E. L. Smith, Miss Lucy Simpson, Mrs. H. Clinton Allnutt, Mrs. Chesley, W. W. Stockberger, Mrs. Henry L. Wells, Eugene F. Stevens, Judson C. Welliver, Dr. Wm. L. Lewis, and Dr. John L. Lewis.

Rev. T. Davis Richards will observe his 25th anniversary in the ministry on next Sunday, the 25th, at the Neelsville Presbyterian Church.

June 27, 1913:
Misses Estelle Ricketts and Lillian Sage have been appointed teachers in the public schools.

Miss Pansy Cecilia Carlin and Ira V. Moore were married on Wednesday of last week.

Mary A. Chapman died on Saturday.

Geo. W. Shaw died last Saturday at his home near Oakdale.

Thomas Perry Thompson died last Saturday at the home of his sister, Mrs. Cornelia Bean, near Derwood.

Mrs. Sarah E. Stabler, widow of Charles Stabler, died last Friday at her home, 'The Cottage', at Sandy Spring.

Mrs. Isabella Ann Isherwood, widow of Robert J. Isherwood, died on Thursday of last week.

Mrs. Sallie A. Darby, wife of Lawrence A. Darby, a former Judge of the Orphan's Court, died last Tuesday.

Commencement exercises at the Briarley Hall Military Academy were held June 11th. Names of Montgomery County students mentioned are Henry Ralph Williams, John Franklin Carlisle, William Harmong Lamar.

July 4, 1913:
The Board of Supervisors of Elections has named the following registration officers:
Cont'd. on next page.

July 4, 1913, cont'd:
     Laytonsville: Luther M. Duvall, Z. M. Waters, Jr.
     Clarksburg district: William W. Dronenburg, Webster V. Burdette.
     Poolesville district: Charles V. Willard, Joseph N. Darby.
     Rockville district, first precinct: Wilbur S. Day, George P. Henderson. Second precinct: John M. Heagy, Claiborne H. Mannar.
     Colesville district: Henry C. Chaney, Wilson G. Johnson.
     Darnestown district: J. William Garrett, Julian Griffith.
     Bethesda district, first precinct: Lewis Keiser, Warren V. Magruder; second precinct, Clarence E. Dawson, Jesse Nicholson.
     Olney district, first precinct: George H. Jones, Francis Snowden; second precinct, Charles R. Hartshorne, Laureson B. Riggs.
     Potomac district: John L. Hall, Carter Clagett.
     Barnesville district: W. W. Hodges, R. Frank Lewis.
     Damascus district: Wm. H. Burdette, Richard M. Stanley.
     Wheaton district, first precinct: Charles E. Dwyer, Lewis B. F. Graeves: second precinct, Edward W. Birgfeld, William E. Anderson.
     By order of Thomas Vinson, Maurice M. Browning, William H. Wade, supervisors.

The School Commissioners have confirmed the appointment of Charles H. Gibson, of Church Creek, Md., as principal of the Kensington grammar school, vice E. Barrett Prettyman resigned. The resignation of Miss Mary E. Clark was also announced. The appointment of the following assistant teachers was announced: Roberta P. Higgins, Landella Etchison, Katherine Hughes. Josephine Chaney has resigned as assistant at the Laytonsville school.

John W. Williams has been selected to go to St. Louis, Mo. to 'look after' the weighing of the mails west of the Missouri River.

Miss Frances C. Grimes and Joseph Albert Moulden were married last Wednesday, in Rockville.

Cont'd. next page.

July 4, 1913, cont'd:
Miss Katherine Miller, of Sandy Spring, and John Casamir Dahl, of Brooklyn, N. Y., were married last Saturday.

Prof. Myrick Hascall Doolittle died last Friday at his home in Linden.

Charles Gassaway Porter, age 94, died on Thursday of last week.

A memorial to Gen. Edward Braddock was unveiled on the Courthouse lawn on July 9$^{th}$. The names mentioned in connection with the program are Judge Edward C. Peter, Rev. J. T. Coolahan, Mrs. Croxall, Mrs. Cora Bacon-Foster of the N.S.D.A.R., Mr. C. C. Magruder, Jr., Hon. William P. Borland, Hon. David. J. Lewis, Lillian Fields, Marie Talbott, Rebecca Fields, Rev. T. A. Haughton-Burke, Maj. William J. Barden, and Lt. Cdr. Chester Wells.

A chapter of the Society of Daughters of the War of 1812 has been formed in Montgomery County. The names of Montgomery County members are Mrs. Martha Ray Keys, Miss Agnes Fenwick, Mrs. Samuel N. Barker, Miss Laura Walker, Mrs. E. L. Bullard, Miss Ida Dove, Miss Marie Talbott, Mrs. Joe Dade, Mrs. W. E. Wall, Mrs. F. P. Stone, Miss Lillian Miller, Mrs. M. L. Croxall, Mrs. J. Frank Wilson, Mrs. Samuel N. Barker, Mrs. Wm. B. Saul. See also item in issue of following week.

July 11, 1913:
Mrs. Eugene Jarboe, Randolph Luhn, and Wm. Williams have been appointed trustees of the school at Sugarland.

Miss Mary E. Dawson, daughter of the late James M. Dawson, died Tuesday.

Miss Catherine Victoria Welsh and Russell Scott Magruder were married last Saturday.

John A. Riggs, age 81, died on Wednesday of last week at his home near Brookeville.

Mrs. Evaline Hopkins Marlow, widow of Julius Marlowe, died last Sunday at her home in Fairland.

An interview with John T. Hoyle, age 90, was published. Mr. Hoyle is a resident of near Boyds.

July 18, 1913:
William R. Fulks, of Gaithersburg, died last Sunday
Cont'd. on next page

July 18, 1913, cont'd:
Funeral services for Mrs. Harriet J. Iddings, widow of Dr. C. E. Iddings, of near Sandy Spring, were held last Saturday.

The members of the Montgomery Club, of Rockville, have elected the following board of governors: Robert B. Peter, Edwin S. Hege, Robert G. Hilton, Samuel E. Eastburn, Roland Wootton, John Brewer, F. Hazel Cashell, Randolph Mason, Randolph Talbott, Theodore S. Mason, Edward S. Dawson, Darby Bowman, Charles M. Jones, Julian W. Whiting, Dr. Geo. E. Lewis. Robert Peter was then elected President; John Brewer, first vice-president; Julian W. Whiting, secretary; Edwin S. Hege, treasurer; Darby Bowman, chairman of the house committee.

Mrs. Mary S. Winsor, a native of Montgomery County, died on Wednesday in Lexington, Mo.

The role of the battalions of Confederate cavalry known as the 'Commanches', under the command of Col. E. V. White, was recalled by Magnus S. Thompson. Others named include Lt. Joshua R. Crown, and Capt. Samuel Means.

John L. Easton died June 21$^{st}$, at his home near Layhill.

July 25, 1913:
The school commissioners have received the resignation of Prof. W. K. Burgee as principal of the school at Hyattstown.

Irving L. McCathran and Miss Sarah. A. Osborne, both of Washington Grove, were married last week.

Miss Pearl E. Offutt and Harry E. Smith, both of Gaithersburg, were married - no date stated.

John Marshall Hebbard, a former resident of Rockville, died last Sunday.

The following judges and clerks of election have been appointed:

Laytonsville district: Henry H. Griffith, Ledoux E. Riggs, judges; Garrison Bell, Lloyd C. Colliflower, clerks.

Clarksburg district: J. William Johnson, William E. King, judges; James F. Purdum, Robert L. Hickerson, clerks.

Poolesville district: Usher Charlton, William E. Compher, judges; William J. Compher, Edgar B. Chiswell, clerks.

Rockville district, first precinct: J. Somerville Dawson, Winfred E. Berry, judges; Duncan Smith, George A. M.

Cont'd. on next page.

July 25, 1913, cont'd:
Kelchner, clerks. Rockville district, second precinct: J. Gardiner Darby, Thomas N. Bailey, judges; Urban N. Wagner, Clifford H. Robertson, clerks. Colesville district: Samuel S. Bond, Edmund C. Davis, judges; Francis S. McLeod, Lawrence E. Harding, clerks. Darnestown district: Preston L. Snyder, Charles G. DuFief, judges; Reuben F. Martin, Thos. D. Darby, clerks. Bethesda district, first precinct: Alexander A. Braddock, M. Wilson Offutt, judges; Edward E. Crockett, Leroy Lochte clerks. Second precinct: Thomas E. Robertson, William J. Callahan, judges; Evans Browne, W. Lyle Offutt, clerks.
 Olney district, first precinct: Clarence B. F. Carroll, Samuel P. Thomas, judges; R. Roland Moore, Nicholas R. Griffith, clerks. second precinct, Lafayette M. Dwyer, Francis B. Musgrove, judges; J. Janney Shoemaker, William P. Jones, clerks.
 Gaithersburg district: Eldridge D. Kingsley, Samuel B. Briggs, judges; Harold L. Kingsley, Edmund L. Amiss, clerks.
 Potomac district, Charles R. Stone, Thomas E. Jackson, judges; John W. Lynch, Harrison Myers, clerks.
 Barnesville district: A. Clinton Brown, Isaac N. Emmert, judges; Charles O. Robertson, Daniel T. Shreve, clerks.
 Damascus district: Samuel V. Broadhurst, James B. Hawkins, judges; Jas. W. Burdette, Archie W. Souder, clerks.
 Wheaton district, first precinct: Gerald H. Warthen, Frank D. Stubbs, judges; Leroy Smith, William A. Fidler, clerks. second precinct, Causin Condict, Walter E. Thompson, judges; James F. Benedict, Oliver H. P. Clark, Jr., clerks.
 Thomas M. Hulings died suddenly last Friday, in Baltimore, at the home of Miss E. F. Magruder. His mother and sister still live in Rockville. See resolution of respect in same issue, adopted by directors and executive committee of Continental Trust Co., of Baltimore.

August 1, 1913:
 It is announced that Miss Emma Lucile Crigler and Ross Heiskell Henson will be married on August 12$^{th}$.
 The engagement of Miss Martha [ ? ] Brown, of Richmond, and Robert Barnard Higgins, formerly of Rockville, was announced.

August 8, 1913:

Mrs. Laura Riggs, formerly of Cedar Grove, and Frank Wilkins, of Washington, were married on July 31$^{st}$, in Rockville.

The Silver Spring Water Co. has been incorporated. The names mentioned are Blair Lee, Montgomery Blair, Wm. W. Jordan, Frank L. Hewitt, and James H. Cissel.

Miss Corrie V. DeVilbiss has resigned as teacher at the Gaithersburg High School.

The school board has awarded scholarships to the State Normal School to Misses Maude England, Joy Fulks, and Marian [?] Howard.

August 15, 1913:

Miss Lee Athey has been appointed stenographer at the Montgomery County National Bank, in Rockville.

Roland Garrett, of Rockville, has been appointed to a position in the U. S. Forestry service.

Attorney Webster Spates has been appointed to a position in the Dept. of Justice, in Washington.

The School Commissioners have appointed the following named to trusteeships of the public schools: W. H. Baxton, Montrose; John H. Jones and Norman Wootton, Dickerson; Mrs. Jesse R. Thompson and Albert H. Gurley, Garrett Park; Maurice Beall, Cedar Grove.

Geo. R. Braddock, son of A. A. Braddock of Friendship Heights, has been placed in charge of work in the state of Wyoming 'connected with the government and offices in Washington'.

Mrs. Mary Catherine Scherrer, widow of Philip Scherrer, died last Saturday at her home near Wheaton.

The annual meeting of the Anti-Saloon League was held in Washington Grove on last Tuesday. The names mentioned are Dr. John L. Lewis, Thomas J. Owen, Alfred Wilson, and A. C. Warthan.

Mary R. Prescott, of Rockville, is among the beneficiaries of a large estate left by Martha S. Hill of Chicago.

A large barn on the farm of W. A. Wimsatt, at Avenel, was struck by lightning last Sunday. The barn was destroyed, along with some horses and a quantity of crops.

Cont'd. on next page.

August 15, 1913, cont'd:

A New York - Washington race between an airplane and a train was held last Friday, with the airplane being the winner, even after the plane was forced to make an unscheduled stop at the farm of John B. Diamond, of this County.

Judges have been named to act in the coming Fair. Names of residents from Montgomery County are Henry Vogt, Wm. H. Holmes, Mrs. Fred. Allnutt, Mrs. James H. Jones, Judge E. C. Peter, Mrs. Henry H. Miller, and Mrs. O. B. Williams.

August 22, 1913:

Mrs. Leta R. Wood, wife of Charles J. Wood, died last Sunday. She was the daughter of the late Samuel Riggs of R.

James F. Lyddane, a native of Rockville, died last Sunday. He was a retired District of Columbia policeman.

Raymond Watkins, son of Noah Watkins of Cedar Grove, died last Saturday of injuries suffered the prior Monday when he fell from a horse pulling a wagon, and was then run over by the wheels of the wagon.

About 2000 persons attended the annual tournament of the St. Mary's Catholic Church, Barnesville. The names mentioned in connection with the event are Ernest Holland, in charge. Preston B. Ray delivered the charge to the knights, and J. Dawson Williams delivered the coronation address. A. B. Shreve was chief marshall, assisted by Bradley Shreve. Creighton Jones, Thomas Gott, Lloyd Jones, and Edward Brosius also assisted. Judges were Henry Black, Silas Ward, and Charles Smoot. Winning riders were William Clements, Clarence Offutt, John Offutt. Lillian Hoyle was crowned Queen of Love – her maids were Mrs. Wm. Clements, Mrs. Clarence West, Miss Marie Jones. Other riders were Hatton Brown, Weller Hammond, Samuel Terrell, Lewis Monard, and Raphael Offutt.

The full primary ticket of the Democrat candidates for the various offices named is as follows:

State Senate: J. Dawson Williams, Eugene Jones.

House of Delegates: J. Furr White, Andrew J. Cummings, Eugene H. Waters, Francis Snowden, Alfred M. Earp, Alfred Wilson, Donald McA. Bowie.

Sheriff: W. Frank Gaither, James P. Gott, Benjamin P. Whalen, Thomas L. Lechlider, William T. Warfield, William Bradley

Cont'd. on next page

August 22, 1913, cont'd:
Carr.

County Commissioner for various districts named: Crittenden H. Walker, Wm. H. Griffith, Robert E. Kanode, James D. Young, John R. Lewis, Eugene A. McAtee, Clarence M. Griffith, Hazel W. Cashell, Odorion W. Robey.

Surveyor: Charles J. Maddox, W. Ernest Offutt.

Delegates to State Convention: G. Rust Canby, R. Bentley Thomas, Richard C. Drum-Hunt, Claude W. Owen, Harry C. West, John W. Henderson, Frederick A. Allnutt, George F. Bonifant, H. Latane Lewis, Lewis W. Poole.

State Central Committee: Preston B. Ray, Robert G. Hilton, David R. Hershey, Alexander G. Carlisle, Richard E. Darby, Robert B. Peter. Having no opposition, the following will be certified as winners, and the names will not appear on the ballot: Thomas F. Hawkins, William L. Aud, Thomas C. Keys, Douglass M. Blandford, John A. Hall, George E. Nicholson, Charles F. Brooke, William H. Wade, Lawrence A. Chiswell, Archie W. Souder. There will be only two County Commissioner contests, as follows: in the Clarksburg district, .Elias Dorsey King and John Gardiner will oppose each other; and in the second precinct of the Bethesda district, Robert E. L. Yellott and R. Ashby Leavell will oppose each other.

In the Republican Progressive party, the following will be certified as having complied with the registration requirements: Charles F. Kirk, Mortimer O. Stabler, Clarence E. Dawson, C. Parker Weller, Frederick W. Page, Thomas Dawson, C. Scott Duvall, William Johnson, Galen L. Tait, D. William Baker. William T. S. Curtis, John A. Butler, and Ormsby McCammon.

At a joint meeting of the Republicans and the Progressives, a fusion ticket has been nominated for the coming general election. The names mentioned are: for State Senate, Charles F. Kirk; for House of Delegates, Edwin S. Hege, James M. Mount, Mortimer O. Stabler, Clarence E. Dawson; for Sheriff, Frederick W. Page; for County Commissioners, Luther M. Gue, C. Parker Weller; for Surveyor, Norman E. Jackson.

Mr. C. Leslie Reynolds, a native of Montgomery County, died on Thursday of last week.

The Social Service League acknowledged contributions received from the following named: Social Service Committee, Mrs.

Cont'd. on next page.

August 22, 1913, cont'd:
R. J. Bushee, Mr. & Mrs. E. J. Walsh, Mrs. Ella Anderson, W. T. Easterbrook, Eugene E. Stevens, Dr. W. R. Butler, R. E. L. Smith, Rev. James Kirkpatrick.
Mary Dove, who died August 11, 1910, was remembered.

August 29, 1913:
Cooke D. Luckett has been re-appointed principal of the Rockville Academy, Lewis R. Watson assistant.
Mrs. Jane Truxton, widow of Wm. Truxton, died last Saturday at her home near Wheaton.
Gen. Marion P. Maus, of Rockville, has retired from the U. S. Army after 42 years of service. He graduated at West Point in 1874.
Mrs. Alpha Omega Dufief, daughter of Samuel K. Bready, of the Rockville area, and Robert Lee Saunders, of the Potomac district, were married last Monday in Rockville.
After having been convicted of wife beating, Waverly Hill was sentenced by Justice Arthur Mace to be given 15 lashes. The punishment was administered by Sheriff Howard.
.The will of Henry Bradley was upheld by the verdict of a jury rendered last Saturday. Mr. Bradley died in 1910, and the validity of the will has been in dispute since then. The members of the last jury were Charles L. Townsend, Charles B. Murphy, George F. Leapley, Thomas E. Shaw, Jas. E. Howes, Herbert L. Diamond, Maurice Pheobus, [Phoebus ?] George H. Johnson, Washington J. Purdum, James E. Schrider, Edward Palmer Rabbitt, and Nicholas M. Howes.
The E. V. White chapter of U.D.C. met at the home of Miss Elsie White. Names of local interest mentioned were Nana P. Hays, Mrs. John A. Jones, Mrs. Jones Hoyle, Mrs. Thomas R. Hall, Medora Jones, Clara Price, and Clorine Fletchall.
The picnic and tournament of St. John's Catholic Church, Forest Glen, was held last week. The charge to the knights was delivered by Dr. Eugene Jones. J. Dawson Williams delivered the coronation speech. Douglas M. Blandford was chief marshall, and the judges and timers were W. Bradley Carr, Alfred Ray, and J. E. Kemp.
The second annual Montgomery County Horse and Colt show as held last Monday, on the farm of Benton G. Ray, near Colesville. Owners names mentioned were Miss Annie Miller, Mrs. F. D. Frey,
Cont'd. on next page.

August 29, 1913, cont'd:
Miss Eleanor Jackson, B. Lowndes Jackson, Jr., Mrs. W. S. Sheets, A. G. Carlisle, James Daniels, F. W. Kruhm, Dr. Ryan Devereaux, Mrs. Geo. G. Getty, Wm. Matthews, Maurice Cissel, Spencer T. Windham, Wm. F. Harding, B. F. Saul, Donald Kirk, Javins Bros., Chas. Hopkins, Robert H. Miller, T. Alex Barnesly, Wm. F. Harding, Wm. Matthews, Mrs. Geo. G. Getty, Herbert M. Brown, A. W. Stonestreet, Harry S. Wheeler, Walter Fawcett, Alex G. Carlisle, Louis A. Randall, Thomas L. Hughes, Miss Martha Hopkins, James Forsythe, Tom Hughes, Joseph Devereaux, Madison Fisher, H. W. Owings, and Benton G. Ray.

September 5, 1913:
Mrs. Rachel Mullican, widow of John Mullican, died last Friday at the home of her daughter and son-in-law, Mr. & Mrs. Charles C. Ricketts, at Derwood.

George Philip Hunckel, who once operated a grocery store in Rockville, died last Thursday.

Harry E. Beall, a recent graduate of Western Maryland College, has been appointed to a position as instructor there. He will also serve as director of the gymnasium, and as assistant coach of athletics.

John William O'Brien, the 8 year old son of George O'Brien, of Bethesda, was hit and killed by a delivery truck, on Wednesday.

William J. Fisher has been admitted to bail in the killing of Wm. D. Altdorfer last Friday in Chevy Chase.

The following is a list of prizes awarded at the recent Fair. If a name appeared more than once in a particular category, the repeats are not listed:

Horse show: The next following combines all the categories and sub-categories dealing with horses – duplications of names were numerous, and are eliminated:

Lee Offutt, B. F. Saul, S. W. Magruder, Stacy Belt., Wm. Dorsey, H. L. Diamond, O. T. Stonestreet, W. T. Brown, F. W. Kruhm, R. J. Sellman, L. L. Green, Miss Annie Miller, Frank M. Hallowell, Dr. Devereaux, Milton Easton, H. T. Newcomb, Rosemont Farm, Don Kirk, H. H. Cashell, Charles T. Nicholson, O. B. Williams, W. T. Brown, Alex Carlisle, Alice Cashell, T. T. Hickman, Robert Miller, J. C. Dorsey, J. W. Jones, D. W. Clarke,
Cont'd. on next page.

September 5, 1913, cont'd:
R. L. Ely, J. Benson, F. F. Fraley, Trundle Brothers, Charles Allnutt, J. N. Barnesley, M. P. Gormley, M. B. Montgomery, Harry Beard, Henry Griffith, A. C. Fawsett.

Dairy: Mrs. C. F. Brooke, Mrs. C. I. Gilpin, Wm. J. Hoyle, Myers Bros.

Farm products: R. P. Hines, Urban N. Wagner, J. R. Lechlider, T. L. Offutt, Lillian Fields, George Shaw, Wm. F. Granger, J. I. Barnesley, A. W. Brown, Seth W. Warfield, E. W. Horner, L. M. Muncaster, C. T. Johnson, J. M. Etchison.

Fruit: R. P. Hines, Mrs. J. E. Muncaster, Seth W. Warfield, Mrs. C. W. Prettyman, Mrs. Albert P. Beall, Mrs. Thomas W. Waters, J. W. Graff, Arthur W. Stonestreet, Donald Bowie, Ben Davis, R. B. Thomas, M. A. Merritt, L. W. Barnesley, Amy Robertson.

Peaches, other fruit and melons Mrs. H. L. Wells, Seth W. Warfield, Willis L. Moore, Ida Bolton, Lavinia Jones, F. B. Abert, Margaret Welsh, Beulah Barnesley, Mrs. S. T. Stratmeyer., Mrs Thomas W. Waters, A. W. Stonestreet, Mrs. W. E. Ricketts, Mrs. H. G. Poss, Mrs. H. L. Wells, Ellen Farquhar.

Garden products: R. P. Hines, Jr., Urban N. Wagner, Seth W. Warfield, Beulah Barnesley, Mrs. C. W. Watkins, Mary Welsh, R P. Hines, Ellen Farquhar, J. R. Lechlider, E. W. Monday, Mrs. C. F. Brooke, Albert P. Beall, W. E. Muncaster, Emmett Dove, A. W. Brown, B. Riggs, Mrs. Riddleberger.

Children's department: Hazel C. Burriss, Scott Offutt, Henry Warfield, Ruth Condon, Helen Muncaster, Thomas Shorts, Wm. H. Gilpin, Clara W. Henderson, Mildred Morrison, J. F. Muncaster, Jr., Hazel T. Burriss, J. E. Muncaster.

Works of art: Emma Stabler, Rose Wagner, W. E. Muncaster, Lucile Offutt, Mrs. I. Livermore, L. C. Freeman, E. E. Hall, S. J. Hutton.

Flowers: Ellen Farquhar, Alva Smith, Mary Magruder, Mrs. Emmett Dove, Mrs. W. E. Ricketts, Mrs. Thomas W. Waters, Mary Hurley, Mary Magruder, C. M. Brooke.

Growing plants: Mrs. W. E. Ricketts, Adele Maus, Mrs. Thos. W. Waters, Mrs. James T. Bogley, Wm. H. Talbott, Mrs. H. E. Stratmeyer, Mrs. H. C. Hurley, Wm. J. Hoyle, Mrs. H. G. Poss, Margaret Welsh.

Culinary department: Mrs. R. B. Thomas, Mary Wagner,

Cont'd. on next page.

Sept. 5, 1913, cont'd:
Ellen Farquhar, Mrs. J. N. Barnsley, C. M. Brooke, Mary Gittings, Mrs. A. R. Speare, Helen Gassaway, Mrs. W. Allnutt, Mrs. W. E. Ward, Mr. T. C. McGaha, Jennie Beckwith, Mrs. W. F. Ricketts, Mrs. W. E. Ricketts, Mrs. Geo. H. Lamar, Mrs. D. M. Watson, Edith Hull, Dorothy Brooke, Mrs. Albert P. Beall, Lavinia Wagner, Arlene McFarland, Marion B. Shorts, L. B. Morrison, Mrs. H. C. Hurley, Mrs. Upton Bowman.

Preserves: Mrs. W. E. Ricketts, Mrs. C. S. Duvall, Mrs. Albert P. Beall, Rose Wagner, Jose Higgins, Mabel Shaw, Lonia Ricketts, Adele Maus, Mrs. George P. Henderson, Mrs. A. W. Brown, Katie Shaw, Mrs. C. T. Johnson, Marion Shorts.

Jellies: Edith Hull, Rose Wagner, Mrs. George Henderson, Arie Davis, Lonia Ricketts, Alva Smith, Marion B. Shorts, Mary Hurley, Mrs. C. T. Johnson, Francis Lynch, Mrs. J. M. Ward, Jennie Higgins, Eva M. Burriss.

Canned blackberries: Lonia Ricketts, Arie Davis, Rose Wagner, Mrs. Artemus Sullivan, Mrs. C. T. Johnson, Mrs. George Henderson, Mrs. Albert P. Beall, Mrs. C. S. Duvall, Mrs. M. E. McGregor, Jose Higgins, Beulah Barnsley, Miss C. T. Johnson, Mrs. Donald Bowie.

Miscellaneous culinary: Mrs. A. C. Warthan, Ada Warfield, Mrs. Edwin Monday, Mary Stabler, Lonia Ricketts, Mrs. Albert P. Beall, Sadie Penn, Mary Welsh.

Children's department: Frances Whiting, Helen Gruber, Dorothy Tschiffely, Maggie Shorts, Anna Offutt, Helen Gardner, Annie M. Shults, Miss L. E. Morrison, Mildred Morrison, S. R. Hall, Clyde Griffith, W. W. Offutt, M. W. Offutt, James M. Condon, Margaret Howser, Anna Muncaster, Wm. A. Linthicum, A. L. Offutt, E. Darby, Elma Cunningham.

Class 3: Anna Offutt, Miss A. E. Hines, G. L. Hines, Anna Muncaster, Gertrude Veirs, Margaret Howser, A. M. Shorts, Maggie Shorts, Lona Robertson, A. N. Shorts, Marie Gardner, Agnes Bean, Annie Shorts, George E. L. Burns.

Domestic manufactures: Mrs. E. M. Williams, Mrs. Wm. H. Talbott, Miss E. S. R. Glover, L. C. Truman, Martha Poole, Mrs. R. B. Thomas, Mrs. C. O. Bean, Jose Higgins, Mrs. Warren Anderson, Mrs. T. W. Waters, Miss M. W. Offutt, Mrs. B. M. Williams, Miss E. H. Owens, Mrs. L. L. Nicholson, Miss W. Hite Miller, Catherine
Cont'd. on next page.

Sept. 5, 1913, cont'd:
Poole, Mrs. Thomas Hoskinson, Jane Offutt, Mrs. O. M. Linthicum, Mrs. R. L. Isherwood, E. T. Barnesley, Mabel Shaw, Mrs. A. P. Bell, Lucy Brewer, Mrs. H. W. Talbott, Mrs. Roger Shaw, Mrs. C. B. Nicholls, E. S. R. Glover, Lillian Fields, Jane Yearly, Elizabeth Higgins, Mrs. E. H. Nicholls, Ruth Owens, Mrs. E. Dishner, Mrs. J. T. Bean, Nena Jones, Susie Owens, Mrs. J. S. Genon, W. Hite Miller, Mrs. L. Burch, Irene Isherwood, Marie Talbott, Mrs. L. B. Goldsborough, Emily Glover, Mrs. E. W. Monday, Mrs. F. Keplinger, Mrs. T. R. Hall, Mrs. D. W. Schaub, Mrs. W. B. Trundle, Mrs. Edward Peter, Mrs. L. A. Darby, Jr., Mrs. William Largent, Mrs. Lloyd Brewer, Mrs. J. S. Genon, Mrs. William Reading, Margaret Howser, Mrs. E. L. Bullard, Mrs. A. R. Thompson, Mrs. M. E. McGregor, Mrs. B. W. Allnutt, Wilheimer Hite Miller, Mrs. L. Burch, Mary Hoskinson.

    Process flour: Hickerson Bros.

    Cattle – [all categories and sub-categories]: J. B. Diamond, Charles Veirs, Emory Ricketts, H. L. Diamond, B. F. Saul, F. H. Cashell, C. M. Brooke, H. C. Hurley.

    Sheep: Emory Ricketts, O. B. Williams, B. F. Saul, F. H. Cashell, L. L. Green.

    Hogs: O. B. Williams, B. F. Saul, H. C. Hurley, R. J. Ricketts, Dorsey L. Peters, D. W. Shaub, T. T. Graff.

September 12, 1913:
    The winners of the Democratic primary are:
        Nominated for the U. S. Senate, Blair Lee.
        Nominated for State Senate, Dr. Eugene Jones.
        For House of Delegates, J. Furr White, Eugene H. Waters, Andrew J. Cummings, Francis Snowden.
        For County Commissioners, Crittenden H. Walker, John R. Lewis, Odorion W. Robey.
        For Sheriff, Benjamin P. Whalen.
        For County Surveyor, W. Ernest Offutt.
        For delegates to the State Central Committee, Robert G. Hilton, Alexander G. Carlisle, Richard E. Darby.
        For delegates to the State convention, Frederick A. Allnutt, George F. Bonifant, H. Latane Lewis, Lewis W. Poole, R. Bentley Thomas.

                          Cont'd. on next page.

September 12, 1913, cont'd:
    Miss Susie Frances Sullivan and Samuel Philip Perrel, both of Poolesville, were married last Saturday.
    Richard H. Lansdale, Jr., and Miss Olivia C. Lindsay were married on Wednesday of last week.
    Wm. J. Daymude died on Thursday of last week at his home near Beane.
    The residence of Mr. Jos. A. Burdette, near Browningsville, was destroyed by fire on Wednesday of last week.
    Miss Clara Lillian Harrison and Carroll A. Warthan, both of Kensington, were married last Saturday. A reception followed at the home of Mrs. William D. Thomas, mother of the bride.
    Miss Ella Wootton died on Thursday of last week.
    Edward H. Brown, a native of Montgomery County, died last Saturday at his home in the District of Columbia.
    Mr. & Mrs. Leonard L. Nicholson celebrated their third wedding anniversary on last Saturday with a party at the Montgomery Country Club.

September 19, 1913:
    The engagement of Miss Elizabeth Walker and William Rodney White was announced, the wedding to be on October 15$^{th}$.
    The engagement of Miss Beatrice Helen Dailey and Hilleary Lyles Offutt, Jr., was announced, the wedding date not stated.
    Harry Raymond Savage, age 8 months, son Mr. & Mrs. Harry R. Savage, died September 6$^{th}$.
    The Gaithersburg High School opened September 8$^{th}$, with 208 pupils attending. In related news, the Waverly Literary Society was reorganized, with 45 members. The officers are Mary White, President; Marjorie Plummer, Vice President; Marguerite Welti, Secretary; Erma King, Treasurer; corresponding secretary; Grace Eury; sergeant-at-arms, Donald Snyder. Others mentioned are Dorothy Hoyle, Miss Henderson, Loraine Williams, R. Monred, Ralph Etchison, Ida Kemp, Olive Selby, Nora Grimes, Ianthe Ward, Guy Meem, Sarah Gray, and Miss Welsh.
    Jas. R. Howes, of Clarksburg district, was killed accidentally on Thursday of last week.
    At a meeting of the directors of the Social Service League held Saturday, it was decided to incorporate. The names mentioned are
                        Cont'd. on next page.

September 19, 1913 cont't:
Joseph Janney, R. E. L. Smith, Rev. John R. Henderson, Judge Joseph Reading, Rev. James Kilpatrick, Asa Stabler, Mrs. G. H. McGrew, Mrs. J. N. Buck, Mrs. John B. Brewer, Mrs. H. J. Finley, Mrs. O. H. Tibbott, Mrs. J. W. Stewart, Dr. John Lewis, Mrs. Wm. Mobley, Mrs. Archibald Small, Mrs. Bernardine Means, Mrs. H. C. Allnutt, Miss Bell, and Mrs. William C. Beck.

The Prohibition Party held a convention last Saturday, and nominated the following individuals for the offices stated:
    For State Senate, Albert E. Shoemaker.
    For House of Delegates, John T. Baker, Samuel O. W. Beall, J. R. Parsley, John F. Boyer.
    Sheriff, Vernon D. Watkins.
    Surveyor, Alburn H. Watkins
    County Commissioner from the 2d. district, Richard C. Beall.

September 26, 1913:
    Miss Myrtle E. Walter and Ambrose C. Kingsbury, both of Rockville, were married on September 10th.
    Miss Pearl Brandenburg and Ray Watkins, both of Damascus, were married on Thursday of last week, in Rockville.
    Miss Beatrice Helen Dailey, of Washington, and Hilleary L. Offutt of Garrett Park, were married last Tuesday.
    Harold Quinby Rowdybush died September 15th.
    In news from the Gaithersburg High School: the number of high school students has increased during the past week to 47. The Waverly Literary Society met on September 19th, with a program in which the following were mentioned: Loraine Williams, Alice Leitch, Mary Ward, Edw. Henry, Marjorie Waters, Marjorie Plummer, Ida Kemp, Alverda Cooke, Guy Neel, Mary Waesche, Donald Snyder, Mary White, Anna Williams, Grace Eury, Marguerite Welti, Eleanor Darby, and Margaretta Henry.
    Burial places of some Montgomery County veterans of the War of 1812 were listed. Names mentioned are Col. Robert Dade, James Mears Allnutt, Joseph N. Dawson, William Dyson, William Poole, Turner Veirs, Richard Rawlings Waters, Maj. Lloyd Dorsey.
    Gertie E. Miller, who died September 16, 1913, was remembered.

                                      Cont'd. on next page

October 3, 1913, cont'd.

Charles Clinton Reed, of Martinsburg, and Miss Anna Maria Allnutt, of Wesley Grove, were married in Rockville last Saturday.

Mr. & Mrs. Wallace Forloine Brown, of Richmond, Va., announced the engagement of their daughter Marie Helena to Robert Bernard Higgins, of Rockville.

Mrs. Elizabeth Ann Hawkins died recently at her home near Clarksburg.

Mrs. George G. Getty, daughter of Joseph Burr, of Colesville, a native of Montgomery County and a noted horsewoman, was accidentally killed on Monday when the carriage in which she was riding overturned and she was thrown to the ground.

Campaign expenses in connection with the recent election were reported as follows: Dr. Eugene Jones, $252.75; J. Dawson Williams, $659.82; Andrew J. Cummings, $186.50; Eugene H. Waters, $94; J. Furr White, $79.45; Francis Snowden, $48; Benjamin P. Whalen, $280; W. Bradley Carr, $693; W. Frank Gaither, $76; James P. Gott, $131.93; John R. Lewis, $35; Crittenden H. Walker, $104.10; Wm. H. Griffith, $102; Odorion W. Robey, $146; W. Ernest Offutt, $25.

An account of the battle of Bladensburg and the defense of Washington, as told by Richard R. Waters to Geo. T. Waters, was published.

The officers of the 1914 Rockville Chautauqua have appointed committees, and named members as follows: Ticket-selling, James T. Bogley, Clifford H. Robertson, William C. Bean, Thomas Vinson, John F. Collins; Reception and Entertainment, Mrs. Wm. H. Welsh, Mrs. Wm. H. Beard, Mrs. S. Duncan Bradley, Mrs. Berry E. Clark, Mrs. Geo. P. Henderson; Platform and Decorations, Chas. W. Prettyman, Mrs. Winfred E. Berry, Mrs. Charles Norman Bouic, Mrs. Wm. H. Talbott, Mrs. R. P. Stansbury.

John Swain, keeper of lock # 14 on the C. & O. Canal, drowned last Saturday at his lock, of unknown cause. His body was discovered by his wife. The drowning was ruled to be accidental.

Mary Elizabeth Nicholson, who died August 19, 1913, was remembered.

October 10, 1913:

J. Floyd Cissell has resigned as cashier of the national

Cont'd. on next page.

October 10, 1913, cont'd:
bank at Silver Spring, and has accepted a position with a New York auditing company.

Eugene H. Cissell, a clerk in the office of the county treasurer, and Miss Cecil Eunice Tschiffely were married last Saturday.

Judge Jas. B. Henderson has resigned the vice presidency of the Montgomery County National Bank for health reasons, and R. H. Stokes has been appointed his successor.

Galen L. Tait has been chosen to be Secretary of the Republican State Central Committee for Maryland.

Miss Amy C. Peters, of Glen, and Newman E. Lynn, of Agnewville, were married on Thursday of last week, in Rockville.

Miss Edith L. Purdum and Ellwood E. Barr were married at Clarksburg – no date stated.

Mrs. Mary Canby Berry, a native of Montgomery County, died September 25th; and her sister, Mrs. Eliza Canby Jackson died October 2$^{nd}$. Both were born near Colesville.

The death of William Edward Butt, who died August 26, 1913, was noted.

October 17, 1913:
Milton W. Strother and Miss Mary I. Austin were married October 8$^{th}$.

The burial place of George Walter Fletchall, a participant in the War of 1812, was noted.

Celestine Maxwell and Florence Anderson have resigned as teachers at Gaithersburg High School. Mrs. Henrietta Rich will succeed Miss Maxwell at the Gaithersburg school.

Mrs. Edna Blizzard, wife of Bertram W. Blizzard of the Potomac district, and daughter of S. Wade Magruder, died by suicide on last Wednesday.

Allan F. Frost, son of Mr. & Mrs. William W. Frost of Friendship Heights, died last Thursday, in Portland, Oregon.

It was announced that Miss Virginia Walker, daughter of Mr. & Mrs. Crittenden H. Walker, and George Plummer will be married November 19$^{th}$.

Miss Emma Louise Alexander and Edward Winsor Offutt were married on Wednesday of last week.

James H. McKenney, Clerk of the U. S. Supreme Court for
Cont'd. on next page

October 17, 1913, cont'd:
the past 35 years, died last Monday at his home in Kensington.

George Parker, of Bethesda, died last Friday, as a result of having been struck by an electric car on the Rockville-Georgetown line.

William A. Allen, who died October 9th, 1913, was remembered.

October 24, 1913:
The Democratic nominees in the coming election are: For U. S. Senate, Blair Lee; for Comptroller, Emerson C. Harrington; for Clerk to the Court of Appeals, Caleb C. Magruder; for State Senate, Eugene Jones; for House of Delegates, J. Furr White, Eugene H. Waters, Andrew W. Cummings, Francis Snowden; for County Commissioners, Crittenden H. Walker, John R. Lewis, Odorion W. Robey; for Sheriff, Benjamin P. Whalen; for County Surveyor, W. Ernest Offutt.

According to the *Sentinel*, the total of the registered voters in Montgomery County is 8038; of which 6005 are white, 2033 colored.

Charles Washington Donaldson and Miss Sarah Elizabeth Young, both of Bethesda, were married on last Monday.

Thomas H. Ward died last Monday at his home near Barnesville. He was 86 years old.

Mrs. Lida W. Ray, widow of John Ray and only child of Judge John E. West, died October 18th.

Miss Mary Elizabeth Walker and William Rodney White were married on Thursday of last week.

Last Monday fire destroyed the dwelling at Brookeville owned by Mrs. Seth W. Griffith and occupied by Dr. I. B. Iddings.

Robert Barnard Higgins, formerly of Rockville, and Miss Marie Helena Brown, of Richmond, Va., were married on Wednesday of last week, in Richmond.

Henry M. Clagett died last Sunday. He was buried in St. Mary's Catholic Church cemetery, Rockville.

Jurors have been drawn to serve during the coming term of the Circuit Court, as follows: Laytonsville district, Thomas G. Griffith, Edward F. Riordan, Thomas Owings; Clarksburg district, Theodore McAtee, Robert L. Hickerson, Chas. C. Waters; Poolesville district, Stephen D. Willard, Mansfield White, Henry Allnutt, Edward Darby;

Cont'd. on next page.

October 24, 1913, cont'd:
Rockville district, Joseph Reading, Wm. Henry Hoskinson, Wm. C. Veirs, Alexander Garrett, Samuel K. Bready, Elijah T. Bean; Colesville district, Louis F. Hobbs, Robert Aitchison, James H. Anderson, Walter Fawcett; Darnestown district, John U. Leaman, John T. Higdon, James H. Offutt; Bethesda district, Chas. C. Bohrer, Benjamin A. Leavell, Frank Welsh; Olney district, Washington B. Chichester, David F. Oland, Wm. Grafton Holland, Samuel Edward Riggs; Gaithersburg district, John E. Clagett, George W. Day, Stanley D. Gaither, Robert A. Young; Potomac district, Charles H. Creamer, Wm. P. Stallsmith, Samuel T. Case; Barnesville district, Thos. G. Mossburg, Octavius Baker, Marcellus E. Wade; Damascus district, Claude G. Mullinix, Crittenden King, James R. King; Wheaton district, David T. Bready, Benjamin R. Hardesty, Wm. J. Umstead, H. Edson Rogers, Chas. R. Wright, Jr.

October 31, 1913:
It was noted that Richard P. Spates, a veteran of the War of 1812, is buried in the old Methodist burying ground in Poolesville.

Samuel W. Briggs died on Thursday of last week at his home near Bethesda.

Miss Lillia May Bosley and Edward W. Luhn were married on Wednesday of last week at the home of the bride.

James N. Benton, age 78, died last Saturday. He had served as a County Commissioner for two terms.

John Bonifant, of Silver Spring, was accidentally shot last Saturday, and died on last Monday.

Miss Marie Helena Brown and Robert Bernard Higgins were married yesterday. They will live in Richmond., Va. The announcement of their engagement appeared August 1st. in the *Sentinel*.

Nominees for election in Montgomery County by parties other than the Democratic party are: for House of Delegates, John T. Baker, Samuel O. W. Beall, John F. Boyer, Clarence E. Dawson, Charles T. Johnson, James M. Mount, Wilbur O. Parsley, Mortimer O. Stabler; for State Senator, Charles F. Kirk; for County Commissioner, Charles T. Day, Hezekiah Day, Hiram W. Harvey, Roger Parsley, Bradley Watkins, C. Parker Weller; for Sheriff, Frederick W. Page, Vernon D. Watkins; for County Surveyor, Alburn H. Watkins.

November 7, 1913:

Abraham Buckingham, of Washington, and Miss Adelia E. Norris of Poolesville, were married last Saturday, in Rockville.

Capt. Truman S. Post died last Saturday, at his home in Chevy Chase. He was a veteran of the Civil War, and for the past 43 years had worked in the auditor's office of the U. S. Treasury.

Miss Julia B. Hewitt and Raymond Harriss were married on Thursday of last week.

It was announced that Miss Florence Veirs and Franklin Bache Abert will be married November 19th.

It has been learned that Mrs. Amanda G. Thomas, one of the pioneer residents of Takoma Park, died last Friday, at Mason, Nev.

The funeral of Fenton Howes was held Tuesday, at Mt. Carmel Methodist Church, near Unity. Date of death is not stated.

Mrs. Minnie A. Houghton, for many years a resident of Glen Echo, died on Thursday of last week.***

The following have been drawn to serve as jurors in the coming term of the Circuit Court, to replace others who were drawn previously but who have been excused: Frank Dwyer, Joseph G. Howes, Henry Smoot, Putnam F. Brian, Eugene Bean, William H. McCrossin, Hattan A. Waters, Daniel P. Morgan. Wm. L. Myers, Levi Houser, Henry M. Lindig, Arthur L. Jones, George A. Wilson. Those excused were Thomas D. Griffith, Chas. C. Waters, Mansfield White, Walter Fawcett, Robert Aitcheson, James Offutt, John T. Higdon, Charles C. Bohrer, J. Edward Riggs, Samuel T. Case, Octavius O. Baker, Marcellus Wade, and Charles R. Wright, Jr.

Cooke T. Luckett, Principal of the Rockville Academy, died last Monday, at his home in Rockville. The item traces his life and career.

The results of the general election for Montgomery County are published. They show that Blair Lee won the U. S. Senate race; the winners of the House of Delegates races were Andrew J. Cummings, Francis Snowden, Eugene H. Waters, and J. Furr White; the State Senate race went to Eugene Jones; the successful County Commissioner candidates were John R. Lewis, Odorion W. Robey, Crittenden H. Walker; The Sheriff race was won by Benjamin P. Whalen; and the County Surveyor race was won by W. Ernest Offutt. The top vote-getter in the local races was W. Ernest Offutt.

The death of Henry Morton Clagett on October 19th was noted. He was buried in St. Mary's Cemetery, Rockville.

November 14, 1913:

Mr. J. Heath Dodge, of Bethesda, and Miss Dorothy Summers of Westwood, Md. were married November 7$^{th}$.

The trustees of the Almshouse have re-elected Philip J. Case overseer, John E. West clerk, and Dr. Edward Anderson as physician, each to serve one year.

Paul Y. Waters, of the Rockville bar, has been appointed referee in bankruptcy for Montgomery County.

Charles E. Bell, age 64 years, died recently - date not stated.

Miss Cuyler D. Dwyer and Russell E. Duvall were married - no date stated.

Miss Madge Lucile Mullinix and Sterling Elwood Day were married - no date stated.

William Randolph Beall, Jr., died – no date stated.

Miss Virginia Rebecca Walker and George Pope Plummer were married last Saturday.

The hay and straw bailing establishment of Thomas I. Fulks, in Washington Grove, was destroyed by fire last Monday.

November 21, 1913:

Pete Mills, of Derwood, has been appointed to a position in the postoffice in Washington.

Miss Bedia F. Cornell, of Virginia, and John W. Earp, of Germantown, were married last week in Rockville.

Miss Bessie May Allnutt and Raymond Lafayette Warfield were married Wednesday in Rockville.

The new barn on the farm of Simon P. Knill, near Barnesville, was destroyed by fire on last Friday.

Dr. James G. Townsend has been recommended for appointment as assistant surgeon in the public health service of the United States. Of 25 physicians who took the examination, Dr. Townsend stood second

Mrs. Florida Higgins, widow of Charles A. C. Higgins, died on Wednesday of last week at the home of her daughter, Mrs. Clinton Dorsey.

Mr. Laurason B. Riggs, of Brookeivlle, and Miss Alverda Owings, of Simpsonville, Howard County, were married on Wednesday of last week at the home of the parents of the bride.

Cont'd. on next page.

November 21, 1913, cont'd:
Miss Florence Veirs and Franklin Bache Abert were married on Wednesday.

November 28, 1913:
The following named have been appointed Trustees of the County Home: Harry Riggs, Henry B. Gardiner, Wm. V. Robertson, and Eleazar Ray. A still-vacant seat will be filled later.

Mrs. Mary Curtin, widow of Thomas Curtin, died on Thursday of last week, at her home near Montrose.

Mrs. Charlotte H. Farquhar, wife of Allan Farquhar, died on Thursday of last week.

The trial of Wm. J. Fisher for the murder of Wm. L. Altdorfer ended on Thursday when the jury failed to agree.

Mrs. Ann Louise Taney, formerly clerk to the County Commissioners of this County for a number of years, died on November 23. She was buried in the cemetery adjoining St. Rose's Catholic Church, Clopper.

William E. Burford, a native of Montgomery County, and a graduate of Maryland Agricultural College, died last Friday.

The engagement of Miss Margaretta Edna Ward and Hermon C. Briggs was announced last Saturday at a 'smoker' given by Mr. Briggs at his home, 'Briggs Manor', near Gaithersburg.

December 5, 1913:
John Bonifant, of near Silver Spring, is planning to go to Colorado for his health.

Prof. Samuel D. Gray has resigned as Principal of the agricultural courses at the high schools of Sandy Spring and Brookeville.

Raymond Guinn Brown and Miss Josephine E. Ray were married on Wednesday of last week.

It is announced that Raymond B. Graves and Miss Edna Mary Hall were married recently.

Fulton Clay Davis and Miss Margaret Bell Cordell were married on Thursday of last week.

Miss Jennie E. Unglesbee and Wm. Wachter were married last Saturday.

Morris J. Clagett, of near Linden, died last Friday
Cont'd. on next page.

December 5, 1913, cont'd:
The newly elected County Commissioners, John R. Lewis, Odorion W. Robey, and Crittenden H. Walker were sworn in last Tuesday. Richard T. White was elected President, Berry E. Clark was elected clerk and treasurer, John A. Garrett, attorney. The old office force, consisting of Wellington W. Welsh, Eugene H. Cissell, Arthur B. McFarland and Octavia B. Wood, was reappointed to their old jobs.
Dr. Wm. R. Tatum, a veterinary surgeon, was accidentally killed last Monday.

December 12, 1913:
George A. Lamphear, of Middlebrook, died last Sunday.
Harry U. Duvall, formerly a resident of Montgomery County, died last Sunday.
The flour mill of Joseph M. Mullinix, at Derwood, burned last Monday, along with a stable and several out-buildings It had been built in 1887, and was once owned by Gaithersburg Milling Company, and later by Mr. Mullinix. See also Jan. 24, 1913.

December 19, 1913:
Mrs. Rebecca Pyles, of Hyattstown, age 35, died suddenly a few days ago. She was a Miss Heffner and was a lifelong resident of Montgomery County.
Samuel D. Byrd has been appointed to the board of Trustees of the alms house.
Dr. Joseph V. Selby, of Rockville, and Miss Bertha C. Clausen, of Baltimore, were married on Thursday of last week.
The funeral of Charles W. Smoot took place on Thursday. No date of death stated.
The Democratic State Central Committee has endorsed Oliver H. P. Clark and M. M. Wolfe for appointment as postmaster of Silver Spring and Forest Glen respectively.
Mrs. Elizabeth Griffith died suddenly last Friday at the home of her daughter, Mrs. Edwin Waters, near Goshen.
The following named have been appointed deputies by Sheriff Whalen: Wm. E. Viett, Aaron R. Hewitt, Artemus Sullivan, E. C. Ramey, Clarence E. Anders, J. Melvin Etchison, Thomas E. Hampton, Edward S. Wise, Eugene Fling, William Fidler, Maurice
Cont'd. on next page.

December 19, 1913, cont'd:
T. Cissell, Randolph Luhn, Miel Linthicum, Robert L. Saunders, Irving Ray, Dean Darby, Preston Hewitt. Wm. P. Trail will be retained as turnkey at the jail.

Mr. Charles B. Rozier, a former resident of Montgomery County, died on Thursday of last week.

December 26, 1913:
The County Commissioners have appointed Mareen Darby constable for the Laytonsville district.

H. S. Koehler has been appointed director of the agricultural schools at Sandy Spring and Brookeville.

Oscar W. Larman, of Bethesda, and Mrs. Grace Eugenia Scheutze, of Washington, were married on Friday, in Rockville.

Dr. Frank H. Manakee, formerly of Rockville, died recently.

It is announced that Miss Priscilla Beall Dawson and R. Watt Farmer will be married in January.

It is announced that Miss Margaret Howard Riggs and Harry Griffith White will be married January $3^{rd}$.

The jury award of $10,000 obtained in 1908 by D. W. Baker against B. H. Warner has been set aside and a new trial ordered.

January 2, 1914:
'For rent. Nine room dwelling, 12 acres, horse and cow stable, and other outbuildings, good orchard, fine water, half a mile from the B.& O. R. R. Station, Gaithersburg, Md., Rent $200 per year, payable monthly. Immediate possession.'

The County Commissioners have appointed Hugh O'Donnell a constable for the Wheaton district - vice Wm. A. Fidler resigned.

Sheriff Whalen has appointed Wm. A. Brooke, Jas. W. Cummings, Hugh F. O'Donnell, and Perry Ensey deputy sheriffs.

Wm. H. Linkins, of the Wheaton district, died suddenly last Tuesday at his home near Aspen.

Mrs. Maria C. Lynch, wife of John H. Lynch, died at her home. No date of death stated – her funeral was on Tuesday.

Mr. J. D. Sponseller, of Boyds, died last Tuesday after having been thrown from the buggy in which he was riding.

John Caleb Bentley died last Saturday at his home, 'Cloverly', near Sandy Spring. See also January 30, 1914.

January 2, 1914, cont'd:
   Miss Ruth Adelaide Snouffer and Joseph Gorman Butler, both of the Potomac area, were married December 22, in Baltimore.
   Miss Ethel Warfield and Elisha Warfield, both of the Damascus area, were married recently at the home of the bride.
   Miss Annie E. Ray and Wm. S. McGaha, both of the Rockville area, were married on Wednesday.
   Miss Emma Elizabeth Conaway, of Carroll County, and Henry Magruder Gilliss, of Warren, Ohio, were married on Wednesday.
   Miss Lula McQuiddy Lillard and George Harrison Braddock were married last Friday.
   The annual Children's Christmas Party of the Rockville Methodist Church was held last Tuesday. Mentioned are Edith Lamar, Miriam Talbott, Lea Athey, Guy Hicks, Russell Howser, Lucile Lamar, Hughes Monday, Margaret Darby, and Betty Wilson.

January 9, 1914:
   Miss Margaret Howard Riggs and Harry Riggs White, both of the Laytonsville area, were married last Saturday.
   Miss Goldie Dwyer and Eli Leisear were married last Saturday.
   Miss Mary Florence Conroy and Raphael Thomas Offutt were married in Rockville on Wednesday.
   Miss Priscilla Beall Dawson and Robert Watts Farmer were married last Wednesday.
   The annual meeting of the Ridgley Brown chapter of U. D. C. was held last Wednesday. The following names are mentioned: Miss F. May Sellman, Mrs. Jed Gittings, Mrs. J. Frank Wilson, Miss Mable Tschiffely, Mrs. Charles C. Waters, Mrs. Wm. H. Talbott, Mrs. L. I. Hays, Miss Nan Tolson, and Mrs. D. H. Warfield.

January 16, 1914:
   Mrs. Achsah Dutrow, widow of Philip Dutrow, died Wednesday. Ten children survive her.
   Gen. M. P. Maus and Mrs. Maus. will spend about a year in Italy and southern France.
   W. H. Thoms has been appointed Principal of the agricultural departments of the Sandy Spring and Brookeville High Schools. He succeeds Prof. Samuel R. Gray, retired.
                                                   Cont'd. on next page.

January 16, 1914, cont'd:

Warren Adams, of Kensington, has signed a contract to play baseball with the Milwaukee team, and will report for practice in March.

Funeral services for Chas. Meyer, of Woodside, were held last Saturday. Date of death is not stated.

Everett Cartwright Hobbs, formerly a resident of Browningsville, died recently in Spokane, Washington.

Miss Mildred Newman, of Silver Spring, and Dr. S. Munson Corbett were married on Thursday of last week.

Fire destroyed the home of Harry C. West, near Seneca, on last Monday.

Robert L. Veitch, of the Colesville district, died as a result of injuries he received when a tree which he was cutting fell on him. Date of death is not stated. His funeral was held on last Friday.

Miss Elsie Day, of Gaithersburg, and Edwin Earl Mossburg were married January $5^{th}$, in Rockville.

Funeral services for Mrs. Elizabeth J. Wilson, widow of Michael Wilson, were held last Friday. Date of death is not stated.

Edward Sellman, of Boyds, accidentally shot himself to death last Sunday, at his home.

The stockholders of the Montgomery County National Bank of Rockville held their annual meeting last Tuesday. Directors elected were Spencer C. Jones, Wm. B. Mobley, James E. Williams, Lawrence Allnutt, Wilson B. Tschiffely, Joseph T. Moore, Richard E. Stokes, Frederick P. Hays, Wm. T. Griffith, Lee Offutt, Perrie E. Waters, and Thomas Vinson. Officers elected were Spencer C. Jones, President; Richard H. Stokes, Vice president and cashier; George M. Hunter, assistant cashier; Russell Brewer, teller; George P. Henderson, note clerk; J. Gardner Darby, correspondence clerk; Lea Athey, stenographer.

Superintendent of schools Earle B. Wood's resignation was accepted by the School Commissioners, and Edwin W. Broome was named acting superintendent.

The large frame dwelling house on the farm of George C. Fry, near Rockville, was destroyed by fire on last Tuesday night.

The annual meeting of the Montgomery County Agricultural Society was held last Wednesday. The following were elected directors: Josiah W. Jones, Lee Offutt, Chas. Veirs, Charles F. Kirk,

Cont'd. on next page.

January 16, 1914, cont'd:
David H. Warfield, Wm. H. Fawcett, Francis Javins, Wm. B. Trundle, Perrie E. Waters, Wm. K. Jones, Charles W. Fields, and John B. Diamond, Jr.

Andrew J. Cummings, a member of the Legislature from Montgomery County, and Miss Zelpha L. Contner, of Washington, were married on Thursday of last week.

January 23, 1914:

Miss Madeline Thompson and Roger D. Nicholls were married on Thursday of last week, in Rockville.

Mr. M. Rawlings Austin, of the Bethesda district, died on Thursday of last week.

Lee Offutt has been elected president of the board of directors of the Montgomery County Agricultural Society; Chas. F. Kirk, Vice president; James T. Bogley; secretary; John J. Higgins, treasurer.

The residence and store of Mrs. Hattie Plummer, Gaithersburg, and the adjoining house belonging to Thomas I. Fulks, burned last Friday.

The stockholders of the First National Bank of Gaithersburg have elected directors as follows: John B. Diamond, James Anderson, H. Maurice Talbott, Thomas I. Fulks, John W. Walker, Zadoc M. Cooke, Clarence H. Hoskinson, Wm. B. Windsor, A. F. Meem, E. C. Etchison, Robert B. Moore, Joseph C. Higgins, Samuel R. Plummer, and Nathan Cooke. Mr. Diamond was elected President, Jas. Anderson, Vice president; Robert B. Moore, cashier; and Frank B. Severance, assistant cashier.

'The Last Supper', painted by Gustavus Hesselius in 1721 for St. Barnabas' Church in Prince Georges County, which had been 'lost' for a number of years and which is presently owned by Mrs. John H. Gassaway of Rockville, has recently been determined to be of considerable value. Mrs. Gassaway has declined a private offer of $30,000 for it because she wants it to go to a museum. Her father, Mr. O. Z. Muncaster, bought the painting at a public sale in about 1839, and left it to Mrs. Gassaway. The ownership of the painting from about 1773, when St. Barnabas Church relocated, until 1839, is unknown.

The following named from Montgomery County have been appointed to positions in the Legislature: John Hardy, John A. Burriss, Leroy Lochte, Samuel P. Thomas, and George McAtee.

January 30, 1914:

Brooke Lee, son of Sen. Blair Lee, has organized a military company in Silver Spring.

Sheriff Peyton Whalen announced the appointment of Henry W. Crismond as a deputy.

A fine lot in Gaithersburg, site of the former Summit Hotel, has been given by Mr. John B. Diamond for the erection of a Catholic Church there.

John T. Carey, for many years a resident of Montgomery County, died last Sunday.

The funeral of Mrs. Ethel Austin was held last Thursday at Boyds. Date of death is not stated.

Miss Della P. Bartgis, of Poolesville, and Remus R. Darby, Jr. were married on Saturday, January 24$^{th}$, in Baltimore.

Judge David Griffith died last Wednesday at his home near Redland. He had served two terms as County Commissioner, 12 years as a judge of the Orphan's Court, and was a veteran of the Confederate Army.

A tribute of John C. Bentley, a former member of the House of Delegates from Montgomery County, was adopted by the House of Delegates and published in the *Sentinel*.

Dr. Edmund L. Amiss died Thursday of last week at the home of his son-in-law and daughter, Mr. & Mrs. Wm. D. Robertson, Gaithersburg. See issue of Feb. 6$^{th}$. for memorial.

The Mutual Amusement Co. announced that it will show movies in Rockville, Gaithersburg and Kensington on a regular schedule.

Geo. C. Fry expressed his appreciation to those who came to his help when his home burned. Also see issue of January 16$^{th}$.

February 6, 1914:

There are 25 people in Rockville who are sick with typhoid, or a typhoid-like illness. There have been earlier cases of typhoid in Rockville this winter, but no fatalities. Medical experts have been called to Rockville to try to establish a cause and to report to town officials. Among those presently sick are Mrs. Lee Offutt, Mrs. Edward Peter, Mrs. Frederick N. Henderson, Misses Margaret Higgins, Julia Fearon, Blanche Nicholson, Lydia Almoney, Ailees Hewitt, Klara Markley; also Jos. Hamilton, William Riggs, Graham

Cont'd. on next page.

February 6, 1914, cont'd:
Riggs, Harry Dawson, Jr., Frank Higgins, Jr., Paul Brunett, and Harmong Lamar.

Miss Mary Hyatt, of Kensington, has been appointed to a clerkship in the office of the commissioners of the public schools.

Miss Nettie E. VanHorn, and William Palmer Beall, both of the Layhill area, were married several days ago.

Mr. Winfred E. Berry has been named postmaster of Rockville, succeeding Willis B. Burdette.

Arthur P. Nicholson and Miss Susie V. Oland were married on Wednesday of last week, at the home of the parents of the bride.

Mr. & Mrs. Edward G. Ward, of Hunting Hill, celebrated their 25th. wedding anniversary last Friday, with a party at their home.

Mr. & Mrs. Arthur Plummer expressed their thanks to those who helped them when their home burned on January 16th.

The *Sentinel* devoted an entire column to an explanation of the reasons why the automobile would never replace the horse.

February 13, 1914:
Garrett Cooley has been appointed constable for the Clarksburg district.

Douglass C. Edwards, of Bethesda, and Miss Ella E. Johnson, of the Rockville area, were married last Saturday in Rockville.

Robert E. Blundon, of Sligo, and Miss Emma Ivy McClure, of Washington, were married on Thursday of last week.

Mr. F. Barnard Welsh, son of Wallace Welsh of Rockville, has been chosen County Attorney in Mesa County, Colo., where he has been practicing law for the past several years.

Miss Ada Duvall and Frederick A. Riley were married on Thursday of last week, in Washington.

Philip Glesner died on Thursday of last week.

Allen Bowie Thomas, a native of Montgomery County, died on February 4th.

The stockholders of the Washington & Rockville Electric Railway, and the Washington Woodside & Forest Glen Railway Cos. have elected as directors the following: Milton E. Ailes, Woodbury Blair, Clarence F. Norment, Clarence P. King, Wm. F. Ham, George Truesdale, Larkin W. Glazebrook, Charles J. Bell, and William B. Hibbs.

Cont'd. on next page.

February 13, 1914, cont'd:

During the past week, three more cases of typhoid have been reported in Rockville, namely of Clements Offutt, son of Lee Offutt, Mrs. Albert Moulden, and Kenneth Lyddane. Young Offutt is regarded as seriously ill. The report of the medical experts, pointing to contaminated water supply and the lack of sewage disposal system also appears. The report also describes, in some detail, the general conditions prevailing along the streets of the town regarding the ditches into which waste water is discharged.

The legislation which later led to the creation of the Washington Suburban Sanitary Commission was introduced in the Legislature by Delegate [Andrew J.] Cummings.

Annie Briggs Small, who died February 10, 1910, was remembered.

John C. Power, who died February 13, 1913, was remembered.

February 20, 1914:

A marriage license has been issued in Washington to Maurice F. Stup and Bessie A. Dasher, both of Derwood.

Rev. George W. Atkinson, Jr., rector of Christ Episcopal Church, Kensington, has resigned in order to become rector of Christ Church, Georgetown.

Rev. Samuel R. White, of Rockville, celebrated his 80th birthday a few days ago.

Prof. and Mrs. William P. Mason, of Rockville, announced the engagement of their daughter, Shirley Carter Mason, to Alexander Fullerton Prescott, the wedding to take place in May.

Miss Alice M. White, of Norbeck, and William Barnsley, of Avery, will marry February 25th.

Edmund L. Amiss was the subject of a resolution of respect by the K. of P. of Gaithersburg.

Mary C. Boswell, who died February 15, 1911, was remembered

February 27, 1914:

Lucy Frances Hickerson, infant daughter of Mr. & Mrs. Lindsay R. Hickerson, died last Friday.

Virginia L. Darby, widow of John W. Darby, died last Sunday.

Cont'd. on next page.

February 27, 1914, cont'd:
Samuel L. English, of Rockville, died last Monday.
John R. Abel, of Ashton, died a few days ago.
There was a meeting on Wednesday, attended by about 300 citizens, to consider ways to improve the sanitary conditions in Rockville. The names mentioned are Chas. W. Prettyman, Robert B. Peter, R. H. Stokes, Dr. Linthicum, Dr. Mannar, W. W. Welsh, and Martin Heim.

The Governor has made the following appointments of residents of Montgomery County: School Commissioners, Charles T. Johnson, William J. Williams; Justices of the Peace, Edward O. Brown, Charles T. Day, Charles B. Murphy, Robert L. Hickerson, Charles F. Elgin, Arthur M. Mace, Carey Kingdon, John A. Hall, E. P. B. Margerum, Preston I. Snyder, Cyrus Keiser, Roscoe M. Roach, Alfred Wilson, Clarence E. Dawson, Alfred F. Fairall, Leonard Weer, R. M. Murphy, H. C. Andrus, Charles H. Grimes, J. W. Burdette, John H. L. Snyder, L. Doan Faher; Notaries, Thomas Dawson, Jr., George M. Hunter, F. Bache Abert, Smith L. Putman, Frank L. Hewitt, William A. Kroll, Edgar B. Gue, Frank B. Severance, J. Janney Shoemaker, Virginia M. Rice, Mary M. Willard.; Supervisors of Elections, Thomas Vinson, Maurice M. Browning, Julian Griffith.

List of Jurors: Jurors for the coming term of the Circuit Court are Perry Ensey, Ledoux E. Riggs, Alton C. Bell, John Rome, Randolph Windsor, Henry B. Gardiner, Benjamin F. Shreve, Richard F. Spates, Harry L. Willard, Thomas R. Hall, William H. Beard, Aaron R. Hewitt, John H. Mills, Charles Lyddane, John S. Gilliss, Conrad F. Maught, Phillip H. Ray, Jos. T. Bond, Benjamin H. Kelley, Edgar B. Ray, Harry C. West, Wm. B. Vincent, Lucien T. Walters, Julian Hite Miller, George W. Cronise, Chas. S. Shafer, Alban Brooke, Samuel B. Wetherald, Montgomery W. Cashell, David S. Craver, William T. Ridgeway, Walter M. Magruder, Porter G. Ward, John W. Briggs, John W. Duley, Otho C. Ward, Matthew O'Brien, William H. Lawson, William C. Brown, Benjamin F. Robertson, Ernest D. Duvall, Columbus W. Day, Arthur R. Burns, Frank A. Ray, James P. Gill, John W. Lucas, James T. Atwood, J. Frank Wilson.

March 6, 1914:
The Governor has appointed George B. Remsburg a Justice of the Peace for the Poolesville district.

Cont'd. on next page.

March 6, 1914, cont'd:

The engagement is announced of Miss Lillian C. Miller and Lieut. Gordon Whiting MacLane. The wedding will be in June.

Miss Alice M. White and William Barnsley were married on Wednesday of last week.

The County Commissioners have appointed the following named assessors:   Z. McC. Waters Jr., W. W. Pyles, Alfred Ray, Philip H. Ray, J. F. Whalen, Leonard Weer Jr., John E. Clagett, Millard C. Fisher, Wm. T. Lynch, F. D. Stubbs.

Jacob Rubel died at Boyds on Wednesday of last week.

Richard H. Bowman died March 5th, at the home of his son, J. Darby Bowman, Rockville. Death was attributed to typhoid pneumonia.

Directors as follows were elected by the stockholders of the Montgomery Mutual Loan Association:   F M. Webster, Eugene Jones, Herbert Wright, H. O. Trowbridge, B. H. Warner Jr., Parker L. Weller, Albert S. Gatley, W. D. Nicholls, A. S. Dalton. Mr. Webster was elected President; Mr. Jones, Vice president; Mr. Gatley, Treasurer; Mr. Trowbridge, assistant treasurer; Mr. Dalton, secretary and manager; and Mr. Proctor, attorney.

A picture of Miss Frances E. Willard was presented to Gaithersburg High School by Mrs. Granville Farquhar, President of the Montgomery County W. C. T. U. Others mentioned are Frank Severance and Dorothy Haddox.

The citizens of Rockville, at a mass meeting, have decided to install a sewer treatment system. The Town Council is authorized to make the necessary plans so that an estimate of cost can be obtained.

March 13, 1914:

E. D. Warfield has been appointed assessor for the second district; N. C. Rice has been named assessor for the sixth district; and Noah Watkins will be the assessor for the twelfth district.

Winfred E. Berry has been appointed postmaster of Rockville.

Col. Edward Haywood died last Monday at his home near Washington Grove.

The following previously drawn jurors have been excused: Conrad Maught, Jos. Bond, Samuel B. Wetherald, John W. Lucas. Their places will be taken by Wm. E. Selby, Hazel W. Cashell, Reuben T. Baker, and Thos. B. Brooks.

Cont'd. on next page.

March 13, 1914, cont'd:
The resignations of Miss Elizabeth Knight and Miss Ella B. Brown has been received and accepted by the School Commissioners. Alexander L. McMillan has resigned as trustee of the school at Garrett Park.
Lemuel Clement Offutt, son of Mayor [of Rockville] and Mrs. Lee Offutt, died last Monday of typhoid fever.
Prof. Thomas Story died March 5th at his home in Barnesville.
The citizen's committee report concerning the sanitary conditions in Rockville was published. The committee members signing the report were Charles W. Prettyman, O. M. Linthicum, C. H. Mannar, Robert B. Peter, Richard H. Stokes, W. W. Welsh, and Martin Heim.
Ida C. Atwood, who died March 10, 1913, was remembered.

March 20, 1914:
Walter Fawcett has been appointed dog-tax collector for the Colesville district.
Hezekiah Morgan, of near Bethesda, died on Thursday of last week, in a hospital in Washington.
George V. Crouse, of Gaithersburg, died on Thursday of last week. Death was attributed to pneumonia.
It is announced that Miss Elizabeth Sommerville Wilson and E. Brooke Lee will marry on April 13th.
Thomas Waters of S., a native of Montgomery County, died on Thursday of last week.

March 27, 1914:
The engagement of Miss Emma Marie Schafer, of Washington, and Claude Worthington Owen, is announced.
It is announced that Miss Margaret Waters and Smith Allnutt will be married March 28th at the home of the parents of the bride, in Spencerville.
Miss Minnie May Gray and Roland Page, both of Travilah, were married in Potomac – no date stated.
Mr. & Mrs. Emory E. Mullinix, of the Damascus area, celebrated their 15th wedding anniversary a few days ago.
Miss Edna C. Clagett and Roy I. Marth were married on Wednesday.

Cont'd. on next page.

March 27, 1914, cont'd:

Rev. Thomas S. Childs died last Saturday at his home in Chevy Chase.

George A. Selby died suddenly last Monday at his home in Glen.

It is announced that Miss Ethel Warthen will marry Carroll F. Duvall on April 8th next.

Miss Elsie Cunningham and Elden Hartshorne will marry April 14th.

Miss Lydia Norris and George R. Buck will marry in the latter part of April.

A roster of the members of Company D, White's Battalion, was published.

April 3, 1914:

Luther F. Johnson, of Comus, and Miss Marian E. Holland, of Washington, were married on Monday, in Rockville.

Herman Kenney and Miss Edna May Thompson, both of Germantown, were married last Friday in Rockville.

Miss Margaret E. Waters and Smith Allnutt were married last Saturday, at the home of the bride.

Mrs. Martha A. Beard, widow of Henry Beard, died on last Saturday at her home in Washington. She was a resident of the Rockville vicinity for a number of years.

Herbert Bennett, son of Titus Bennett of Clarksburg, died on Wednesday of last week.

Reuben A. Burriss died on Thursday of last week at his home near Gaithersburg.

Lester B. Funk, of Barnesville, was killed last Saturday when he was hit by a train.

Alexander Wilson, of Gaithersburg, died on Thursday of last week at his home

April 10, 1914:

Judge [Edward] Peter has appointed Robert L. Warfield an examiner in chancery.

A. H. Osmond has been appointed Constable and dog-tax collector for the Darnestown district.

Cont'd. on next page.

April 10, 1914, cont'd:

James Moody Ray, of Oakdale, and Miss Beatrice Rebecca Bowman, of Norbeck, were married on Wednesday of last week, in Rockville.

M. Donaldson Knight has been re-elected county road superintendent, to serve for the next 4 years.

Wm. J. Williams has declined to be appointed a School Commissioner to succeed Milford Offutt, and the Governor has appointed Dr. John Gardiner, of Clarksburg, in his place.

Charles H. Creamer, of near Potomac, died on Thursday of last week at his home.

Charles F. Elgin, of the Poolesville district, died last Sunday.

At the annual election of the Cropley Presbyterian Church, the following officers were elected: Trustees: Levi Hill, W. H. Bolton, P. E. Redden, Odie Lynch, C. F. Bodine, A. F. Hill, G. E. Ricketts; Treasurer, Miss Dora V. Redden; Sunday School Superintendent, Miss I. R. Redden; Assistant superintendent, Mrs. W. H. Bolton; Secretary, Mrs. Arthur F. Hill; Teachers, Mrs. T. Bissett, Mrs. G. E. Ricketts, Mrs. Joshua Lynch; Organist, Miss Dora V. Redden; Flower committee, Mrs. S. R. Pennefill; Ushers, Russell Redden, Walter Schley, Herbert Redden; Mite Society, Mrs. I. R. Redden, Superintendent, Levi Hill, assistant; Secretary, Mrs. Oscar Hill; Treasurer, Mrs. A. F. Hill; Deaconesses, Mrs. Pennifill, Mrs. Redden, Miss Redden.

At the annual election of officers of the Hermon Presbyterian Church, the following were elected: Trustees, F. P. Stone, J. M. Harrison, J. P. Vaughn, W. E. Hamilton, W. B. Myers, L. W. Moore; Treasurer, F. P. Stone; Deaconesses, Miss Margaret Harrison, Mrs. Arthur Myers, Miss Betty Tschiffely, Mrs. P. E. Redden, Mrs. Susan Harper, Mrs. Emma Stearn, Mrs. Frank Embrey, Mrs. Alice Kinney, Mrs. E. E. Crockett, Mrs. F. P. Stone, Mrs. R. W. Stone; Sunday School Superintendent, Mrs. F. P. Stone; Mrs. Stearn, assistant; Teachers, Mrs. Stone, Mrs. Kinney, Mrs. Stearn; Music, Miss Carlisle, Miss Collins, Mrs. Stone, Mrs. Stearn, D. Stone, E. Stearn, H. Saunders, L. Kinney, C. Brown.

April 17, 1914:

Delegate A. J. Cummings, of this County, has been selected

Cont'd. on next page.

April 17, 1914, cont'd:
to be one of the Maryland representatives at the California exposition which will be held next year.

George E. Darby, father of Herbert S. Darby and J. Gardiner Darby of Rockville, died on Wednesday.

Walter Fawcett has resigned as constable of the Colesville district, and Harry Easton has been appointed in his place. The Commissioners have also appointed Wm. S. Tyler a constable for the Wheaton district.

The Governor has pardoned Nicholas D. Offutt, Jr. after Mr. Offutt has served 5 years of an 18 year sentence.

The board of directors of the Montgomery County Agricultural Society met last Tuesday, and made the following appointments: J. C. Dorsey to be chief marshall; Artemus Sullivan to be chief of police; Charles C. Waters to be advisory director for the $2^{nd}$. election district, replacing Perrie E. Waters; Joseph H. Bradley to be advisory director for the $4^{th}$. election district; Dawson Trundle to be advisory director for the $6^{th}$ district; John G. Stone to be advisory director for the $10^{th}$ district, replacing Wm. K. Jones; O. H. P. Clark, Jr., to be advisory director for the $13^{th}$. district; Hon. P. L. Goldsborough to be advisory director at large; Hon. David J. Lewis to be advisory director from Allegheny County; Hon. Edwin Warfield to be advisory director from Howard County. The Board also appointed Mrs. Josiah W. Jones, Mrs. Mary A. Greene, Miss Mary Waters, Mrs. Edward P. Schwartz, and Mrs. L. A. Darby, Jr. to revise the premium list of the household department. The Board also decided to abandon the horse show feature of the Fair. Other names mentioned are J. W. Jones, Francis Javins, Wm. H. Fawcett, William B. Trundle, Charles F. Kirk, John B. Diamond, Jr., Charles Veirs, J. W. Jones, Charles F. Kirk, C. W. Fields, D. H. Warfield, W. K. Jones, J. W. Jones, John J. Higgins, and James F. Bogley.

Miss Elizabeth Somerville Wilson and Mr. Brooke Lee were married last Monday, in the Trinity Episcopal Church at Upper Marlboro.

April 24, 1914:
Miss Bessie Warfield, daughter of Mr. & Mrs. Walter Warfield, of the Damascus vicinity, and Herbert Gosnell, of Baltimore, were married a few days ago in Frederick

Cont'd. on next page.

April 24, 1914, cont'd:
The large new stable of Dr. R. C. Warfield, Rockville, burned last Sunday. An auto stored in the building was saved.
Mr. Elden Bennett Hartshorne, of Kensington, and Miss Elsie Janet Cunningham were married - no date stated.
Miss Bernadine K. Gardiner, daughter of Mr. & Mrs. Bernard Gardiner of Clarksburg, and Oscar Leaman, of Washington, were married on Wednesday of last week at the home of the parents of the bride.
Miss Shirley Carter Mason and Alexander Fullerton Prescott, Jr. were married in Mt. St. Alban's Episcopal Church on last Wednesday.
Mrs. Mary Virginia Yellott, widow of Coleman Yellott, died April 19th.
Mr. W. Burns Trundle died suddenly last Sunday.
Mrs. Clarinda Beecher Hall, widow of Thomas Randolph Hall, died April 21st at her home in Poolesville.
Hanson H. Ricketts, who died April 1, 1914, was remembered.

May 1, 1914:
Charles H. Leizear and Mrs. Laura V. Talbott, of Burnt Mills, were married on last Saturday, in Rockville.
Mr. A. Henson Beane, of the Bethesda district, died on Wednesday of last week.
George Peter, son of Judge Peter, left yesterday to resume surveying for the government in the mountains of Virginia.
The marriage on January 16, 1914, of Ivy Bready and Dr. James B. Morrison, was announced.
Charles Kohlhoss died last Monday at his home in Poolesville.
Mrs. Caroline C. Griffith died at her home last Sunday.
Somerset O. Jones died on Wednesday at his home in Goshen.
The regular business meeting of the Waverly Literary Society of the Gaithersburg High School was held last Friday. The names mentioned are Donald Snyder, Marjorie Waters, Alverda Cooke, Annie Bottlemay, Anna Williams, Lloyd Riley, Lillian Hoyle.
At the annual meting of the Montgomery County Medical Association, officers as follows were elected: President, Dr. John L.
Cont'd. on next page.

May 1, 1914, cont'd:
Lewis; Vice president, Dr. Ernest L. Bullard; Secretary, Dr. C. H. Mannar. Others mentioned are Dr. Stuart B. Muncaster and Dr. Thos K. Conrad.

Oliver Pitt Watkins, a resident of Montgomery County, and a veteran of the Mexican war of 1846-48, reminisced about his experiences.

Prof. Thomas Story, who died March $5^{th}$, was remembered by a resolution of respect of the vestry of St. Peter's Parish, Poolesville.

May 8, 1914:

William A. Carter of the Rockville vicinity, and Miss Mary E. Howes, of near Gaithersburg, were married last Saturday.

The newly-elected mayor and council of Rockville have re-elected John J. Higgins as town clerk and treasurer, and Aaron R. Hewitt, bailiff.

Nicholas D. Offutt, Jr., and Miss Anna H. Bohrer were married last Saturday.

Mr. R. Wm. Vinson, druggist in Rockville, has installed a soda water fountain in his drug store which is unsurpassed by anything in Washington for beauty, cost, and modern style.

Mrs. Emma Virginia Curtis, widow of John M. Curtis, died on Thursday of last week.

It is announced that postmasters have been appointed as follows: in Bethesda, Henry J. Hunt; in Sandy Spring, Samuel B. Wetherald; in Linden, Enos C. Keys; in Kensington, Mrs. Alice I. Exley; in Cropley, Ida H. Bodine; in Ednor, John H. Cuff; in Germantown, Richard I. Waters, and in Poolesville, Arthur Fletchall.

George P. Ward, who was found in February nearly frozen to death, has recovered and has been released from Maryland General Hospital.

Dr. John Gardiner, and Charles T. Johnson, recently appointed as members of the board of County School Commissioners, have taken office. The new Board has elected Dr. Ryan Devereaux as President, Willis B. Burdette, county Superintendent of Schools, and Edwin W. Broome, assistant Superintendent. Thomas Dawson has been named Attorney, and Robert G. Hilton, Auditor.

At the stockholders meeting of the Farmers' Banking and
Cont'd. on next page.

May 8, 1914, cont'd:
Trust Company of Rockville, directors as follows were chosen: Samuel L. Phillips, John Joy Edson, Edward C. Peter, Harry Griffith, J. Dawson Williams, John W. Walker, Horace D. Waters, Jas. E. Deets, Robert G. Hilton, Wm. W. Welsh, Wm. W. Darby, Albert M. Bouic, and Arthur Peter. Others mentioned are Roland Wootton, John J. Higgins, and F. Bache Abert.

    Mrs. Charles G. Griffith was remembered in a resolution of respect passed by the Aid Society of the M. E. Church South of Poolesville.

    In the recent election of the town of Rockville, Lee Offutt was re-elected Mayor, Jos. L. Clagett and Jacob Poss were re-elected; and Willis B. Burdette and Edwin S. Hege were elected councilmen.

    In Kensington, Edgar W. Moore was elected Mayor, John T. Williams and John W. Saxon were elected Councilmen.

    In Gaithersburg, Richard H. Miles was re-elected Mayor, and John W. Walker, A. F. Meem, Carson Ward, and J. C. Phoebus were re-elected Councilmen.

    In Takoma Park, Stephen W. Williams was re-elected Mayor, and L. R. Grabill, E. E. LaFetra and H. F. Taff were elected Councilmen.

    In Glen Echo, Wm. H. Roach was elected Mayor, and James D. Riley and Thomas Henley were elected Councilmen.

    In Barnesville, Arthur L. Jones was elected Mayor, and Clagett C. Hilton and Charles R. Darby were elected Councilmen.

    In Poolesville, B. W. Walling, T. R. Hall, L. R. Cruitt, Howard W. Spurrier, and H. L. Willard were elected Commissioners.

May 15, 1914:
    Benjamin F. Sparrough, a native of Montgomery County, died last Sunday, in Washington.

    Southard P. Warner, U.S. consul at Harbin, Manchuria, died there last Saturday. He is a son of Mr. & Mrs. Brainard H. Warner.

    Richard Hawkins, age 14 years, has been committed to jail and charged with burning the home of W. M. Magruder at Goshen.

    The new Board of Elections, composed of Thomas Vinson, Maurice M. Browning, and Julian Griffith, has elected Mr. Vinson President, Thomas Dawson, attorney, and Carey Kingdon, clerk.

Cont'd. on next page.

May 15, 1914, cont'd:

Edgar W. Moore, the newly elected Mayor of Kensington, has appointed Dr. Wm. L. Lewis health officer, and Preston B. Ray town attorney. Mr. Ray succeeds J. Dawson Williams, who resigned. Dr Eugene Jones, Dr. T. A. Geddes and Alfred C. Warthan were named members of an advisory board created in accordance with a law authorizing a bond issue for the construction of a water and sewage treatment system for the town.

Mrs. Ella Anderson, widow of Thomas Anderson, died last Sunday. She had lived in Poolesville for most of her life.

May 22, 1914:

Gov. Goldsborough has commissioned Smith S. Putman and Nevis S. Burrier notaries public for Montgomery County.

Mrs. Lottye Ward Briggs, of Gaithersburg, has bought a Case roadster, which she intends to operate herself.

Henry Howard has been appointed postmaster at Brookeville, and Bessie Brake has been appointed postmaster at Washington Grove.

Principal Lewis R. Watson was re-elected by the trustees of the Rockville Academy to serve during the school year 1914-1915.

William Columbus Bowman, a well known farmer of the Cedar Grove neighborhood, died suddenly a few days ago.

Arthur Williams has sold his mercantile business at Kensington, but will continue to reside there and superintend the operation of his farm near Dawsonville.

It is announced that J. Dawson Williams, of Montgomery County, and Miss Molly Z. Pessou were married on May 14th, in Mt. Pleasant, Tenn.

Miss Mary Scherrer, daughter of Wm. Scherrer of Montrose, and Garnett Koiner were married last Saturday in Baltimore.

Gen Jacob Coxey and an 'army' of 7 members passed through Rockville last Tuesday on their way to Washington.

May 29, 1914:

Miss Isabel Burroughs and William Brown Nicholson were married on Thursday of last week, in Rockville.

Miss Bessie Banks Woodward and Oliver M. Duvall were married last Friday, in Spencerville.

Cont'd. on next page.

May 29, 1914, cont'd:
   Mrs. Eliza Earley Lindsey, wife of Dr. John H. Lindsey and daughter of Capt. and Mrs. James Anderson of Rockville, died last Tuesday at her home in Falls River, Mass. See also June 5, 1914.
   A chamber of commerce has been organized in Kensington. The names mentioned are Cornelius W. Clum, Eugene Jones, Merritt O. Chance, Charles R. Rowdybush, George Peter, Brainard H. Warner, Jr., Wm. L. Lewis, J. Phillip Herrman, Lewis Knapp, Wm. P. Hay, Ralph H. Chappell, H. O. Trowbridge, Wm. M. Terrell, and W. H. Ronsaville.
   'Education Day' was held in Rockville on May 22. Among the names mentioned are A. Dawson Williams, William F. Prettyman, Berry E. Clark, E. S. Prescott, Guy Neel, Jonathan J. Baker, Wightman Smith, Paul Twomby, Edgar Harbaugh Logan, Claude W. Owen, Clifford Robertson, Robert Warfield., Mrs. Stella Thomas, Miss Mary Welsh, Miss Marie Boadman, and Miss Helen Schwartz.
   Geo. S. Mills has been committed to jail, charged with killing C. Edward Lowe. Both men are residents of the Derwood area.

June 5, 1914:
   St. John's Episcopal Church, near Bethesda, burned completely last Friday. The fire is thought to have been caused by defective wiring.
   Miss Mildred Esther Allison, daughter of Mr. & Mrs. Horatio C. Allison of Bethesda, and Hugh Granville Myers, of Park Lane, Va., were married – no date stated - in Rockville.
   The graduation exercises of the Brookeville High School will be held this evening, June 5th. The graduates will be Bertha Virginia Brown, Mildred Augusta Kemp, Isabel Edward Brian, Daisy Cornelia Higgins, Martha Lavinia Leishear, Alice Dorsey Owings, Helen Louise Higgins, and Roland Brewer Easton.
   The Rockville High School commencement was held last night. The names mentioned are Rev. John R. Henderson, Frank D. Day, E. Stedman Prescott, Charles W. Prettyman, W. B. Burdette, Mary Margaret Karn, Harriet Elizabeth Higgins, Annie Elizabeth Dawson, Glenna Elizabeth Fisher, Avice L. Rabbitt, Margaret Early Houck, Ellen Patton Offutt, Louise Frizzell, Edward S. Prescott, and Franklin D. Day.

June 12, 1914:
Miss Geneva Walters, daughter of Prof. Julian F. Walters, head of the Brookeville High School, graduated at Maryland State Normal school on Thursday.

The barn on the farm of Benjamin Kelly near Burnt Mils, was struck by lightning on Thursday, and burned completely.

Mrs. Eliza Ellen Warfield, widow of Caleb N. Warfield, died at the home of her daughter, Mrs. Charles E. Dwyer. No date.

June 19, 1914:
During the severe windstorm of Wednesday of last week, the barn on the farm of Titus W. Day was blown down, and 4 cows were killed.

Jas. O. Cubitt, a resident of near Barnesville, died on Thursday of last week.

Miss Flora Margaret Dill, of Olney, and Forrest Purdum Hall were married on Wednesday, in Rockville.

Mrs. Sarah E. Kisner, of Alta Vista, and Jacob Jacobson were married on Thursday of last week, in Rockville.

Clarence B. F. Carroll, of near Norwood, died by suicide on last Friday.

The annual closing exercises of the Rockville Academy were held last Wednesday. The graduates were Josephine Watson and Robert Peter. Others mentioned are Otis Hicks, Lewis Watson, John A. Garrett, Charles W. Prettyman, and Judge Edward C. Peter.

Flag Day was celebrated in Montgomery County by the Janet Montgomery chapter of the D.A.R. by planting small flags on the graves of the following named revolutionary soldiers and patriots: Maj. Nathan Musgrove, Dr. Richard Waters, Ignatius Waters, Maj. Richard Green, Sgt. Henry Leeke, Col. Richard Brooke, Dr. Thomas Sprigg Wootton, James Anderson, Gen. Jeremiah Crabb, Dr. Joseph Hall, Thomas Davis, Joseph Hall, Capt. Samuel Griffith, Henry Griffith, Maj. Philemon Griffith, Robert Doyne Dawson, Robert Willson, Rev. Townsend Dade, Nathan Talbott, Samuel Wade Magruder, Daniel Carroll, Maj. William Hempstone, Capt. Gleeson, William Larman, Allen Bowie, Henry Hilleary, and John Courts Jones.

Miss Lillian Cannon Miller, of Alta Vista, and Lieut. Gordon Whiting MacLane were married June 10$^{th}$, in Washington.

June 26, 1914:
Dennis Touhey has been appointed postmaster at Cabin John; and Wesley A. Maxwell has been appointed postmaster at Comus.

The residence of Carey Soper, near Potomac, was completely burned a few days ago.

Last Sunday a fire of unknown cause broke out in the store of John Welch, at Avery, and destroyed the building and the contents.

Michael J. Murphy, a lifelong resident of the Olney district, died last Sunday.

Miss Selena Wilson, daughter of Mr. & Mrs. Charles G. Wilson of Layhill, and Harry Theron Peters, of Washington, were married last Wednesday.

At a meeting of the School Commissioners, the following teacher appointments were announced: Estelle Ricketts, Lillian Bennett, Elizabeth Defandorf, to be assistants at Rockville High School; Ruby Robertson to be assistant at Montrose; Florence V. Corson to be assistant at Darnestown; Kate Frizzell to be assistant at Germantown; Landella Etchison to be assistant at Washington Grove. Resignations of J. F. Walters, Cecelia Kilgour, Frank Pearre, Helen L. Barnes, Emma Offutt, and Hadassah J. Moore were accepted.

Mrs. Elizabeth Peter, widow of William Thomas Peter, died last Saturday at her home near Bethesda.

Miss Belle Bond, of Baltimore, and William F. Prettyman, of Rockville, were married Tuesday.

Joseph Henderson died on Thursday of last week at his home near Germantown.

Miss Laura Annetta White and William Beattie Hammond were married on Thursday of last week.

Miss Florence A. Gering and Dr. Irving M. Cashell were married June 17$^{th}$.

Edward Lowe, who died May 224, 1914, was remembered.

July 3, 1914:
Mrs. Katherine Griffith, widow of Frank Griffith, died last Sunday. She was the daughter of the late Artemus Riggs.

The Court of Appeals has recently decided the Henry Bradley will case, which has been in the courts for nearly three years. The ruling means that the widow gets the entire estate.

Cont'd. on next page.

July 3, 1914, cont'd:

    Miss Nellie Josephine Miller, daughter of Mrs. Seth W. Griffith, of Brookeville, and Ernest Wiggins, of Washington, were married last Saturday, in Brookeville.

    The Governor has appointed J. Ezra Troth a Notary Public.

    Chairman Philip D. Laird has resigned from the Public Service Commission. The article traces his career.

July 10, 1914:

    The County Commissioners have organized themselves into the Montgomery County Drainage and Sewerage Commission, and have elected Richard T. White chairman, and Berry E. Clark secretary.

    Mr. L. S. Witherow has been elected assistant teacher at the Rockville Academy.

    Miss Sarah Veirs, daughter of the late S. Clark Veirs, died on Wednesday of last week at her home near Beane.

    An explosion of gasoline in an automobile started a fire which destroyed the barn on the farm of H. E. Sands, near Potomac.

    Mrs. Katie L. Schaeffer died last Tuesday. See July 17th.

    Henry H. Chick died Monday at his home near Potomac.

    Maj. Alexander Hunter died on Tuesday of last week at his home in Silver Spring. He was a member of Mosby's Rangers.

    Miss Margaret C. Ashbridge and Harvey H. Rabbitt were married on Thursday of last week, in Washington.

July 17, 1914:

    Thaddeus J. Maloney has been appointed postmaster at Brinklow.

    Mrs. Lillian F. Bardroff and Frank A. Weiner, both of the Glen Echo area, were married last Friday, in Rockville.

    Messrs. Watts Farmer and Clarence Hoskinson have bought the general merchandise store of T. M. Hoyle, at Derwood, and will conduct the business there in the future. [retracted –see July 24th]

    It is announced that Miss Mary Bertha Maus and John W. Cross will marry in September.

    It is announced that Miss Sarah Ray Wilson and Richard Laurence Waters will marry in the early fall.

    Certificates to teach have been issued to Laura Frizzell,

    Cont'd. on next page.

July 17, 1914, cont'd:
Margaret Karn, Frank Day, Mary White, and Chancellor Brown.
Scholarships as follows have been awarded: to State Normal School, Delma E. Sauder, Avice L. Rabbitt, Margaret Houck, Glenna E. Fisher, Elizabeth Dawson; to Western Maryland College, E. Ray Warfield; to Blue Ridge College, Carlton Burdette; to St. John's College, E. Otis Gardner.

The School Commissioners have appointed Dr. Wm. E. Pratt, Howard Fawcett, and Edward Atwood trustees of the new school near Potomac; Garrett Cooley and James B. Smith, trustees at Kingsley; George M. Kephart, trustee at Avery; Wm. L. Griffith, trustee at Etchison; John J. Burdette, trustee at Woodfield; Mrs. Frederick Keplinger, Rev. Jas. Kirkpatrick, and Dr. James T. Morris, trustees at Bethesda.

John Connell died on Thursday of last week.

Thomas Levin Magruder died on Tuesday of last week.

Dr. William F. Magruder died last Monday at his home near Olney.

The following named have been appointed school teachers: Lucy Hughes, Orpah Ashby, Nora J. Rabbitt, Derelle Kilpatrick, Helen Redden, Grace Watkins, Geneva Walters, Ida L. Isherwood, and Maude Carlisle. Resignations have been received from Clark F. Brown, and Anna Hurley.

Wilson B. Tschiffely died on Wednesday of last week at his home near Seneca.

Eugene H. Waters, of Germantown, has been appointed an examiner by the Interstate Commerce Commission.

Three buildings, memorials to Clara Barton, will be built in Glen Echo. Most of the money needed has already been raised.

The Supervisors of Election have appointed the following named to be doorkeepers in the coming elections: James H. Barber, Benjamin F. Allnutt, A. B. Thompson, Geo. W. Norwood, Roy L. Wright, Wm. T. Hoskinson, Wm. Skillman, Ulysses M. Ricketts, Michael Conroy, Edward V. Robey, Newton Stabler, Charles E. Lechlider, Weller Hammond, Chas. H. W. Pennyfield, Joshua E. Broadhurst, Daniel P. Morgan, Reimy Springirth, Charles E. Marlowe, John R. Boswell, Wm. O. Giddings, Geo. W. Nicholson, Carl T. Brown, Jacob Gartner, Gideon T. Briggs, Edward C. Ricketts, Levi Hill, Charles C. Orme, Chas. F. Holland, Darius F. Watkins,

Cont'd. on next page.

July 17, 1914, cont'd:
Nicholas E. Burns, N. M. Howes, Wm. T. Gray, Frank VanNess, John E. Thompson.
  Charles N. L. Howes, who died July 13, 1911, was remembered by his parents.

July 24, 1914:
  Mrs. Tavie Anderson, wife of James Anderson, formerly of Rockville, died last Sunday in Shreveport, La.
  Mary Louise Parsly and Dr. Ernest Clyde Fishbaugh were married July 16$^{th}$, at the home of the bride's parents, in Brookeville.
  The *Sentinel* printed a speech by Senator John Walter Smith describing the events leading to the bombardment of Ft. McHenry and the writing of the Star Spangled Banner.

July 31, 1914:
  Mr. E. Lloyd Fawcett has been appointed supervisor of assessments for Montgomery County.
  The explosion of a coal oil stove on Monday, in the home of John Burriss, in Gaithersburg, started a fire which resulted in the complete loss of the house and contents.
  Wm. J. Corrick, of Kensington, and Miss Gertrude Prinz, of Washington, were married last week.
  Wm. O. Reid, of the vicinity of Boyds, died on Tuesday.
  Hardy S. Cissell died last Tuesday.
  Frank S. Duff died on Friday of last week.
  Miss Blanche Fawcett has transferred as principal of the school at Colesville and is now principal of the school at Burtonsville; and Miss Effie Ternant has been appointed principal of the grammar school at Hyattstown.
  Mrs. Hatttie Miller, a native of Montgomery County, widow of Rev. John Miller, died Tuesday.
  John T. Kelley died on Thursday of last week at his home near Darnestown.

August 7, 1914:
  Miss Mary Elizabeth Beall and George W. Pennifield, both of the Travilah area, were married on Thursday of last week.
  A family reunion was held last Sunday at the home of Mr.
           Cont'd. on next page.

August 7, 1914, cont'd:
Franklin Mace to celebrate his 83$^{rd}$. birthday. The names mentioned are Mr. & Mrs. Frank Mace, Mr. & Mrs. Samuel Mace, Mr. & Mrs. William G. Counselman, Mr. & Mrs. Winifred Berry, Charles R. Mace, Arthur M. Mace, Miss Doree G. Holland, and James D. Holman.

Mr. Alexander A. Gassaway died last Sunday at his home near Darnestown. He was 58 years old.

The Montgomery County Sunday School convention was held last week in Washington Grove. The names mentioned are E. Wilson Walker, Columbus W. Day, Isabel Kingdon, Jos. Reading, Bessie Woodward, Mrs. Preston L. Snyder, Warren Choate, Mrs. Eliza Crawford, Rev. O. C. Barnes, Amanda Wilson, and J. B. Ely.

Judges have been named to act in the coming Fair. Those from Montgomery County are Wm. T. Griffith, Miss Mary Darby, Mrs. C. C. Waters, Mrs. Clarence Gilpin, Hon. E. C. Peter, and Mrs. Wm. H. Holmes.

The first annual dance under the auspices of Co. K., Md. Nat. Guard, will be held August 12, at the new armory in Silver Spring. The names mentioned are Brooke Lee, Frank L. Hewitt, Basil Boykin, H. F. O'Donnell, Cliff Howes, W. H. Fidler, Gerald Warthan, Oscar McKay, Paul Clark, Mrs. Ben Ray, Mrs. Ormsby McCammon, Mrs. George Chandler, Mrs. Wm. T. Brown, Mrs. Enos Keys, Mrs. William Wimsatt, Preston Ray, Dawson Williams, Rust Canby, George Bonifant, Ben Ray, Enos Ray, Robert Hilton, B. H. Warner, Jr., B. F. Clark, Ormsby McCammon, Arthur Peter, Alexander Carlisle, Clinton Allnutt, Norman Bouic, Albert M. Bouic, Peyton Whalen, George Bradley, J. Bond Smith, Frank Birgfeld, Dr. Wright, Rev. George W. McGrew, B. R. Gammon, W. A. Kingsbury, J. E. Benedict, G. H. Holmes, Edson Olds, Joseph Childs, Rev. C. O. Rosensteel, William Matthews, Allen Farquhar, Samuel Thomas, J. H. Cissel, Ira C. Whitacre, Mark Stearman, R. E. Yellott, Harry Martin, W. P. Wilson, T. S. Gaddes, W. Currtis, E. W. Byrn, C. W. Clum, Charles Wright, Ray Wright, Charles McKenny, R. W. Rapley, J. Enos Ray, Hampton Magruder, Capt. O. Y. Gregor, Robert Wells, Frank Blunden, William Holmead, George Mullen, Homer Guerry, A. J. Corry, Frank Fidler, Judge. J. L. H. Sawyer, C. A. Burns, Jack F. Moss, P. H. Gormley, James Patterson, Perry Patterson, Woodbury Blair, H. H. Buck, Douglas Blandford, Dr.

Cont'd. on next page.

August 7, 1914, cont'd:
Israel Warfield, Edward Aytono, Fred. L. Thomas, Eugene Waters, A. J. Cummings, Blair Lee, W. B. Jackson, W. S. Sheets, S. W. Waters, C. W. Fairfax, B. F. Myers, W. F. Columbus, Arthur Thall, Theo. Rover, Walter Plant, Frank B. Myers, Dr. S. Ren Howard, Montgomery Blair, and W. H. Rapley.

    The annual picnic and tournament of St. John's Catholic Church at Forest Glen was held on Wednesday of last week. It was attended by several thousand people, and there were 15 riders. The names mentioned are Douglas M. Blandford, Wm. Rapley, Robert Wimsatt, James E. Kemp, John N. Kelly, Theodore Freeman, Brainard H. Warner, Jr., Philip Love, A. D. Langley, Wm. Aitcheson, J. L. Aitcheson, and Miss Gertrude Ellis.

August 14, 1914:
    At the Howard County horse show held last Saturday Wallace Ricketts, of Rockville, won first prize for the fine performance of his saddle horse, ridden by Miss Alice Cashell.

    Dr. Israel Warfield has been appointed to a position at the Customs House, Georgetown; and W. Frank Gaither has been made a deputy U. S. Marshall.

    Lightning set fire to the barns on the farms of James Moxley and Tobias Watkins recently, and both buildings and their contents were lost.

    The Social Service League will station members in the rest rooms at the coming Fair. The names mentioned are Mrs. Helen Gassaway, Mrs. Henry J. Finley, Mrs. O. H. Tibbott, Mrs. J. Frank Wilson, Mrs. U. D. Nourse, Mrs. Horace B. Haddox, Mrs. James H. Giddings, Mrs. Bernadine Means, Mrs. R. E. L. Smith, Mrs. John B. Brewer, Mrs. John J. Higgins, Mrs. Mary J. Spencer, Mrs. Wallace W. Welsh, Mrs. Robert W. Lyddane, Miss Caroline Henderson, Miss Isabel Kingdon, and Miss Ida S. Dove.

    Mrs. Laura Victoria Ward, widow of Henry C. Ward, died last Sunday.

    The annual meeting of the Anti-Saloon League was held last week in Washington Grove. The following are mentioned: Rev. Oscar W. Henderson, Thomas J. Owen, Miss Isabel Kingdon, Rev. J. E. Fort, J. Wesley Boyer, Howard G. Spurrier, W. E. Ward, Reuben T. Baker, Newton C. Rice, Albert E. Shoemaker, Mordecai T. Fussell.

    Cont'd. on next page.

August 14, 1914, cont'd:
E. Wilson Walker, W. W. Hodges, Max Wenner, W. W. Hodges, Columbus W. Day, Charles G. Wilson, Mrs. Sarah T. Miller, Caleb C. Lawson, Willis B. Burdette, J. Henning Purdum, R. Bentley Thomas, and Frank Higgins.

August 21, 1914:
The Governor has commissioned A. W. Simmonds as forest warden for Montgomery County.

The engagement of Miss Ray Wilson, of Kensington, and Richard L. Waters, of Germantown, was celebrated at a party given by Miss Helena Webster, in Kensington.

Trujean Aud has been appointed a division Deputy Collector of internal revenue at Washington.

The barn on the farm of brothers John and Charles Javins, near Colesville, was destroyed by fire on Thursday of last week.

Mr. A. O. Appleby, a well known wheelwright, died suddenly last Saturday at his shop near Germantown.

Residents of Montgomery County who won prizes at the recent Colesville Horse and Colt show are Miss E. Johnson, Wallace E. Ricketts, William Matthews, William W. Moore, Jr., Florence Hogg, Mrs. W. Sheetz, Alexander G. Carlisle, James Daniels, William T. Brown, John H. Ray, Mary R. Bradley, William T. Brown, F. W. Kruhm, Joseph H. Bradley, George G. Getty, Betty Ray, Lucy Newcomb, Spencer Windham, Maurice E. Cissel, Mrs. F. D. Frey, Albert Stabler, Eli Bready, Donald Kirk, George F. Bonifant, Robert H. Miller, Thomas A. Barnesly, R. G. Bliss, Charles C. Jones, Hugh O'Donnell. S. J. Cochran, and Elgar Stabler.

Marian Estella Boyd, daughter of Mr. & Mrs. J. Allen Boyd, of Lancaster Co., Pennsylvania, and Thomas Trundle Graff, of Derwood, were married August 12, at the home of the bride's parents.

An item concerning the Montgomery County Fair contains an extensive comment regarding 'Pleasant Fields', the farm and home of Charles C. Waters on the Frederick road about 3 miles north of Germantown.

August 28, 1914:
Frank E. Huffman, son of Mr. & Mrs. John W. Huffman, died last Saturday, of typhoid.

Cont'd. on next page.

August 28, 1914, cont'd:

    Messrs. Charles G. Griffith, Charles J. Lyddane, M. Wilson Offutt, John R. Lewis, and Horace D. Waters have filed certificates of their candidacy to be delegates to the Democratic state convention.

    The following have been selected to be delegates to the Republican state convention: Charles F. Kirk, Thomas Dawson, Arthur M. Mace, John W. Lynch, and Galen L. Tait.

    Albert I. Hall, of Rockville, died last Sunday.

    Leonard G. Pearce, age 18 years, and Miss Edna Estelle Watkins, age 17 years, were married last Friday.

    Richard Pyles, of the Bethesda district, committed suicide last Saturday.

    Samuel Elsworth Stewart died on August $18^{th}$.

    The barn with all contents, on the farm of Edward Beall, near Derwood, burned completely on last Monday, after having been set afire by lightning.

    Horace Young was shot and killed by Jacob Gue last Wednesday. The men were neighbors in the Damascus area, and had argued about Mr. Gue failing to vacate a property which he had been renting from Mr. Young. See also Sept. $4^{th}$. and November $27^{th}$.

    Miss Anna Hartshorne and Carroll T. Brown were married last Saturday at 'Hill Crest', the home of the parents of the bride, near Brighton.

September 4, 1914:

    Prof. William Nicholson has resigned as principal of the high school at Darnestown, and T. W. Darnell has been appointed to fill the vacancy.

    William H. Wade, of near Cabin John, died on last Tuesday at his home.

    B. H. Warner, Jr., has withdrawn from the race for the Republican nomination to Congress from the $6^{th}$ district.

    Marie Ward, age 17, of Rockville, and Smith Linthicum, of Gaithersburg, eloped to Washington on Thursday of last week and were married there, while her parents were attending the Fair.

    The annual Fair, recently concluded, was marred by inclement weather, and has resulted in a financial loss to the Society. The following named were awarded premiums:

    Pure bred Durhams, Benton G. Ray

                             Cont'd. on next page.

September 4, 1914, cont'd:
    Holsteins: J. B. Diamond, Jr., W. F. Ricketts, Charles Veirs.
    Jerseys: B. F. Saul, H. L. Diamond.
    Guernseys: F. H. Cashell, Harry Beard, H. C. Hurley.
    Ayrshires: F. H. Cashell.
    Local grades: H. C. Hurley, Chas. Veirs, W. F. Ricketts.
    Hogs – Berkshires: O. B. Williams, F. C. Hutton.
    Large Yorkshires: D. W. Shaub.
    Duroc-Jerseys: D. W. Shaub.
    Essex: D. W. Shaub.
    Small Yorkshires: D. W. Shaub.
    Victorias: D. W. Shaub.
    Suffolk: D. W. Shaub.
    Mixed breed: J. W. Graff, D. W. Shaub, Thomas Graff.
    Sheep – Shropshire: B. F. Saul.
    Southdown: H. B. Witter.
    Oxford Down: H. B. Witter, F. H. Cashell.
    Hampshire Down: F. H. Cashell.
    Cheviot: H. B. Witter.
    Mixed breed: F. H. Cashell.
    Farm products: Mrs. Minnie Wagner, Jos. E. Janney, T. A. Barnesley, J. R. Lechlider, George Shaw, Hal. Dawson, Seth W. Warfield. L. M. Muncaster, John E. Muncaster, G. Nicholson, Charles F. Johnson, J. M. Etchison, R. P. Hines.
    Garden products: Emma T. Stabler, Frank Cashell, J. R. Lechlider, Mrs. Bernard Poss, Ellen Farquhar, Seth Warfield, Jos. E. Janney, J. W. Barnesley, R. P. Hines, Jr.
    Garden products #2 A. E. Burriss, R. P. Hines Jr., Ellen Farquhar, Mrs. Minnie Wagner, T. A. Barnesley, Joseph Reading, D. H. Horner, N. P. Hines, B.C. Hughes, Brownell Riggs, Seth Warfield, Emma T. Stabler, Richard Torpin, Helen Riggs, J. R. Lechlider, Jacob Poss, Frank Cashell, J. C. Bean.
    Culinary: Rose Wagner, Bertha Hughes, Mrs. W. U. Bowman, Mrs. Seth W. Warfield, Ellen Farquhar, Emma T. Stabler, Mary M. Stabler, Louise Larcombe, Mrs. Anna Welsh, Mrs. C. F. Brooke, Miss A. W. McFarland, Mrs. Frank Higgins, Marie Ward, Mabel C. Ward, Mrs. W. E. Ricketts, Mrs. J. C. Bean, Mrs. G. H. Lamar, Ada Warfield, Mrs. Albert P. Beall, Lelia Morrison, Mrs. Albert Johnson, E. C. Hull, Miss I. Wagner, Marion B. Shorts,
                                          Cont'd. on next page.

September 4, 1914, cont'd:
Dorothy Brooke, Ellen Brewer, Edith E. Hull, Mrs. L. R. Bowman, Mrs. S. A. Clagett, Mrs. A. C. Warthen, Mrs. J. Darby Bowman, Mrs. Edwin W. Monday, Mrs. Geo. C. Fry, Lizzie Pumphrey, Hanna B. Stabler, Mrs. C. L. Hickerson, Mary Welsh.

 Hams: Mrs. J. W.Barnesley, Joseph Janney.

 Butter: R. P. Hines, Eva Burriss.

 Honey: W. J. Hoyle.

 Preserves, canned fruit, jellies: Mrs. Wallace E. Ricketts, Mrs. Albert B. Beall, Mrs. C. T. Johnson, Mrs. George P. Henderson, Edmonia Gardiner, Mrs. Roger Shaw, Josie Higgins, Mrs. W. E. Bowman, Mrs. C. S. Duvall. Mrs. C. C. Johnson, Marion B. Shorts, Mrs. J. W. Barnesley, Miss A. V. McFarland, Edgar Higgins, Mrs. A. H. Ward, Edith E. Hull, Anna Hurley, Sally Hill, Jennie Higgins, Harry Davis, Mrs. J. H. Ward, Adele Maus, Mrs. G. W. Davis, Mrs. Emma Sullivan, Emma Johnson, Mrs. James P. Brown, Mrs. Samuel Leizear, Mrs. A. T. Hull.

 Fruits: Pearl Cashell, Richard Torpin, R. P. Hines, Mrs. Thomas Waters, Mrs. A. P. Beall, A. W. Stonestreet, Seth Warfield, Donald Bowie, Mrs. W. U. Bowman, Mrs. T. T. Barnsley, R. B. Thomas, Mrs. Willis Moore, H. E. Stratmyer, Alice Binder, Margaret Welsh, Mrs. B. C. Hughes, Margaret Plummer, Mrs. T. A. Barnsley, J. R. Lechlider, H. C. Williams, Thomas Waters, Claudia Robertson.

 Works of art: Emma T. Stabler, Miss M. F. Moran, Rose Wagner, Miss L. L. Dodge, Mrs. Russell Brewer, Edmonia Gardiner, Mrs. C. A. Spates, Anna Yearley, L. R. Hall, Mrs. Donald Bowie, M. Brown, Miss Pumphrey, W. S. Ward, J. Darby Bowman, Letha Edwards.

 Domestic manufacture: Bertha Hall Talbott, E. Winslow, Mrs. Jas. T. Bogley, Josie Higgins, Marion B. Shorts, Mrs. C. O. Bean, Mary B. Stabler, Mrs. Wm. Reading, Marie Talbott, E. S. Slaymaker, Mrs. T. R. Hall, Elizabeth Higgins, Mrs. Rebecca Scherrer, Mrs. Roger Shaw, Mary Almoney, Mrs. A. C. Schirer, Lillian Fields, Mrs. A. P. Beall, Mrs. Wm. B. Trundle, Wilhelmina Heitmuller, Mrs. J. S. Gruver, Mrs. L. Burch, Edith E. Hull, Ida S. Dove, Julia Anderson, Mrs. Lloyd Brewer, Mrs. E. W. Monday, Mrs. A. R. Speare, Katherine Poole, Lucile Priest, Mrs. George L. Banes, Mrs. S. B. Hege, Mrs. Thos. Hoskinson, Mrs. Ada Thompson, Mrs. Thos. R. Hall, Mabel Ward, Elizabeth Keys, Sophia Higgins, Mrs. E.

           Cont'd. on next page.

September 4, 1914, cont'd:
W. Cissel, Helen Pumphrey, Mrs. Lila Dodge Goldsborough, Mrs. C. T. Johnson, Mrs. M. E. McGregor, Mrs. Lawrence Flack, Daisy Magruder, Alton Beall, Mrs. S. F. Slaymaker, Miss M. S. Poole, Maddie Saxton.

Children's department: Matilda Prescott, Isabelle Stabler, Helen Gruver, Annie May Shorts, Helen Gardiner, Fannie Oldfield, Margaret B. Shorts, Mildred Morrison, Palmer Beall, Stonestreet Lamar, Heath D. Goldsborough, J. S. Moulden, Margaret Howser, Elizabeth Darby, Gertrude Hines, Gertrude Veirs, Miriam Johnson, Mary Reading.

Children's garden products: Charles F. Hines, Lillian Morrison, John W. Warfield, Hazel C. Burroughs, H. B. Witter, John E. Muncaster, Jr., J. A. Higgins, Wm. Morrison.

Display of vegetables: Charles F. Hines, J E. Muncaster, Jr.

Chickens: There were prizes awarded for many different breeds of chickens. The winners, all breeds included, were as follows: Mrs. Norman Bouic, A. E. Burriss & Sons, George C. Gorsuch, J. H. Shorts, Wm. S. Becker, Dr. C. N. Etchison, Enoch G. Johnson, Mrs. R. P. Hines, J. F. Defandorf, Pine Groves Poultry Farm, R. E. Lee, J. M. Heagy, E. W. Monday, Lewis R. Watson, R. C. Drum-Hunt, S. E. Ferran, Henry Hunt, R. D. Lilly, Reuben P. Hines, Jr., J. C. Heitmuller, D. P. Smith, Enoch G. Johnson, C. Norman Bouic, O. F. Hicks, Jos. Dawson, Wm. L. Gates, W. V. Wilson.

Flowers: Mrs. W. R. Lyddane, Ellen Farquhar, Mrs. W. E. Ricketts, Mrs. H. Beard, Mary Hurley, Mrs. Thomas Waters, Mrs. Kate Umstead, Mrs. A. C. Warthen, Ada Warfield, Mrs. S. A. Clagett, Estelle Ricketts, Wm. H. Talbott, Mrs. Albert P. Beall, Margaret Welsh.

Heavy draft Percherons: Trundle Bros.

Heavy draft horses: J. B. Matthews, W. K. Jones, C. M. Williams, Trundle Bros., A. D. Trundle, C. T. Nicholson, D. B. Diamond, B. F. Saul.

Jacks: Geo. Mills.

Teams: Trundle Bros., Rich'd. Lansdale, W. E. Wilt, C. T. Nicholson, W. E. Ricketts, Wallace Cashell.

Thoroughbred horses: F. C. Hutton.

Saddle horses: J. W. Barnsley, F. M. Hallowell, C. T.

Cont'd. on next page.

September 4, 1914, cont'd:
Nicholson, W. E. Ricketts, Wallace Cashell.
   Standardbred horses: F. H. Cashell, Javins Bros., O. T. Stonestreet.
   Quick draft horses: O. T. Stonestreet, Geo. E. Nicholson, Cecil Allnutt, J. S. Bolton, D. W. Clark, F. C. Hutton, H. L. Diamond, C. T. Nicholson.
   Teamster's prize: Tobias Holland.
   Ponies: Rosemont Farm, Josephine Esputa, Alton Bean.
   Miss Lavinia Gassaway Dawson and John H. Henderson were married September $2^{nd}$, in Rockville.

September 11, 1914:
   Misses Edmonia Gardner and Marie Gardner have left for Canada to pursue their studies at Loretta Academy, Niagara Falls, Ontario.
   John B. Diamond has started the construction of a flour mill in Gaithersburg.
   Miss Myrtle M. Sponseller and Robert L. Murphy were married last Friday.
   Miss Fannie Virginia Flore, daughter of Mr. & Mrs. Frederick Flore, of Howard County, and John T. Thompson, of Ednor, Montgomery County, were married last Saturday in Olney.
   James M. W. Briggs died last Saturday at his home near Gaithersburg.
   Benjamin C. Hughes and George E. Wheatley have been commissioned forest wardens for Montgomery County.
   Jack Bentley, pitching for the Nationals, was the object of commendation by the Washington Star, reprinted by the *Sentinel*.
   Rachel Mullican, who died August 29, 1913, was remembered by her daughter.
   Kate V. Howes, who died September 14, 1908, was remembered.

September 18, 1914:
   Miss Isabel Bissett, daughter of David Bissett of Garrett Park, has been appointed to a scholarship in the State Normal School, and Frank R. Griffith, son of Artemus Griffith of Unity, has been appointed to a scholarship at St. John's College.
                              Cont'd. on next page.

September 18, 1914, cont'd:
>Mrs. Lillian J. Abbe, daughter of Mrs. A. F. Prescott and the late A. F. Prescott, died on Tuesday, in New Orleans.
>
>Carl M. Reed, of Colesville, died - no date stated – and was buried on Thursday of last week.
>
>Miss Rosemary Heenan of Washington, and Clifton Hershey Norris, of Boyds, were married on Wednesday of last week.
>
>Miss Dorothy W. Kinney and Alfred Lloyd Fraley were married on Thursday of last week, in Rockville.
>
>Dr. Harry G. Offutt has been appointed an assistant surgeon in the U. S. Army. He had the best score of the 32 candidates examined.
>
>Lemuel Thomas Beall, age 73, of Bridgewater, Va., and Miss Emma V. Maxwell, age 62, of Comus, were married on Wednesday of last week.
>
>Miss Marie Wood and Eugene S. Murphy were married on Wednesday of last week.
>
>Mr. J. Sprigg Poole died last Friday at his summer home near Rockville.
>
>By examination, Otis Price has been awarded a scholarship to St. John's College, and Margaret Karn has been awarded a scholarship to Western Maryland College.
>
>Mrs. Marian Felka, wife of Albert W. Felka and daughter of Mr. Jacob Poss, of Rockville, died suddenly on Thursday of last week.
>
>The barn and outbuildings on the property of Harry T. Newcomb at Alta Vista burned on Thursday of last week.
>
>Miss Sarah Ray Wilson and Richard Lawrence Waters were married on Wednesday, in Kensington.
>
>Miss Mary Bertha Maus and John W. Cross were married on September 9$^{th}$, in Washington.
>
>A paper read at the Woman's Club of Poolesville by M. Gertrude Hoskinson described the early mail and stage routes in Maryland. See also September 25$^{th}$.
>
>Gertie E. Miller, who died September 9, 1913, was remembered.

September 25, 1914:
>Mr. Cloe E. Meem died last Monday in a Washington

Cont'd. on next page.

September 25, 1914, cont'd:
hospital. He was a resident of Gaithersburg.
   Susie Thompson, of near Slidell, shot and killed Joseph Fish at her home. She says that she acted in self defense. There will be a preliminary hearing soon.
   Mr. T. Edward Aud, a native of the Poolesville district, claims to have invented a life-saving suit to be worn in cold water in case of an accident, which will prevent the user from freezing.

October 2, 1914:
   Harry Dawson, of Rockville, has resigned his government job in Washington, and intends to practice law in Rockville.
   Mrs. Mary Helen S. Hopper, wife of Dr. George S. Hopper, died on Wednesday of last week at her home in Garrett Park.
   Louis Allison, a long-time resident of Montgomery County, died recently at Soldier's Home, at Hampton, Va.
   William Perry Stallsmith committed suicide last Saturday.
   Miss Corrie V. Devilbiss and Bennie O. Woodward were married on Thursday of last week, in Gaithersburg.
   Fire recently completely destroyed a house under construction belonging to Walter C. Shaw, of Glen Echo. A 'merry-go-round' organ was also lost in the fire.

October 9, 1914:
   Albert T. Marlowe, of Colesville, has been appointed an assistant to the supervisor of assessments.
   E. J. Stillwell has been appointed a deputy forest warden.
   Miss Elizabeth Barrett Prettyman and Alexander Kilgour were married last Saturday at the home of he mother of the bride.
   The home of J. T. Thompson in Alta Vista burned last Tuesday. The contents were also lost.
   C. C. Hughes has been named a tree warden for the
Rockville vicinity, to act under the provisions of a new State law.
   The Waverly Literary Society of the Gaithersburg High School held its regular meeting last Friday. The names mentioned are Blanche English, Lillian Day, Virginia Moore, Elizabeth Fulks, Alverda Cooke, Oscar Gaither, Clements Gloyd, Frances Gloyd, Marguerite Arnold, Annie Trundle, Erma King, Annie Bottlemay, Ruth Fulks, Loretta Snyder, Findley Pollock, Miss Buxton, Miss
                              Cont'd. on next page.

October 9, 1914, cont'd:
Henderson, Miss Wenche.
Maryland Agricultural College is now completely State-owned. by reason of the purchase of an outstanding interest in some of the land on which the College is located.

October 16, 1914:
George W. Meem, a former judge of the Orphan's Court, died Tuesday at his home in Gaithersburg.
Richard H. Hewitt died on last Monday, at the home of his son, Frank L. Hewitt, in Silver Spring. He was a native of England, but had lived here for nearly 50 years.
Simeon G. Gowan shot and killed his wife last Saturday in Washington, in view of 'hundreds' of busy shoppers.
The *Sentinel* welcomed Richard H. Frasier into the Poolesville area, where he has bought a farm upon which he intends to live.
The Woman's Club of Poolesville met on October 8$^{th}$ at the home of Mrs. George Willard. The other names mentioned are Margaret Perry, Mrs. Wm. Hempstone, Helen Louise Johnson, Mrs. James Darby, Mrs. Thomas F. Chiswell, Mrs. Howard Griffith, Della Young, Mrs. J. T. Williams, Nannie Poole, and Mrs. T. R. Hall.
The Waverly Literary Society of the Gaithersburg High School held a meeting last Friday. The names mentioned are Donald Snyder, Ruth Fulks, Samuel Berry, Lula McBain, Ravenel Monred, Ida Kemp, L. Fulks, Anna Williams, Anna Bottlemay, Alverda Cooke, Marjorie Waters, Eleanor Darby, Blanche Golden, Mary Ward, andMargaret Welti.

October 23, 1914:
George Thomas Barnesly, a well known farmer of the Olney district, died on Wednesday of last week. He was a life-long resident of Montgomery County.
Harry L. Butler was found dead last Saturday, lying near the track of the Georgetown-Rockville Electric Railway between Halpine and Montrose. The cause of his death remains unknown.
Miss Mary Edna Noyes and Roger Joseph Whiteford were married on Wednesday of last week, in Washington.

cont'd. on next page.

October 23, 1914, cont'd:
It is announced that Miss Sarah H. Hersperger and A. Hempstone Griffith will be married on October 28th, at the Poolesville Presbyterian Church.

October 30, 1914:
Mrs. Mary M. Snouffer, widow of G. Fenton Snouffer of Gaithersburg, died Monday.
Miss Mary Alice Mossburg and Jesse A. Brown were married on Thursday of last week, in Rockville.
Mahlon F. Mobley and Mrs. Bertie Edwards, both of the Dickerson area, were married recently.
Rudolph L. Heley died Sunday.
Miss Ivy Alice Phillips, of Rockville, and Arthur R. Garrett, of New York city, were married on Thursday of last week.
Requests for changes in voter registration were considered by the Circuit Court last Saturday. The names mentioned are Henry S. Bean, Spencer J. Bean, Arthur C. Houghton, Addison H. Flournoy, Edmund S. Flournoy, Benjamin C. Flournoy, Harvey Ricketts, Zadoc Ricketts, and John E. Hilton.
Jurors have been named to serve in the Circuit Court during the coming term of court. The names mentioned are Hugh C. Townsend, James S. Bolton, Geo. W. Mobley, John P. Harris, Jas. E. King, James B. Maughlin, Wm. L. Aud, Wm. J. Williams, Harry M. Williams, Carroll A. Shreve, William R. Lyddane, Charles C. Ricketts, Urban N. Wagner, Millard W. Belt, Wm. W. Welsh, Hilleary W. Offutt, Howard McC. Marlowe, Wm. Z. Tolson, Wm. P. Waters, Columbus Brashears, Charles H. Thrift, Thomas H. Offutt, James Small, Leonidas L. Green, John W. Bogley, Edward C. Boswell, John E. Muncaster, Jonathan D. Barnesly, Nicholas R. Griffith, Frank M. Hallowell, John H. Nicholls, Wm. C. Crawford, Samuel R. Plummer, Horton G. Thompson, Milton F. Embrey, Edward P. Atwood, Arthur Myers, F. Leonard Hays, Charles G. Griffith, Wm. G. Brewer, William E. Watkins, Rufus K. King, Richard H. Stanley, Arthur Williams, Chas. T. Cooley, Geo. H. Bean, Daniel W. Barnes, and Oliver B. Clark.
Dr. Wm. E. Magruder, who died July 13, was remembered by resolution of the Montgomery County Medical Society.

November 6, 1914:

Wm. S. Mansfield, a long-time resident of Montgomery County, was found Friday lying dead in a field on the farm of Edward Wallace, near Germantown. The date of his death is not stated.

Miss Sarah Amelia Poole and Jesse H. Burns were married on Thursday of last week, at the home of the parents of the bride, in Damascus.

The granary on the farm of I. T. Fulks, near Gaithersburg, burned down on last Wednesday, of an unknown cause.

Mrs. Jos. T. Moore, Jr., of Sandy Spring announced the engagement of her daughter, Mary Gillingham, to Brainard H. Warner, Jr. The wedding will take place about the middle of November, and will be private.

Mrs. Mary M. Welsh, wife of Asa H. Welsh, died last Friday.

The following named jurors previously selected, have been excused, namely: John P. Harris, James E. King, William P. Waters, John H. Nicholls, Edward P. Atwood, Harry M. Williams, Nicholas R. Griffith, Samuel R. Plummer, and Rufus K. King. They will be replaced by Joshua L. Riggs, Eugene A. McAtee, Alfred M. Earp, Chas. E. Becraft, John W. Lynch, Marion F. Beall, Charles T. Nicholson, Alexander G. Carlisle, and Henry L. Clay.

Mrs. Elizabeth H. Offutt, of Rockville, has announced that her daughter, Elizabeth Hulings, will marry Bertram Neynoe Garstin on November 28th, in Christ Episcopal Church, Rockville.

S. Lavinia Warfield, who died October 8th [year not stated] was remembered.

The Children's Club gave a Halloween party on the evening of the 30th, at the home of Mrs. L. G. Gardiner. The names mentioned are Mary Reading, Lucille Lamar, Helen Gardiner, Clara Henderson, Myrtle Rabbitt, Katherine Monday, Mary Simpson, Mrs. Louis Watson, Dorothy Clark, Bettie Wilson, Nancy Watson, Mildred Gardiner, Billy Prescott, Lloyd Howes, Hugh Reading, John Maddox, Milbourne Ward, Thomas Anderson, Edward Peter, Reuben Riggs, Wm. Linthicum, Hilton Darby, John Reisinger, Harry Dawson, John Dawson, and Louis Watson.

Miss Sarah Marcylean Hersperger and Armistead Hempstone Griffith were married on Wednesday of last week, at the Presbyterian Church of Poolesville.

November 13, 1914:

Edgar H. Cashell, formerly of Montgomery County, has been elected a member of the State legislature in Montana.

Samuel B. Holland, a long-time resident of the Damascus district, died Monday at his home.

Henry Miles, of the Beallsville area, died last Friday.

Benjamin Crown died last Saturday at his home.

Miss Bessie Louise Ridgley and William T. Ray were married last Tuesday at the home of the parents of the bride, in Unity.

Miss Ruth B. Corrick and Lester G. VanFossen were married on Wednesday of last week at the home of the bride's parents in Kensington.

Charles Mossburg, of Seneca, died last Sunday of injuries received in an automobile accident on Friday.

James Cummings, a deputy sheriff of Montgomery County, has been charged with homicide after he shot and killed Harrison Weaver as Weaver was attempting to flee after having been arrested by Cummings for shooting craps.

A double wedding took place on last Saturday at 'Bai Nola', the country home of Mr. & Mrs. S. Wade Magruder, of Rockville, when Miss Effie Virginia Magruder, daughter of Mr. Magruder, was married to Edward H. Frease, and Miss Alma Virginia Petty, daughter of Mrs. Magruder, was married to Arthur L. Ball.

November 20, 1914:

Miss Laura B. Huffer, daughter of Mr. & Mrs. Edwin M. Huffer of Laytonsville, and Edward C. Gaither, also of Laytonsville, were married on Thursday of last week, in Rockville.

The Commissioners have appointed the following Trustees of the Poor, namely: Harry Riggs, Henry B. Gardiner, Samuel D. Byrd, W. T. Pratt, and Eleazar Ray.

Mrs. Anna Gilpin Lea died recently at her home.

Wm. Wright died last Saturday at the Starmont Sanatorium in Washington Grove.

Elsie Charlotte Turner, daughter of Wm. and Bessie Davis Turner, died November 4th.

James W. Cummings, of Bethesda district, who was in jail on a charge of having killed Harrison Weaver, a negro, was not indicted by the grand jury. Upon the failure of the grand jury to

Cont'd. on next page

November 20, 1914, cont'd:
return an indictment the jury was criticized by Judge Peter.
 Miss Elizabeth Hulings Offutt, daughter of Mrs. Elizabeth H. Offutt, of Rockville, and Bertram Neynoe Garstin, of Baltimore, were married last Wednesday, in Rockville.
 Miss Mary G. Moore and Brainard H. Warner, Jr., were married last Saturday at the home of the mother of the bride near Sandy Spring.

November 27, 1914:
 Berry E. Clark, County Treasurer, announced that taxes will be received at the following places:
  Laytonsville: J. C. Higgins' store.
  Clarksburg: Levi Price's store.
  Poolesville: Poolesville National Bank.
  Colesville: T. R. Cissel's store.
  Darnestown: R. B. Beall's store.
  Bethesda: A. Wilson's store.
  Sandy Spring: First National Bank.
  Gaithersburg: First National Bank.
  Barnesville: A. L. Jones' store; Poole's store.
  Potomac: Stone's store.
  Damascus: Beall's store.
  Silver Spring: Silver Spring National Bank.
 At a special meeting of the Mayor and Council of Rockville, Preston L. Hewitt was elected bailiff of Rockville, to fill out the unexpired term of his late father, A. R. Hewitt.
 Patrick J. Leahy of this County, and Miss Katherine M. Lyons, of New York city were married on Wednesday of last week.
 Andrew Glorius, age 96, died on Wednesday of last week at the home of his nephew, Henry Nolte, in Silver Spring.
 Thomas Sampson, of Garrett Park, and Miss Wilhelmina C. Joubenall, of Washington, were married Wednesday. It is the third marriage for the groom.
 Lewis Payne was killed on last Saturday when he was struck by a train at Boyds.
 Lawrence A. Darby died last Sunday. He had been a judge of the Orphan's Court. See also Dec. 4, 1914.

Cont'd. on next page.

November 27, 1914, cont'd:

    Aaron R. Hewitt, bailiff of Rockville, died on Thursday of last week. as a result of injuries inflicted by Franklin C. Boswell after Boswell had been reprimanded by Mr. Hewitt.

    At the Maryland Horticultural Society's annual exhibition held in Baltimore this week, prizes were awarded to Marjorie L. Waters, of Gaithersburg, and to Allen F. Brooke, of Sandy Spring.

    Dr. Charles W. Shreve died last Tuesday at the home of his son, Wm. A. Shreve, in Washington. He had lived for most of his life near Dickerson.

December 4, 1914.

    Miss Myrtle B. Garst, of Frederick, and Robert R. Rhoderick, of Chevy Chase were married last Saturday.

    Miss Rosa Virginia Peters and Jesse Herbert Veitch were married on Wednesday of last week. at the home of the bride, in Burnt Mills.

    Mrs. Mary H. Lyddane, formerly a resident of Rockville, wife of Stephen B. Lyddane, died December 2, in Washington.

    Henry Dwyer, a native of Montgomery County, died on Wednesday of last week.

    A granary, some agricultural implements and some grain, harnesses, etc., on the farm of Thompson Williams near Cedar Grove, were burned on Thursday of last week. It is thought that the fire may have been intentional, and a suspect has been arrested.

    Joseph W. Buck, of Kensington, died at his home last Monday.

    The completion of the construction of the road from Rockville to Potomac was celebrated by a banquet at the school building in Potomac. Among the names mentioned are Dr. and Mrs. Wm. T. Pratt, Mrs. John G. Stone, Miss Sallie Kilgour, Mrs. Willis L. Moore, Mrs. Darius Clagett, Miss Jackie McDonald, Mrs. Carter Clagett, Mrs. Frank P. Stone, Miss Cecelia Kilgour, Mrs. George G. Bradley, Jr., Mrs. Walker, Mrs. Samuel Case, Mrs. Harry Myers, Mrs. Robert Saunders, Prof. Willis L. Moore, Andrew J. Cummings, Preston B. Ray, and Geo. G. Bradley.

December 11, 1914:

    The Governor has named F. M. Webster and A. M. Thomas

                                        Cont'd. on next page.

December 11, 1914, cont'd:
to serve as forest wardens for Montgomery County for two years.

The trustees of the Alms House have elected Harry Riggs President, John E. West clerk, and Dr. Edward Anderson, physician.

Sheriff Whalen has appointed Dr. L. W. Glazebrook and Robert D. Weaver deputies.

Wm. M. Davis, of Rockville, died last Thursday at his home.

Mrs. Laura V. Ward, who died August 9, 1914, was remembered.

Field trials of the Montgomery County Foxhunters Association were held on Thursday of last week, starting before daybreak. The names mentioned are A. J. Cummings, Samuel Ross, Chas. A. Clagett, John Magruder, W. O. Spates, Z. M. Waters, E. C. Davis, Geo. Gates, Richard F. Spates, Wm. Riggs, Joseph Howes, Clay B. Edwards, Edward Umstead, Robert Curran, Arthur M. Mace, George Edwards, Artemus Sullivan, Howard Marlowe, Roger Spates, Douglass Edwards, Mr. Chambers, Mr. Berry, George Kelchner, and Cecil Allnutt.

The newly organized Darnestown Literary Society held its third meeting on Friday. The names mentioned are Neoma Butts, Josephine Wolfe, Mrs. Charles Allnutt, Mildred Lewis, Mr. & Mrs. Darnell, Margaret Darby, Julia Lewis, T. W. Darnell.

December 18, 1914:
John W. Whiteside, of Brookeville, died last Saturday.

George A. Garrett, formerly a resident of Montgomery County, died last Monday in St. Joseph, Mo.

It is announced by Mr. & Mrs. A. Austin Braddock that their daughter Tabitha Austin and Deatherage Leslie Daniel of Oklahoma City, Ok. will be married the latter part of this month.

Miss Cecelia F. Margerum and John J. Johnson, both of the Burtonsville area, were married on Thursday of last week.

The funeral of Miss Mary Magruder, daughter of Mrs. Laura Magruder and the late Bradley Magruder, was held on Thursday of last week. Date of death is not stated. Interment was in Rockville Union Cemetery.

Miss Bessie E. Price and Arthur P. Luhn both of the Poolesville neighborhood, were married on Wednesday of last week.

Stevens J. Musgrove, of Damascus, and Miss Nora M. Beall
Cont'd. on next page.

December 18, 1914, cont'd:
were married on last Saturday.
    Miss Erma Helen Bogley and Leland Lawrence Fisher, both of Rockville, were married on Wednesday of last week.
    Joseph T. Moore, of 'Norwood', Sandy Spring, died on Thursday of last week. He had served as a Maryland State Senator, and as a director of the Montgomery County National Bank, The National Park Bank of New York, and was one of the organizers of the Savings Institution of Sandy Spring.

December 25, 1914:
    Miss Sarah A. Day, of Clarksburg, and Thomas E. Luhn, of Comus, were married on Thursday of last week.
    At the annual election of officers of the Olney Grange, Calvin Bready was chosen Master; Samuel P. Thomas, Overseer; Rev. Henry H. Marsden, lecturer; Mary E. Thomas, secretary, and Elizabeth T. Stabler, treasurer.
    Miss H. Delma Young and James W. Burdette, both of Damascus, were married on Thursday of last week.
    The large barn on the farm of Harry M. Boland, near Germantown, burned on Thursday of last week.
    Mrs. Annie Burdette, wife of Nathan J. Burdette, died on Wednesday of last week at her home near Damascus.
    John W. Whitesides, who died last Sunday, was remembered.

January 1, 1915:
    The death of John L. Brunett, and the appointment of Preston B. Ray to succeed him as Clerk of the Circuit Court was reported. In a separate item, the death of Mr. Brunett on Friday of last week was reported.
    Mr. & Mrs. Samuel Thomas Briggs, of Quince Orchard, celebrated their golden wedding anniversary on Tuesday of last week.
    Harry Dawson Jr. won an automobile valued at $450. raffled by Parker, Bridget &. Co., of Washington.
    Miss Blanche Fawcett and Henry Lamar Benson were married on Wednesday.
    George S. Garrett, a native of Montgomery County, died December 13, 1914, in St. Joseph, Mo.

                              Cont'd. on next page.

January 1, 1915, cont'd:
> Miss Tabitha Austin Braddock, daughter of Mr. & Mrs. A. Austin Braddock, and D. Leslie Daniel were married on Monday.
> Miss Frances Walter, daughter of Mr. & Mrs. Frank Walter, and William Dake Campbell were married on Thursday of last week at 'Ravenswood', the country home of the bride's parents, near Rockville.
> The death of Elmer Vincent Beall on November 24, 1914, was noted. He was the son of Mr. & Mrs. Elbridge Beall.

January 8, 1915:
> Mrs. Marian Holland, widow of S. Benton Holland, died suddenly last week at her home in Damascus.
> Mr. & Mrs. William V. Beall announce that their daughter, Ellen Louise, will marry Harry Franklin Baker on January 16.
> Joseph Stabler, of the Sandy Spring area, died last Sunday.
> Thomas L. Dawson, of Rockville, has passed the bar examination and will be admitted to the practice of law.
> Wm. H. Burdette died last Monday as a result of injuries sustained about two weeks ago when his house was destroyed by fire.
> Miss Clyta Mullinix and Leslie W. Woodfield, both of the Damascus area, were married recently.
> Preston B. Ray, the new Clerk of the Court, has announced the appointment of Adrian L. Brunett, eldest son of the late John L. Brunett, to a vacant deputy clerkship in the Clerk's office.
> Miss Blanche D. Jones, of Linden, and Michael F. Keating, of Washington, were married last Wednesday.
> Mrs. Mary Augusta Hutton, widow of W. R. Hutton, died last Monday at her home, 'Woodlands', near Clopper.
> W. H. Lamar has signed a contract to play baseball with the Washington Nationals. He will begin training in March, in Charlottesville, Va.
> In news from the School Board, it was announced that Miss Josephine Batson has been named principal at the school at Spencerville, to succeed Miss Blanche Fawcett. Miss Gertrude Fawcett will take Miss Batson's former job. Miss Dorothy Brooke has resigned as a teacher at Sandy Spring High School and has entered Swarthmore College. Mrs. Philip Robison has been appointed in her place. Also, Miss Daisy Cecil has been recommended for a
> > Cont'd. on next page.

January 8, 1915, cont'd:
certificate to teach.

    Miss Nettie G. Ward and Charles A. Boyer were married December 29.

    Mrs. Margaret A. Green, widow of the late T. W. Green, and for many years a resident of Bethesda, died December $8^{th}$, 1914.

January 15, 1915.

    Mrs. Margaret S. Cator, widow of Holland S. Cator, died last Tuesday.

    Frank Lewis died last week at his home near Browningsville.

    Amos W. Bean, formerly of Montgomery County, died on Wednesday of last week.

    Amos S. Young died last week at his home near Comus.

    James H. Massey died on Thursday of last week at his home at Kensington.

    Directors as follows were elected at the recent annual meeting of stockholders of the Montgomery County National Bank, namely: Spencer C. Jones, Wm. B. Mobley, Jas. E. Williams, Lawrence Allnutt, Richard H. Stokes, Frederick P. Hays, Wm. T. Griffith, Perrie E. Waters, Lee Offutt, Thomas Vinson, H. A. Waters, and J. H. Parsley. Mr. Jones was then elected President; Mr. Stokes, vice president; Geo. M. Hunter, assistant cashier; Russell Brewer, teller; Geo. Henderson, discount clerk; Gardner Darby, bookkeeper; and Miss Leigh Athey, stenographer.

    The following were elected directors of the Montgomery County Agricultural Society at the annual meeting on Wednesday, namely: Lee Offutt, Chas. Viers, Chas. W. Fields, David H. Warfield, Wm. K. Jones, Chas. F. Kirk, Perrie E. Waters, John B. Diamond, Jr., Wm. B. Trundle, N. H. Ward, and W. H. Fawcett.

    The Janet Montgomery chapter of the D. A. R. met on January 5 at the home of Clara Barton. The names mentioned are Mrs. Wm. Hyde Talbott, Mrs. Loughborough, Mrs. Ernest L. Bullard, Mrs Nora Sellman Meem, Maj. Richard Sprigg, Mrs. Frank P. Stone, Maj. Richard Brooke, Charles Kirk, Mrs. Heiron, and Clara R. Wilson.

    Miss Martha Marie Jones and John Bernard Offutt were married last Saturday, in St. Mary's Catholic Church, Barnesville.

January 22, 1915.
> Miss Blanche May Walker, of Concord, and Charles N. Pugh, of Friendship Heights, were married on Tuesday, in Rockville.
> M. I. Kingsbury, son of C. T. Kingsbury, died last Saturday.
> Miss Elizabeth B. Nicholson and George H. Johnson were married last Saturday.
> The County Commissioners have entered into contracts with several hospitals in Washington, by which the hospitals will be paid to care for the indigent sick admitted from Montgomery County. The following named physicians are authorized to issue entrance permits, namely: Drs. Vernon H. Dyson, James E. Deets, Upton D. Nourse, C. H. Mannar, J. R. Batson, Chas. H. Nourse, John L. Lewis, J. W. Bird, Horace D. Haddox, Wm. T. Pratt, Jos. M. White, Geo. M. Boyer, and Eugene Jones.
> Miss Margaret Louise Peddicord and Charles Edwin Myers were married last Saturday.
> John L. Brunett, former Clerk of the Circuit Court, who died December 25, 1914, was remembered.
> The School Commissioners have adopted a plan to appoint 'examination boards' the function of which will be to prepare examination questions to be used in the public schools. The names mentioned are Willis B. Burdette, Mary Easton, Frances English, Ruby Robertson, Mary Brewer, Frances Horner, Helen Neel, Virginia Brewer, Edna Hawke, Elberta Rice, Charles G. Myers, Thomas W. Troxall, and Wm. K. Klingaman.
> Miss Ellen Louise Beall and Harry Franklin Baker were married January 16, 1915 at the home of the parents of the bride.
> The stockholders of the First National Bank of Gaithersburg have elected the following named directors, namely: John B. Diamond, James Anderson, H. Maurice Talbott, Ignatius T. Fulks, Nathan Cooke, Clarence H. Hoskinson, John W. Walker, Zadoc M. Cooke, R. B. Moore, Jas. S. Windsor, Samuel R. Plummer, Jos. C. Higgins, Elisha C. Etchison, and A. F. Meem. The directors then elected Mr. Diamond president; Mr. Anderson, vice president; Robert B. Moore, cashier; John A. Stover, assistant cashier; Frank B. Severance, bookkeeper, and Louis C. Beall, clerk.
> The newly elected directors of the First National Bank of Sandy Spring are Alban G. Thomas, Asa M. Stabler, Allen Farquhar, Chas. F. Kirk, Frederick L. Thomas, Josiah W. Jones, Geo. W.
> Cont'd. on next page.

January 22, 1915, cont'd:
Bready, Tarlton B. Stabler, Francis Thomas, W. L. Cashell, and T. L. Jackson.

January 29, 1915.
Miss Katherine Moore has been appointed assistant teacher at the Unity school.
Miss Jane Adele Riggs and Wm. L. Ray were married on Wednesday of last week.
Mr. & Mrs. John B. Pumphrey celebrated their 50$^{th}$ wedding anniversary on Wednesday of last week with a dinner party at their home in Derwood.
Capt. Joshua Davis, son of the late Joshua Davis of Rockville, died last Saturday. He was a Confederate veteran.
Mrs. Selina D. Wilson, of Woodside, died January 19$^{th}$.

February 5, 1915.
Jacob Umstead has been reappointed superintendent of the fair grounds at Rockville, a position which he has held for several years.
Nicholas Brewer has been placed in charge of the Hagerstown office of the New York Life Insurance Company, and will move to Hagerstown shortly.
Miss Minnie G. Clark and Ashton S. Fox were married on Wednesday of last week at the home of the bride's parents.
James H. Holland died last Sunday at his home near Norwood.
Miss Mabel Anderson Spencer, of Washington, and J. Alby Henderson of Rockville, were married on Wednesday.

February 12, 1915.
Joseph T. Moore was remembered by a resolution adopted by the board of directors of the Montgomery County National Bank of Rockville.
The Rockville circle of King's Daughters celebrated the 25$^{th}$ anniversary of its organization in an open meeting held last Friday. The names mentioned are Mary Brewer, Isabel Kingdon, Mrs. George H. Lamar, Mrs. John B. Brewer, Rev. Frank M. Richardson, Rev. O. W. Barnes, Mrs. J. Somervell Dawson, and Miss Lydia Almoney.
Mary Katherine Boswell, who died February 15, 1911, was remembered by her daughter, Sarah Hill.

Cont'd. on next page.

February 12, 1915, cont'd:

Miss Elsie M. Kingsbury has been appointed postmistress at Boyds, succeeding Edward D. Lewis.

Miss Isabel Parsley has resigned as assistant teacher at the Brookeville High School.

Mrs. Sarah E. Bean, wife of J. Clarence Bean, died on Thursday of last week.

Mrs. Martha Jane Etchison, wife of J. Melvin Etchison, died last Saturday at her home in Gaithersburg.

The Janet Montgomery chapter of the D. A. R. met on February $2^{nd}$. at the home of Mrs. Frank Wilson. Other names mentioned are Marie Talbott, Maria Elizabeth Waters, Col. Wm. Hempstone, Mrs. Wm. H. Talbott, Mrs. J. F. Wilson, Mrs. Ernest L. Bullard, Mrs. Edgar W. Moore, Mrs. Alfred Ray, Mrs. Jas. Loughborough, Mrs. Jas. Adams, Mrs. E. J. Hartshorn, Miss Virginia Wilson, Mrs. Frank P. Stone, Mrs. Harry Cunningham, and Mrs. Richard L. Waters.

February 19, 1915.

Mr. & Mrs. Elisha Riggs announced the engagement of their daughter, Marguerite duMeste Riggs to Thomas A. Ridgley.

The County Commissioners have appointed Clarence H. Wright and Wm. H. McCrossin constables for the Colesville and Darnestown districts respectively.

Miss Eloise Walters recently won a prize at the Washington City Technical High School for her rifle shooting.

The set of china offered as a prize at the weekly movies shown at the Masonic Hall in Gaithersburg, was won by Perry A. Gloyd.

Benjamin W. Allnutt, a prominent resident of the Poolesville district, died last Tuesday.

Mr. & Mrs. Joseph H. C. Hoyle celebrated their $60^{th}$. wedding anniversary last Saturday.

There was a Valentine's Day dance last Friday, given by the young men of the Germantown area. The names mentioned are Misses Josephine Boland, Alice Waters, Virginia Wilson, Mr. & Mrs. Perrie E. Waters, Mr. & Mrs. Richard L. Waters, Mrs. H. M. Boland, Mrs. Bowie F. Waters, Mrs. D. W. Baker, Mrs. James H. Jones, Mrs. John Henderson, and Mrs. R. L. Waters.

Annie Briggs Small, who died February 10th, 1910, was remembered.

February 26, 1915.
Louis B. Scholl has been commissioned a notary public.
Miss Katherine Baker, sister of Mr. D. W. Baker, died last Monday at her home near Germantown.
Mrs. Lucinda Bean, widow of Cornelius Bean, died last Wednesday.
Mrs. Marie Oland, age 18, died last Friday of pneumonia.
Mrs. Elizabeth Schaeffer, widow of Dr. T. H. Schaeffer, died on February 16th.
An effort is being made to establish a public library in Rockville. The names mentioned are Miss Mary Farr, of the State Library Commission, and Mrs. Wm. H. Talbott, Mrs. H. C. Allnutt, and Mrs. O. M. Linthicum.
Jurors as follows have been drawn to serve during the coming term of the Circuit Court: Laytonsville district, Basil T. Warfield, James H. Barber, Granville S. Haines; Clarksburg district, John W. Henderson, Julian B. Walters, Benjamin D. Duvall; Poolesville district, Paul Dyson, Charles B. Sellman, Randolph Luhn, Walter W. Pyles; Rockville district, Charles O. Bean, Harry Kengla, Henry Dwyer, Wm. A. Harmon, Wm. B. Waters, Martin F. Heim; Colesville district, George T. Windham, Geo. L. Lusby, Osborne Crawford, Geo. F. Phair; Darnestown district, Lewis Reed, Millard L. Rice, Jas. H. Giddings; Bethesda district, Wm. T. Owens, John W. Huffman, Joseph F. Whalen; Olney district, Walter H. White, Douglas H. Riggs, Josiah W. Jones, Allan R. Brown; Gaithersburg district, George S. Dorsey, John B. Diamond, Joseph B. Schwartz, George Mills; Potomac district, Edward T. Ricketts, Henry T. Mobley, Jos. H. Bodine; Barnesville district, Charles R. Darby, Richard C. Carlisle, Clarence O. Warfield; Damascus district, Samuel R. Molesworth, Archie W. Souder, Sebastian M. Mullinix; Wheaton district, Jno. A. Cannon, Parker L. Weller, Jason P. Warthen, Wm. G. W. Leizear, Edwin W. Birgfeld.
Benjamin Allnutt was remembered by resolution of the Dawsonville Woman's Club.
John C. Power, who died February 13th, 1913, was remembered.

March 5, 1915:
The new flour mill recently established by John B. Diamond,
Cont'd. on next page.

March 5, 1915, cont'd:
in Gaithersburg, is now operating and producing flour.

Henry Bussard died on Wednesday at his home near Dickerson.

Joseph J. Stearn died last Sunday.

Mrs. Ann America Walters, widow of Richard H. Walters, died last Tuesday.

Miss Mary Aud and Edwin Barbour Hutchison were married on Wednesday of last week.

March 12, 1915.

Frank H. Darby has been appointed a constable for the Damascus district.

It was announced that Miss Ethel Douglass Graves and George Kelchner have been married - no date stated.

The following named have been appointed forest wardens for Montgomery County, namely: Rufus H. Davis, of Barnesville; I. E. Riggs, Laytonsville; Z. M. Waters, Jr., Goshen; J. M. Etchison, Gaithersburg; and John N. Kelley, of Garrett Park.

Fire of unknown origin destroyed the barn on the farm of Thomas Hyde, near Sandy Spring. Five horses died in the blaze.

The young people of the Linden and Woodside area have organized a club to be known as the Hi Si. The following names are mentioned: Elizabeth Chandler, Margaret Fry, Marian Olds, Elizabeth Engle.

The Home and School Association of Kensington has elected William P. Hay, president; Mrs. L. P. Boynton, vice president; Victor Haugaard, treasurer. Members of the executive committee are the officers, plus Mrs. W. W. Bishop, Mrs. James B. Cook, Rev. Henry Rumer, Chas. H. Gibson, and Edmund Noyes.

The following jurors last drawn to serve in the coming term of the Circuit Court have been excused, namely Basil T. Warfield, John W. Henderson, Paul Dyson, Harry Kengla, Wm. A. Harmon, Samuel R. Molesworth, John A. Cannon, and Jason P. Warthen. Their places will be taken by George R. Howes, Amos Whipp, Nathan H. Metzgar, Samuel K. Bready, Noah Watkins, Wm. G. Gates, and Wm. V. Beall.

Miss Katherine Emily Oxley and Herbert Franklin Lazelle were married last Tuesday at the home of the parents of the bride, Mr. & Mrs. Charles Oxley, of near Poolesville.

Cont'd. on next page.

March 12, 1915, cont'd:

Mrs. Elizabeth Ann Blundon, widow of Charles F. Blundon, died last Tuesday.

Mrs. Mary E. Luckett died last Tuesday.

John W. Loeffler, of Montrose, died last Monday.

Milton Bohrer, son of H. B. Bohrer and the late Alice Bohrer, died last Friday.

Mrs. Anna Hawkins, wife of John T. Hawkins, died last Saturday at her home near Boyds.

Robert A. Cannon, son of John A. Cannon, died on Thursday of last week.

Mrs. Artemesia Gingell, widow of James M. Gingell, died on Thursday of last week.

Dorsey L. Peters died last Saturday following an operation for appendicitis

Wm. D. Baldwin died Monday. His widow was the former Miss Maria Bache Abert, daughter of the late Charles Abert of Montgomery County.

Sheriff B. Peyton Whalen attempted to kill himself in his office in the Courthouse last Saturday. He was taken to a hospital in Washington, where he was operated on, and his condition is said to be improving.

War claims, under a law passed by Congress last week, have been allowed to the following residents of Montgomery County: estate of Alfred C. Belt, estate of Thomas N. Gott; Maria M. Harris, widow of Henry N. Harris; Frank N. Harris, Henry W. Harris, Annie E. Harris, George W. Harris, Alla V. Harris, Annie E. Harris, John W. Harris, Wm. Harris, Thomas D. Harris, being heirs of Henry N. Harris; estate of John L. T. Jones; estate of Wm. D. Poole, estate of Wm. P. Leaman; estate of Richard T. Mitchell; estate of Elijah Thompson; estate of Lewis W. Williams; estate of Zachariah L. Windsor; and to Marion B. Young and Geno D. Weller, heirs of Samuel C. Young.

Roy Osborne Etchison died March 2nd.

Lucinda Bean, who died February 24th, was remembered.

March 19, 1915:

Francis Snowden announced that he would be a candidate for the House of Delegates, subject to the Democratic primary.

Cont'd. on next page.

March 19, 1915, cont'd:

Richard L. Saunders announced that he was a candidate for County Commissioner from the fourth election district, subject to the Democratic primary.

Frank Mobley, recently a resident of Baltimore, died Saturday at Dickerson.

Wm. J. Corrick died last Friday at the home of his parents, Mr. & Mrs. Harry K. Corrick, in Kensington.

Miss Ida A. Gangewer died last Friday at the home of Mrs. Frank A. Spencer, in Rockville. Miss Gangewer had been a resident of Washington for many years, but had lived in Rockville in recent years.

Miss Elizabeth H. Thompson, a life-long resident of Montgomery County, died last Sunday.

Miss Mabel M. Plyer, of the Wheaton district, and Harry B. Nicholls, of Washington, were married on Tuesday.

Fire destroyed the barn on the farm of Mrs. Josephine Harding, near Spencerville, on last Thursday.

Mrs. Harriet A. Cashell, widow of Hazel A. Cashell, died last Friday.

James Graham Pearre, for several years a resident of Rockville, died on Thursday of last week.

The School Commissioners announced the appointment of the following public school teachers, namely: Miss Ola B. Lawson to be principal of the school at Clagettsville; Miss Lillian Spinney assistant at the Woodside school in place of Miss Rose Clark, resigned; Miss Joyce to be assistant at the Brookeville school in place of Miss Isabel Parsley, resigned. The Board also appointed Mrs. H. S. Parsons and Osgood Dowell trustees of the Woodside school, and C. M. Zeitler to be trustee of the school at Unity in place of H. B. Moxley, resigned.

Mrs. Annie Elizabeth Hawkins, wife of John T. Hawkins, died March 5 at her home near Clarksburg.

March 26, 1915.

Mr. & Mrs. John H. Parsley, of Brookeville, announced the engagement of their daughter, Miss Isabel Jackson [Parsley], to Lee Clagett Warfield. The marriage will take place in April.

Warren Choate has been appointed chief clerk of the Federal Trade Commission.

Cont'd. on next page.

March 26, 1915, cont'd:
Wm. A. Shreve died last Saturday at the residence of Charles E. Dwyer, in Glenmont.

The barn and corn house on the farm of Arthur Williams, near Dawsonville, were destroyed by fire last Sunday.

Thomas J. Brown, of the Gaithersburg district, died last Saturday at his home near Brown's Station.

William A. Bogley died on last Wednesday at his home in Rockville.

Thomas A. Ridgley and Miss Marguerite duMeste Riggs were married March 16$^{th}$.

April 2, 1915:
William Walter Mills, only child of W. A. Mills and Ada Weed Mills, died last Sunday.

Judge Stanton J. Peele, of Chevy Chase, has been appointed a school commissioner for Montgomery County.

Mrs. Mary Katherine Shipley, wife of C. Gassaway Shipley, died last Saturday at her home near Cedar Grove.

Mrs. Ruth G. Beall, widow of Edward M. Beall, died last week at her home near Cedar Grove.

Smith Hoyle will begin the erection of a mill at Boyds.

Mrs. May B. Lewis, wife of Wm. J. Lewis, died last week. See also April 7, 1916.

William P. Moxley had his right hand amputated following an accident at a woodworking mill which he was operating.

Charles R. Gray, of Germantown, attempted suicide last Monday. He was worried about the fact that his wife has been missing about two weeks and her whereabouts are unknown.

A large bank barn and other outbuildings on the farm of D. C. Winebrenner, near White's Ferry, burned on Wednesday of last week.

Joseph Reading announced that he would be a candidate for Register of Wills, subject to the Democratic primary

Alfred Wilson announced that he would be a candidate for the House of Delegates, subject to the Democratic primary.

J. Melvin Etchison announced that he would be a candidate for Sheriff, subject to the Democratic primary vote.

W. Frank Gaither announced that he would be a candidate for Sheriff, subject to the Democratic primary.

April 9, 1915:

Col. Spencer C. Jones died on Thursday of last week at the home of his daughter, Mrs. Thomas R. Falvey, in New Orleans, La. The article traces his life.

Columbus Brashears has been appointed constable and collector of dog taxes for the Colesville district.

President Wilson has appointed Harold C. Waters, of Germantown, to the position of consular assistant.

Mr. & Mrs. Mansfield White announced the engagement of their daughter, Elsie Lee White, to William A. Daniel. The wedding will take place on April 27.

Nathan Todd Kinney died April 14th at his home at Cloppers.

The home of Reginald D. Poole, plus the nearby barn and several outbuildings, was destroyed by fire on Monday.

The death of Spencer C. Jones has resulted in the following changes of officers at The Montgomery County National Bank of Rockville: R. H. Stokes has been elected president; Wm. B. Mobley has been elected vice president; George M. Hunter, cashier; and Russell Brewer, assistant cashier.

Rev. Dr. Henry Rumer, pastor of Warner Memorial Presbyterian Church, Kensington, has resigned in order to become pastor at Harmony Presbyterian Church, Darlington, Harford County.

Miss Lora A. Souder and Chas. W. Barnesly, both of the Olney neighborhood, were married Monday.

Miss Pearl W. Hawkins and Clarence E. Green were married last Saturday.

Miss Eleanor Mary Louise Costello and Cyrus Keiser, Jr. were married on last Monday.

Miss Ruby Adelaide Gloyd, of Derwood, and Aubrey Wilson Burdette, of Rockville, were married on Wednesday of last week.

Hugh C. Townsend died last Friday at his home near Unity.

Miss Isabel Jackson Parsley and Lee Clagett Warfield were married on Thursday April 1st.

Franklin C. Boswell was convicted by Judge Urner of manslaughter in the death of Rockville bailiff Aaron R. Hewitt on November 1, 1914. Bailiff Hewitt had reprimanded Boswell, and Boswell then hit Hewitt on the head with a quart whiskey bottle.

Mrs. Mary O. Monday, widow of Bernard Monday, died March 31st. The article traces some of Mrs. Monday's genealogy.

April 16, 1915:

Sheriff Whalen has returned to his duties.

George F. Linthicum has sold his store in Gaithersburg to M. M. Walker, Forrest Walker and Clay Plummer.

Miss Clydia Marie Carlin and Crawford Wade Young were married on Thursday of last week.

A fire in the woods of the farm of Charles T. Brosius near Barnesville burned about 10,000 fence rails and a large quantity of young trees.

The barn and granary on the farm of Clayton Hoyle, at Dickerson, burned last Saturday. It is thought that the fire was caused by sparks from a B. & O. locomotive.

Miss Margaret Owen Magruder and Thomas H. Clark were married on Thursday of last week.

Roy Hargett, 25 year old son of Albert Hargett of Germantown, died on Thursday of last week as a result of injuries sustained when he was kicked by a horse about 3 weeks ago.

Edgar Fulks, of Gaithersburg, struck Charles Louis Robinson with his auto last Saturday in Washington, resulting in the death of Mr. Robinson about 2 hours later. Mr. Fulks will have to appear before the coroner in Washington.

Jacob Meriam Darby, son of Samuel Darby, died last Monday.

Jacob Hager, of the Damascus district, died last Sunday.

Mrs. Lottie Ward Briggs, age 21, wife of Herman Briggs, died last Monday in Providence hospital, Washington, of pneumonia.

Christopher E. Watkins died on Wednesday of last week.

George Washington Murphy died last Sunday at Hyattstown.

Miss Mildred Iglehart, age 19, daughter of Mr. & Mrs. Wm. G. Iglehart, died in a Washington hospital last Saturday, of pneumonia.

Mrs. Alice E. Harris, widow of Richard F. Harris, died last Friday at the home of her son-in-law and daughter, Mr. & Mrs. Perrie E. Waters.

Dr. James Belt Chesley, of Forest Glen, died on Wednesday of last week.

Harry M. Boland, of the Germantown vicinity, died last Friday.

Cont'd. on next page.

April 16, 1915, cont'd:
Dr. Reverdy B. Beall, for many years a dentist and druggist at Darnestown, died Tuesday.

Richard Sewell, a native of Rockville, died on Thursday of last week.

The board of directors of the Montgomery County National bank of Rockville adopted a resolution in memory of Spencer C. Jones, lately President of the Bank.

The Rockville Baptist Church adopted a resolution in memory of Spencer C. Jones.

Miss Addie Lee Saunders and Chesterfield Francis Clagett were married April 7th, at the home of the bride in Washington.

April 23, 1915:
Messrs. Marshall Walker, Frank Beall and Rufus Davis took delivery of Overland touring cars this week.

Mr. & Mrs. L. I. G. Owings, of Glenelg, Howard County, announced the engagement of their daughter, Katherine Owings, to John Arthur England, of Rockville.

Preston B. Ray, Clerk of the Circuit Court, has promoted James T. Bogley to the office of chief deputy, which became vacant by reason of the resignation of Darby Bowman; and has appointed J. Roger Spates to the position vacated by Mr. Bogley.

The alpha chapter of Phi Mu Sigma fraternity has been organized here. The following persons are mentioned, namely Lester Witherow, Edgar Reed, Lewis R. Watson, Frank H. Higgins, Edgar D. Thompson, Wm. F. Prettyman, and Edwin Fry.

Rev. T. A. Haughton-Burke has resigned as Rector of Prince George's parish after having been rector for the past 3 years. He plans to return to New York.

The dwelling, barn, poultry house, blacksmith shop, and other outbuildings on the property of Dr. John R. Batson, Spencerville, were destroyed by fire last Monday. The buildings are said to have belonged to Harry Black.

Robert B. Moore, of Gaithersburg, died of pneumonia on Thursday of last week.

Capt. John C. Delaney died on Wednesday of last week at his home in Chevy Chase.

William Henry Beane died April 15th, at the home of his
Cont'd. on next page.

April 23, 1915, cont'd:
daughter, Mrs. Daniels, near Germantown.
In a letter published by the *Sentinel*, Geo. T. Waters advocated bleeding as a treatment for pneumonia.

April 30, 1915:
John Darby Bowman announced that he would be a candidate for Clerk of the Circuit Court, subject to the Democratic primary.

Wm. T. Griffith of D.P. announced that he would be a candidate for Register of Wills, subject to the Democratic primary.

Winfield S. Magruder announced that he would be a candidate for County Commissioner from the $3^{rd}$ district, subject to the Democratic primary.

Norman Wootton announced that he would be a candidate for County Commissioner from the $3^{rd}$ district, subject to the Democratic primary.

John Ertter announced that he would be a candidate for County Commissioner from the $4^{th}$ district, subject to the Democratic primary.

Thomas C. Groomes announced that he would be a candidate for County Commissioner from the $4^{th}$ district, subject to the Democratic primary.

H. Clay Perry announced that he would be a candidate for County Commissioner from the $4^{th}$ district, subject to the Democratic primary.

Richard L. Saunders announced that he would be a candidate for County Commissioner from the $4^{th}$ district, subject to the Democratic primary.

Bradbury B. Warfield died last Sunday.

Miss Laura V. Soper and Luther E. Musgrove, both of Colesville, were married on Wednesday of last week.

Mrs. Julia Hewitt, widow of Richard H. Hewitt, died on Wednesday of last week.

Harry T. Whalen, brother of Sheriff [Peyton] Whalen of this County, was found dead by gas asphyxiation last Friday.

Montgomery Harris was killed on Wednesday in an automobile accident involving a car driven by Dr. R. C. Warfield, of Rockville.

Miss Margaret Owen Magruder and Thomas Henry Clark were married April $8^{th}$.

May 7, 1915:
In an essay contest, Walter B. Brock, of Bethesda, has been awarded one of the ten prizes offered to church members by the Carnegie Church Peace Union.

Geo. L. Crawford, E. T. Mills, Ed G. Ward, and Geo. F. Garrett have bought automobiles this week.

Walter S. Pratt died last Sunday at his home in Forest Glen.

A boulder with a bronze tablet will be placed by the Janet Montgomery chapter of the D.A.R. to mark the spot of 'Dowdens Ordinary', where General Braddock and his army camped in 1755 while on their way from Washington to Fort Duquesne. The location is on the farm now owned by Dr. James E. Deets, in Clarksburg.

May 14, 1915:
Frank B. Severance has been elected cashier of the First National Bank of Gaithersburg, succeeding Robert B. Moore.

Prof. George W. Walker, of Browningsville, died last Friday at his home.

At a meeting of the stockholders of the Monocacy Cemetery, the following were elected directors, namely: R. R. Darby, F. P. Hays, L. A. White, W. W. Poole, L. A. Allnutt, Jr., W. T. Griffith, L. P. Allnutt. Mr. R. R. Darby was elected president; Mr. W. T. Griffith, secretary-treasurer. The board of directors then adopted a resolution of respect in memory of Lawrence A. Darby, Sr.

Educational Day was held in Rockville – no date stated. There was an oratorical contest, with the prize offered by Brainard H. Warner, Jr., and athletic sports and drills held at the fair grounds. In connection with the oratorical contest, in the high school division the names mentioned were Clarence E. Dawson, first prize winner, Orlando Young, second prize winner, and Jennings Dodd, Leonard Hoyle, Charles Rice, Donald Snyder, Herbert P. Burdette, and Medford Canby. In the oratorical contest in the grammar schools, the names mentioned are Paul Tombly, first prize winner, William Canby, second prize winner, and Owen Knight, third prize winner. Other prizes went to Wightman Smith, and Albert Barber. Judges were Otho W. Talbott, Rev. O. A. Gillingham, Berry E. Clark, Rev. R. G. Koonts, Robert L. Warfield, J. A. Kendrick, Charles H. Gibson, T. W. Darnall, and Nellie Grock

Mrs. Charlotte Briggs, wife of Herman Briggs of Gaithersburg, who died April 9$^{th}$, was remembered.

May 21, 1915:
While assisting raising a barn on the farm of W. Jerome Offutt, near Poolesville on last Saturday, Israel Gibbs was instantly killed when a heavy timber fell on him.

Watson Belt died last Saturday at his home in Avery

William Lycurgus Cashell died last Monday at his home near Norwood. See also June 11, 1915 memorial resolution.

Mr. N. C. Rice has sold his store at Quince Orchard, and will become a minister in the Methodist church.

Mrs. Emma R. Bell, widow of Silas A. Bell, died last Saturday at her home near Laytonsville.

Miss Clara M. McAbee, of Lime Kiln, Frederick Co., has been chosen by the Baltimore News as the prettiest young lady in Maryland.

The graduates of the four Montgomery County high schools this year will be: Rockville, Lafayette Banes, Thos A. Butt, Alice H. Cashell, Nellie D. Duvall, Millard M. Fisher, Nellie H. Grock, Dorothy L. Higgins, Merrill D. Knight, Virginia W. Mullinix, Mary Geneva Reed, Mary E. Waesche, Bradley M. Woodfield. From Sandy Spring, Helen T. Nesbitt, Sarah Chichester, Anna B. Bird, Esther W. Scott, Stanley D. Owings, Allen F. Brooke. From Brookeville, Daisy C. Higgins, Mildred Powell, Mildred I. Burns, Catherine Townsend, Malcolm R. Brown. From Gaithersburg, Blanche Golden, Eleanor E. Darby, Lillian F. Waters, Mary E. King, Annie E. Trundle, Ravenell A. Monred.

Oliver Stonestreet Maus, who died 23 years ago, was remembered.

May 28, 1915:
James N. Barnsley announced that he would be a candidate for election to the House of Delegates subject to the Democratic primary vote.

Preston B. Ray announced that he would be a candidate for election as the Clerk of the Circuit Court, subject to the Democratic primary vote.

Alex. Kilgour announced that he would be a candidate for election as State's Attorney, subject to the Democratic primary vote.

Cont'd. on next page.

May 28, 1915, cont'd:
The following announced that they would each be candidates for Judge of the Orphan's Court, subject to the Democratic primary, namely: John E. West, Alfred C. Tolson, Edward O. Brown, J. Thomas Austin, Winfield S. Magruder.

The following announced that they would each be candidate for election as Sheriff, subject to the Democratic primary vote, namely, Thos. L. Lechlider, Wm. L. Aud, J. Melvin Etchison, W. Frank Gaither.

The Mayor and Council of Rockville has re-elected John J. Higgins and Preston R. Hewitt as town clerk, and bailiff, respectively.

Mrs. Josephine Harding, widow of Jos. Harding, died last week at her home near Ednor.

The annual banquet given by the junior class of the Gaithersburg High school to the graduating class, was held last Friday. The names mentioned are Thomas W. Troxal, Principal, and Miss Alverda Cooke, Donald Snyder, Alice Trundle, Willis B. Burdette, Edwin W. Broome, and Charles W. Prettyman.

June 4, 1915:
Samuel R. Deets, of Clarksburg, and Chas. F. Wedderburn, of Chevy Chase, were among the graduates of the Naval Academy class of 1915.

Robert B. Moore was remembered by resolution adopted by the directors of the First National Bank of Gaithersburg.

Miss Orpha Ashby has resigned as an assistant teacher

R. R. Adams, son of Barry Adams, formerly of Montgomery County, graduated from the Naval Academy in Annapolis, first in his class.

Robert B. Peter has been elected to the board of directors of the Montgomery County National Bank of Rockville.

At the commencement exercises of the Academy of the Visitation, Georgetown, Miss Helen Brunett, of Rockville, received a gold medal and other honors; and Miss Frances Scott Veirs, daughter of Charles Veirs, received a gold medal for scholarship and deportment.

In a popularity contest at the Lyric theater, T. D. Gates was the winner, followed by Artemus Sullivan and Miss Everett Stratmeyer.

Cont'd. on next page.

June 4, 1915, cont'd:

Miss Agnes Noland, a lifelong resident of Montgomery County, died on Thursday of last week.

Mr. & Mrs. George H. Bennett celebrated their $50^{th}$. wedding anniversary last Saturday by a family reunion held at their home.

Miss Mildred Hallowell Bentley and Dr. Karl Miller Wilson were married Tuesday.

Miss Valeria Robertson and Paul M. Lehman were married on May $27^{th}$.

The [Montgomery County] Agricultural Society sponsored a day of sports events at the fair grounds. Horse racing and baseball attracted a large crowd. The names mentioned in connection with the baseball game are Washington Chichester, manager of the Brookeville team, and Calhoun Patterson, manager of the Washington Grove team. In the area of horse racing, the names mentioned are Lee Offutt, F. G. Getzendanner, George Kelchner, Javens Bros., Howard C. Fawcett, Ed Gummell, Jim Brown, Dr. Devereaux, Thomas P. Baldwin, J. A. Jones, Thomas C. Keys, and Frederick W. Page.

June 11, 1915.

Albert M. Bouic announced that he was a candidate for State's Attorney, subject to the decision of the Democratic primary.

Luther A. Hoelman and Miss Etherl A. Elliott were married last Saturday in Washington.

It was announced that Miss Marie C. Bonifant and Thos. McLane Liebig will be married on June $16^{th}$.

It was announced that Miss Ethel Pate will marry J. Hampton Jones in July.

President Wilson has appointed Robert G. Hilton, of Rockville, to the position of subtreasurer at Baltimore. He will enter upon his duties at once.

R. Hugh Stevens died last Friday at his home in Hunting Hill.

E. Wilkerson Jones died last Saturday at his home near Dickerson.

Mrs. Martha Tyson Hopkins died on Thursday of last week at her home 'Grove Hill', in Montgomery County.

Miss Marjorie Snowden and Reuben Brigham were married last Monday at 'Ingleside', the home of the parents of the bride, at Ashton.

Cont'd. on next page.

June 11, 1915, cont'd:
 The annual commencement exercises of the Rockville High School were held last Friday. Certificates of graduation were awarded to Misses Alice Hazel Cashell, Nellie D. Duvall, Dorothy I Higgins, Virginia W. Mullinix, Mary Geneva Reed, Mary Waesche, and to Lafayette Banes, Thomas A. Butt, Millard M. Fisher, Merrill D. Knight, and Bradley M. Woodfield. The grammar school scholarship medal was awarded to William A. Linthicum.
 The commencement exercises of the Gaithersburg High School were held on Thursday evening of last week. The graduates mentioned are Misses Blanche G. Golden, Eleanor E. Darby, Annie M. Trundle, Lillian M. Waters, and Mary E. King, and Ravenell Annesly.

June 18, 1915.
 Miss Margaret C. Bonifant and Thomas M. Lieburg were married on Wednesday.
 At the annual meeting of the Montgomery County Federation of Home and School Associations, officers for the coming year were chosen as follows: President, Eugene E. Stevens; first vice president, Mrs. Josiah W. Jones; second vice president, Howard W. Fisk; secretary, Mrs. H. W. Parsons; treasurer, Charles H. Becker.
 The Florence Crittendon Circle of Kensington elected officers as follows: President, Mrs. J. Philip Hermann; first vice president, Mrs. J. Townsend; second vice president, Mrs. Mary Simpson; recording secretary, Mrs. Chas. Houghton; corresponding secretary, Mrs. Broomall; treasurer, Mrs. West; members of the Washington Board, Mrs. John T. Bready, Mrs. James H. Massey, Mrs. Holt.
 The annual commencement exercises of the Briarley Hall Military Academy have been held. The graduates are Brice P. Selby. Otho Trundle, and Walter G. Taylor. Others mentioned are Huston B. Joyner, Howard P. Preston, John F. Carlisle, Basil B. Coleman, Herbert Dorrence, Wm. F. Walker, W. Mgruder, and Wm. F. Walker.
 Isabella Griffith and Dr. Harvey Kaufman Fleckenstein were married last Saturday.
 Mrs. Martha Pearce Laird Goldsborough died last Saturday.
 Miss Katherine Thomas Owings and John Arthur England were married June $9^{th}$.
 Judge John C. Motter died last Saturday.
Cont'd. on next page.

June 18, 1915, cont'd:
Charles V. Morrison was remembered by resolution of the directors of the Poolesville National Bank.

Isaac Singleton Hendry died May 27$^{th}$. The article traces his career, and part of his ancestry.

R. Hugh Stevens, who died June 4$^{th}$, was remembered.

June 25, 1915:
Dr. J. Lawn Thompson has earned a degree of M. A. from Mt. St. Jospeh's College.

Miss Mary N. Riggs died suddenly on Wednesday.

The installation of the new sewer system in Rockville has now been completed, and owners are connecting.

Miss Stella E. Ball and Elden Henry Leith were married on Wednesday.

Fire last Sunday destroyed the ice house and several other buildings o the farm of Charles J. Maddox near Rockville.

Mrs. Jennie Burriss, wife of John A. Burriss, died suddenly last Friday at her home in Gaithersburg.

Mr. and Mrs. Porter Garrett were guests of honor at a reception given last Saturday by Mr. & Mrs. Alexander Garrett at their home in Hunting Hill.

Mrs. Elizabeth G. Reisinger died last Tuesday at her home in Rockville.

The cornerstone of the Monocacy Cemetery chapel was laid June 17$^{th}$., with about 700 people present. Among those mentioned were Milton W. Brewer, Charles E. Becraft, Wm. A. Waters, Harold S. Kingsbury, Fred F. Grimm, Lutie Griffith, Mrs. Frank Davis, A. H. Griffith, Horace Davis, Julia Belt, Charles R. Darby, Mr. Williamson, Col. Robert E. Lee, Alexander Kilgour, Rev. Gillingham, Nana Hays, Medora Jones, and Lillian Brewer.

July 2, 1915.
The barn on the farm of Ernest Ricketts, near Seneca, was struck by lightning and entirely destroyed by the fire which followed.

The large tenant house on the farm of Herman Briggs near Gaithersburg, burned.

Miss Mary Cecil and Levi Price were married on Wednesday of last week, in Washington.

Cont'd. on next page.

July 2, 1915, cont'd:
    Mrs. Caroline Nicholson died last Saturday, in Washington.
    On last Saturday, Mr. & Mrs. Judson Welliver gave a dance in the new barn on their farm near Rockville. Young people from all over the County attended and enjoyed the novel occasion.
    Nicholas H. Crawford died suddenly on Thursday of last week at his home near Brighton.
    As a result of competitive examinations, scholarships have been awarded as follows:  to State Normal School, Misses Mildred Barnes, Eleze Waesche, Marjorie Waters, Marguerite Waters, Eleanor Darby, and Marguerite Kohlhoss; to Washington College, Lafayette Banes; to St. Mary's Seminary, Miss Virginia Stonestreet.
    G. Raymond Flack died on Thursday June 24, at his home in Washington. He was a native of Rockville.
    John W. Connelly died on June 19th. He was a native of Montgomery County.

July 9, 1915.
    The salary of the postmaster at Forest Glen has been increased from $1400 per year to $1500.
    Wm. O. Orndorf, formerly of Montgomery County, died on Thursday of last week at his home in D. C.
    Misses Annie C. Pace, R. Marie Spates, and Mary White are attending summer school in Knoxville, Tenn.
    Miss Esther Scott, Miss Debora Idings, and Miss Alice I. Spates will attend summer school in Ocean City, Md.
    Miss Frances W. Higgins and Garnett H. Briggs were married on June 2nd.
    The Vestry of St. John's Church, Olney, remembered William Lycurgus Cashell.

July 16, 1915.
    Hon. P. D. Laird, of Rockville, announced his candidacy for the House of Delegates.
    Thomas Miles, of Clarksburg, caught a bass weighing 8 pounds 4 ounces in the Potomac, near the mouth of the Monocacy
    H. C. Allnutt has given to the Woman's Club of Rockville a building lot in Rockville upon which the Club will build a clubhouse.
    Mrs. Annie E. Trail died July 8th.

                              Cont'd. on next page.

July 16, 1915, cont'd:
Miss Margaret Kern Davis and Charles Sweet Trip were married on July 3rd.

Miss Mary Ritchie R. Atkin and John R. Henderson, Jr., of Rockville, were married on Monday.

Albert P. Beall, a lifelong resident of this County, died last Sunday at the home of Thomas W. Waters, near Brookeville.

Clarence E. Owen, formerly of Gaithersburg, has been appointed associate train master of the B. & O. R.R., with headquarters at Camden Station, Baltimore.

Miss Irene Kimler, of Williamsport, Md., and Francis Miller were married recently.

Miss Sallie Welling Simpson died July 1st.

July 23, 1915.
Mr. E. Olin Garrett and Miss Agnes I. Johnson were married recently in Pittsburg, Pa.

Miss Daisy C. Higgins is now attending summer school at Ocean City, Md.

G. Cleveland Johnson and Eva M. Burriss were married July 17th, in Washington.

L. Bates Etchison, formerly of Montgomery County, died on Thursday of last week.

Augustin J. S. Bourdeau and Edwin Julius Andrews were killed Monday when they were struck by a lightning bolt at Takoma Park.

Miss Ethel May Pate and J. Hampton Jones were married on Wednesday.

J. Frank Howes, who died July 24, 1912, was remembered.

July 30, 1915.
Vice Consul Harold E. Waters, of Germantown, will leave for Berlin, Germany, on next Tuesday.

N. Lyde Griffith, of the Laytonsville district, died last Wednesday.

Miss Rose May Powell and Raymond S. Diehl were married a few days ago at the home of the bride, in Bethesda.

There was a baby show in Poolesville on Friday of last week. The prize for the prettiest baby went to Mr. & Mrs. W. W. Williams,
Cont'd. on next page.

July 30, 1915, cont'd:
second prize to Mr. & Mrs. Walter Pyles; and Mr. & Mrs. John Hickman won first prize for the fattest baby.

Frank Walters, who lived on a farm near Rockville, died last Saturday in Baltimore, following an operation for appendicitis.

The Montgomery County Republicans, in a conference on Tuesday, nominated the following for places on the ballot for the coming general election, namely: for Clerk of the Court, Harry A. Dawson; for House of Delegates, Paul Sieman, George D. Curran, Edward D. Lewis, Wm. E. Brown; for County Commissioner from the 3$^{rd.}$ district, Windsor W. Hodges; for Sheriff, Henry Letterner; for Register of Wills, Ormsby McCammon; for State's Attorney, Wilson L. Townsend; for Judges of the Orphan's Court, Henry C. Chaney, John R. Woodfield, Harrison G. Ward; for State Central Committee, C. Scott Duvall, Thomas Dawson, Galen L. Tait, D. W. Baker, Wm. H. Johnson; for Delegates to State convention, Charles F. Kirk, Wm. T. S. Curtis, Brainard H. Warner, Gist Blair, Albert Warfield; alternates, James M. Mount, Bradley H. Dutrow, George M. Williams, George W. Meads, John W. Lancaster.

Mrs. Rosa V. Sands was accidentally shot and killed last Friday by her visiting nephew, at her home near Potomac.

J. Hills Robison announced that he was a candidate for Sheriff, subject to the vote of the Democratic primary

W. Ernest Offutt announced that he was a candidate for County Surveyor, subject to the vote of the Democratic primary.

August 6, 1915.
Miss Mary Elizabeth Fulks, daughter of the late Ignatius Fulks, died Monday.

Miss Julia May Butler and Earl Ulysses Stearn, both of the Potomac areas, were married last Saturday in Forest Glen.

Miss Margaret Welsh, daughter of Mr. & Mrs. Edward E. Welsh of Rockville, and John M. Heagy, Jr., of Rockville, were married Monday.

At the annual convention of the Montgomery County Sunday School Association, the following officers were chosen, namely: President, E. Wilson Walker; vice president, Columbus W. Day; secretary, Miss Woodward, treasurer, Jos. Reading.

Miss Helen Zanette Gingell and Guy Conrad Brewer, both of
Cont'd. on next page.

August 6, 1915, cont'd:
the Bethesda neighborhood, were married last Saturday.

    Frederick A. Allnutt, a merchant at Seneca, died last Saturday. He had been operated on for appendicitis about 2 weeks ago.

    The following named residents of Montgomery County have been chosen to judge the entries submitted in the upcoming Fair, namely: for garden products, Charles Norris; for art, Wm. H. Holmes; Culinary, Mrs. Charles Holland, Mrs. Wm. B. Dawson; preserves, etc.; Mrs. Chas. Jones, Mrs. Jas. H. Jones; hams, Judge E. C. Peter; children's dep't., Mrs. H. H. Miller.

    In School Board news: the school commissioners have accepted resignations of teachers Julian F. Walters, Margaret Screen, Fannie Condon, and Ruby Robertson. They have confirmed the appointment of A. Grace Baker, Mary E. Milburn, Leta Riggs, and Nellie Duvall. Assistant teachers appointed are Lena Ricketts, Virginia Waters, Louise Larcombe, Elsie Soper, Esther Scott, Roberta Higgins, Lillian Morgan, Emma Washington, Elsa Muench, Grace Birgfeld, Deborah Idings, Minnie Carlisle, Mary Reed, Ruby Robertson, Martha Brown, Dorothy Clum, Lillian Sage, Edna Hawke, Josephine Chaney, Helen Schwartz, Florence Barksdale, Effie G. Barnsley, and Edgar Thompson. Landella Etchison has been transferred from Washington Grove to Montrose. Wm. E. Brown, Joseph H. Janney and Arthur W. Brown have been named as trustees of the school at Brighton.

August 13, 1915.

    Mr. & Mrs. R. I. Lamb gave a barn dance at 'Wineth' farm on Wednesday night of last week, with about 150 guests present.

    Mrs. Mary Penn, widow of Ignatius Penn, died on Wednesday of last week at her home in Redland.

    Mrs. Elizabeth Dorsey Blunt, widow of William W. Blunt, died on August 3rd at her home near Goshen.

    There was a meeting of the Ridgley Brown Camp of Confederate Veterans held in Rockville last Saturday, at which officers were chosen as follows: Commander, Elgar L. Tschiffely; Lt. Cdr., John W. Holland; adjutant, David H. Horner; treasurer, Francis S. Kilgour; chaplain, Frank B. Horner; sergeant-at-arms, Wm. F. Boland. The executive committee consists of Benjamin D. Canby, James T. Moore, and Alfred C. Tolson.

                                        Cont'd. on next page.

August 13, 1915, cont'd:

The members of the Rockville Fox Hunt are having a very good season because of the plentiful supply of foxes. They had a recent hunt on the farm of Elijah T. Bean, near Redland. The members mentioned are Judge Edward C. Peter, Artemus Sullivan, Ledoux E. Riggs, Chas. A. Clagett, Charles H. Lyddane, Peyton Whalen, William Riggs, Julian F. Walters, W. O. Spates, Cecil Allnutt, Z. M. Waters, and Harrison England.

The roster of Company K, National Guard was published. The names mentioned are: Richard B. Clayton, E. Brooke Lee, L. Q. C. Lmar, Geo. Landon, Hugh F. O'Donnell, Oliver H. P. Clark, Jas. E. Burdette, Edward F. Shaifer, Charles T. Cooley, Carroll Cissel, Ernest Eslin, Ernest VanHorn, Bert Cowell, Leon P. Shoemaker, Clarence E. Dawson, Jr., Henry Crismond, George Price, Daniel Allen, Terence Brady, George Burdette, Charles Clark, Frank P. Clark, Clarence E. Clements, Louis H. Ely, Henry Eslin, Wm. Fidler, Russell Gill, John Gladmon, James S. Harvey, Frank L. Hewitt, Jos. T. Hewitt, Wm. Howes, Arch Johnson, Oscar Lackoff, Wm. G. Linkins, Wm. Lusby, Oscar McKay, John K. Magee, Frank Murray, Henry Sparks, Wm. S. Tyler, Hugh O. Thompson, Walter Thompson, Geo. VanHorn, Roland C. Williams, Dorsey Jones, Clarence C. Anders, Preston Hewitt, Oscar Hilton, Wm. S. Poss, Cliff Howes, Geo. W. O'Brien, Charles Shoemaker, Ralph E. Sullivan, Rogers P. Tutow, Charles R. Parks, Jr., Leonard W. Lindner, Chas. Purdum, Ernest Purdum, Joseph Savage, Arthur Sabin, Carl B. Springirth, Eugene E. Stevens, Jr., Gerald Warthen, J. Albert Hickey, and Wm. J. Fierstein.

A tribute to Frederick A. Allnutt, who died July 31st., was published. See also September 10, 1915.

August 20, 1915.

The new flour plant of Smith Hoyle, at Boyd's was completed last Friday, and is now running.

The school commissioners have received the resignations of Miss Frances English at Derwood, and Miss Mary Davis at Rockville.

Mrs. Frank Giddings won the set of dishes recently given away by Reisinger's.

The body of William Darne, a native of Montgomery County and a Confederate veteran, was brought from Richmond last Friday

Cont'd. on next page.

August 20, 1915, cont'd:
and buried in the Presbyterian cemetery at Darnestown. He had enlisted at age 16 and served for the entire time of the Civil War.

Miss Nora J. Rabbitt and Jacob T. S. Shalcross were married on Wednesday of last week.

Mrs. Frances R. Carlin, widow of John T. Carlin, died Sunday.

Wm. W. Russell, formerly of Rockville, has been selected by President Wilson to be the Minister to Santo Domingo. He has previously served as Minister to Columbia, Venezuela, and Santo Domingo.

Charles H. Parker died on Thursday at his home at Layhill.

The entries for the races at the coming Fair are listed. Owners from Montgomery County include Clifton Park Stock farm, Fields Bros., W. O. Dosh, R. J. Offutt, C. J. Selvage, H. C. Fawsett, Wm. G. Butler, R. T. Offutt, Mrs. H. L. Diamond, Spencer Magruder, Thomas C. Keys, Joe Umstead, Selby Bros., and J. F. O'Brien.

At the annual meeting of the Montgomery County Anti-saloon League, the following officers were elected: President, Rev. Oscar W. Henderson; vice president, Thomas J. Owen; secretary, Wilson Walker; treasurer, Alfred C. Warthen. Others mentioned are Rev. J. E. Fort, J. Wesley Boyer, Howard Spurrier, Wm. E. Ward, Reuben T. Baker, W. Brooke Vincent, H. Latane Lewis, Mordecai Fussell, Edington Bell, Wesley A. Maxwell, Columbus W. Day, Charles G. Wilson, Mrs. Sarah T. Miles, and Preston L. Snyder.

Mrs. Arabella C. Peele, wife of Chief Justice Stanton J. Peele, U. S. Court of Claims, died last Friday at her home in Chevy Chase.

August 27, 1915.

George T. Windham died last Sunday at his home.

Mrs. Frank Giddings won a fine set of dishes recently given away by Reisingers.

Zadoc Thomas Crown died on Thursday of last week at his home in Hunting Hill.

Claude Nicholson died last Sunday. He was the son of the late L. Baker Nicholson of Dickerson and his wife Elizabeth.

Miss Lucy Eleanor Wright, of Forest Glen, and Americus Dawson Trundle, of the Poolesville district, were married last Sunday, at the home of the bride's parents in Forest Glen.

Cont'd. on next page.

August 27, 1915, cont'd:
Harold Waters, of Germantown, has arrived in Berlin, where he will represent the U. S. as vice consul. He is the son of P. E. Waters.

Thomas Daymude, who enlisted in the U. S. Marine Corps on June 26$^{th.}$ last, is now on duty in Port au Prince, Haiti.

September 3, 1915.
Merritt Chance, of Kensington, became postmaster of Washington last week.

Mahlon H. Austin died on Wednesday of last week at his home near Concord, Bethesda district.

Mr. & Mrs. Charles T. Stearn announced the marriage of their daughter Miss M. Victoria Stearn to Spencer Magruder on Saturday, August 28$^{th}$.

The Postmaster-General has ordered the dismissal of W. E. Berry as postmaster at Rockville, and the dismissal of Oliver H. P. Clark as postmaster at Silver Spring. Mr. Lane Johns, of Washington, has been appointd to succeed Mr. Berry, and President Wilson has named O. B. Clark to succeed his son as postmaster at Silver Spring.

In school board news: The following teachers have been appointed: H. W. White, to Darnestown; Ruth Beall, assistant at Bethesda; Corinne Duff, assistant at Takoms Park; Maud England, assistant at White Oak; Ruth W. Rogers, assistant at Rockville; Evelyn McAtee assistant at Darnestown; Marion True, assistant at Darnestown. Resignations have been accepted from Miss Bruce Colton, DeLos Cissell, Sylva Townsend, Frances English, Mary Davis, Louise Larcombe. Teacher appointments confirmed: Alice L. Spates, Effie K. Ternent, R. Marie Spates, F. S. Gladhill, Stella E. Thomas, Katherine Moore, Violette Murphy, Edith Lindig, Margaret Hall, Daisy Higgins, Claudia Hall, Eleanor Reed, Frances Ricketts.

Edward P. Beall announced that he was withdrawing as a Democratic candidate for election as County Commissioner of the 4$^{th}$. district.

The Fair which closed on last Friday, was a great success. On Thursday there were 15,000 people present. A partial list of the prizes is as follows: In cases where any individual is mentioned more than once in a category, the duplication is not here copied.

Saddle horses: J. N. Barnsley, F. M. Hallowell, A. T. Powell,
Cont'd. on next page.

September 3, 1915, cont'd:
W. E. Ricketts.
Standard bred: Fields Bros.
Quick draft: Dr. W. T. Brown, J. W. Barnsley, J. S. Bolton, W. T. Ridgely, A. T. Powell, Mrs. H. L. Diamond.
Registered Perchrons: Benton G. Ray, Rockville and Potomac Percheron Co.
Heavy draft: Walter Walker, Charles M. Williams, E. H. Peters, Fields Bros., J. W. Graff, W. E. Wilt, H. A. Dawson, Edward P. Beall, Charles T. Nicholson, R. H. Lansdsale, Jr., L. H. Young.
Shetland ponies: Tyler Case, Rosemont Farm, George M. Ash, Josephine Esputa.
Sweepstakes: Walter Walker
Registered Durham cattle: Benton G. Ray
Registered Holstein Fresian: Fields Bros., Charles Veirs
Registered Jersey: Rosemont Farm.
Registered Guernsey: W. Harry Beard.
Grade Holstein: Charles Veirs.
Aberdeen Angus: A. T. Powell.
Hogs: D. W. Shorb.
Large Yorkshire: D. W. Shorb.
Durock Jersey: D. W. Shorb, J. R. Lechlider.
Essex: D. W. Shorb.
Small Yorkshire: D. W. Shorb.
Victoria: D. W. Shorb.
Grade hogs: John S. Gillis.
Sheep: John E. Muncaster, Jr.
Fruit: Mrs. Lillian Robertson, C. W. Barnsley, R. Bentley Thomas, Dr. Francis Thomas, Irving Wagner, Claudia Robertson, Thos. Waters, Seth W. Warfield, R. P. Hines, Minnie Case, Frederick Stabler, Mrs. T. T. Barnsley, Catherine Cowsill, J. Poss, Mrs. W. U. Bowman, Mrs. W. W. Welsh, Mrs. H. E. Stratmyer, T. A. Barnsley, Jennie Higgins, Frederick Stabler, Prof. Willis S. Moore, M. S. Plummer, Arthur Stonestreet, A. W. Brown, Mary Welsh, R. P. Hines.
Garden products: R. P. Hines Jr., Myers Bros., T. A. Barnsley, Seth Warfield, Frederick Stabler, Mrs. Wm. W. Welsh, Lewis R. Watson, Frederick Stabler, Ellen Farquhar, Emma T. Stabler, B. A. Dove, Emmet Dove, Kenneth Barnsley, Urban Wagner, Wm. Gilpin Jr., J. R. Lechlider, Guy Watkins, Mrs. W. E. Ricketts
Cont'd. on next page.

September 3, 1915, cont'd:
Hattie Granger, E. W. Monday.

Farm products: R. P. Hines, T. A. Barnsley, R. P. Hines, Wm. B. Dove, Irving Hoskinson, George Shaw, Myers Bros., C. W. Barnsley, Seth W. Warfield, John E. Muncaster, James R. King.

Dairy: Mrs. A. E. Burriss, Mrs. Geo. P. Hunter.

Honey: Myers Bros., W. S. Ward.

Hams: Mrs. Donald Bowie, Urban Wagner.

Culinary: Margaret Dawson, Addie McFarland, Mary Wagner, Mrs. Seth Warfield, Beulah Barnsley, Hannah V. Stabler, Emma T. Stabler, Mrs. A. G. Kingdon, Mrs. Charles Veirs, Josephine Watson, Mrs. John F. Bailey, Mrs. W. Robert Lyddane, Rose Wagner, Mrs. Geo. H. Lamar, Mrs. Seth W. Warfield, Mrs. W. E. Ricketts, Mrs. W. E. Ward, Mrs. Clarence Hoskinson, Jane Offutt, Rose L. Wagner, Edith Hull, Margaret Higgins, Mary Stabler, Miss L. V. Morrison, Nannie Owns, Lillie Stabler, Mrs. Alfred Ray, Miriam E. Johnson, Miss M. S. Plummer, Lila Goldsborough.

Preserves, canned fruit, jellies: Mrs. W. E. Ricketts, Mrs. C. Scott Duvall, Mabel Shaw, Josie Higgins, Ada Warfield, Mrs. W. Hicks, Mrs. G. P. Henderson, Mabel Shaw, Mrs. T. T. Barnsley, Mrs. W. U. Bowman, Mrs. S. A. Clagett, Mrs. A. C. Warthen, Mrs. G. W. Bready.

Canned goods: Mary Smith, Mrs. Wm. A. Posey, Mrs. G. P. Henderson, Mrs. G. W. Davis, Jennie Higgins, Emma Sullivan, Mrs. C. Scott Duvall, Rose Wagner, W. E. Riley, Mrs. W. U. Bowman, Helen L. Pumphrey.

Jelly: Nellie Long, M. E. Pumphrey, R. P. Hines, Mrs. O. M. Linthicum, Mrs. Irving Hoskinson, Mrs. G. P. Henderson, Katherine Poole, Nannie Owens, Edgar Higgins, Laura V. Shaw, Mrs. J. F. Walters, Mrs. W. E. Riley, Edith Hull, Jennie Higgins, Josie Higgins.

Misc. culinary: Ada Warfield, Mrs. S. A. Clagett, Mrs. B. C. Hughes, Mary Stabler, Mrs. W. E. Ricketts, Helen L. Pumphrey, E. E. Monday, Mrs. S. F. Slaymaker, Mrs. A. C. Warthen, M. S. Plummer, Mary Welsh.

Children's department: Dorothy Tschiffely, Mary Stallsmith, Nettie Shorts, M. E. Shorts, Mildred Gardner, Fannie Oldfield, Nettie Shorts, Mildred Morrison, L. Y. Hall, Helen Moulden, A. E. Beall, Stonestreet Lamar, Heath D. Goldsborough, Fannie Oldfield, Mildred Morrison, C. H. England, Phillips Lee Goldsborough, Annie Shorts,

Cont'd. on next page.

September 3, 1915, cont'd:
Gertrude L. Hines, Catherine W. Hines, Hazel Plummer, R. P. Hines, Elizabeth Bowman, Gladys Hilton, Anna Shorts, George Sullivan.
Children's garden products: Chas. Hines, Hazel Burriss, John F. Warfield, Milburn Ward, Donald Walter, Mildred Morrison, John E. Muncaster Jr., Charles Hines, James Cortland Trundle, Pearl A. Brown.

The E. V. White chapter of United Daughters of the Confederacy held its annual meeting August 18$^{th}$, at the home of Mrs. Jones Hoyle, president. Officers were elected as follows: President, Mrs. Jones Hoyle; first vice president, Mrs. Reginald Darby; second vice president, Mrs. George Jones; recording secretary, Mrs. T. R. Hall; corresponding secretary, Miss Medora Jones; treasurer, Miss Julia Belt; historian, Mrs. John Jones; registrar, Miss Clara Price; educator, Miss Virginia Belt.

September 10, 1915.
George Walters, of Monocacy, died on Wednesday of last week.
Jane Boyd Rice, of Spencerville, and Charles A. Fise, of Chevy Chase, were married on last Wednesday.
The residence of James E. Day was destroyed by fire on Monday.
Miss Mary Agnes Chapin, of Kensington, and Louis Hamilton Willard, of Washington, were married on Wednesday.
Invitations have been issued for the wedding of Mary R. Janney and James Mark Shields, to be held September 21$^{st}$.
The marriage of Miss Frances E. English and Arthur M. McFadden took place on Thursday of last week.
Miss Bessie C. Brake entertained the class of 1913, Gaithersburg High School with a reunion party at her home, on September 6$^{th}$. Those present were Olive Gilliss, Amy Robertson, Mary Kelly, Bessie Brake, Paul Lehman, Gaither Warfield, Nathan White, and Paul Anderson. Also present were Mr. & Mrs. W. H. Brake, Mr. & Mrs. G. S. Brake, Paul Lehman, Mae Wilson, Eleanor Brake, Jos. Brake, and Ralph Bevans.
A new feature of the recent fair was a 'Better Babies Contest'. Babies were brought to be examined by physicians, with examinations conducted by Dr. Curtis Lee Hall, of Massachusetts
Cont'd. on next page.

September 10, 1915, cont'd:
General Hospital, Boston, assisted by nurses from Starmont Sanatorium and from Dr. Bullard's sanatorium. First prize of a pair of crib blankets was won by Mr. & Mrs. W. W. Gingell of Bethesda, Second prize went to the baby of Mr. & Mrs. LeonardNicholson of Rockville. Also mentioned were Mr. & Mrs. Wm. Reuben Pumphrey of Rockville and Mr. & Mrs. Robert Soper of Olney.

The following completes the list of prizes awarded at the recent Fair:

Poultry [all varieties of chickens combined here, even though they were listed individually by variety in the newspaper] F. A. Kerr, E. G. Johnson, Mrs. L. I. Nicholson, R. P. Hines, J. Defendorfer, A. E. Burriss, D. Walter, R. C. D. Hunt, B. E. Hutchinson, J. H. Shorts, Edwin Monday, L. R. Watson, Charles Beard, C. W. Rippey, D. P. Smith, E. G. Johnson, Mrs. L. I. Nicholson, B. F. Hutchinson, Edmund J. Hickey, A. Sullivan.

Turkeys: R. P. Hines

Ducks: [all varieties] Mrs. L. I. Nicholson, A. Sullivan, M. E. C. Allnutt, E. G. Johnson.

Guineas: J. H. Shorts, A. E. Burriss.

Hares: A. Sullivan

Pigeons: R. P. Hines, V. Wilson.

Works of art: Rose Wagner, Mrs. Fred. Keplinger, S. R. Hall, M. E. Moran, M. W. Offutt Jr., Mrs. Donald Bowie, Louise Larcombe, Miriam E. Johnson, Emma T. Stabler, S. P. Wagner, H. Defandorf, Mrs. S. R. Hall, Katherine Sutherland, Florence Snyder, Courtney Stauffer, Helen S. Pumphrey, M. E. Pumphrey, Mrs. C. M. Grubb, J. Darby Bowman, Lethia Edmunds.

Handicrafts: Miss B. A. Dove, Emma Granger, Mrs. O. M. Linthicum, Mrs. Fred. Keplinger, S. R. Hall.

Flowers: Miss B. A. Dove, Ellen Farquhar, Emmett Dove, Mrs. Emmett Dove, Mrs. S. J. Finneyfrock, Mrs. James T. Bogley, Mrs. W. E. Ricketts, E. S. Dawson, Mrs. W. E. Ward, Mrs. W. R. Lyddane, Charles R. Morriss, Mrs. L. I. Nicholson, Mabel Ward, Lucy M. Smith, Mrs. Carey Kingdon, Mrs. James Bogley, Mrs. Leland Fisher, Ada Warfield, Mrs. H. E. Stratmyer, Mrs. Charles W. Prettyman, Eleanor Umstead, Mrs. Jacob Umstead.

Domestic manufactures: Margaret Higgins, Josie Higgins, Mrs. C. O. Bean, Mrs. M. B. Shorts, Mrs. L. G. Gardner, Mrs. M. O.

Cont'd. on next page.

September 10, 1915, cont'd:
Winslow, Mrs. Charles Holland, Mrs. J. C. Patterson, Mrs. J. J. Bussart, Mrs. S. E. East, Leona Rabbitt, Mrs. Bertha H. Talbott, Elizabeth Dawson, Mrs. George P. Henderson, Mrs. Lloyd Brewer, Mrs. Roger Shaw, Mrs. Wm. B. Trundle, Mrs. O. M. Linthicum, Ruth Wilson, Hazel Simmons, Helen Gruber, Mrs. A. R. Thompson, Mrs. L. Birch, Katherine Poole, Mrs. L. Birch, Mrs. J. S. Gruver, Helen Gruver, Maria Hodges, Vera Gravers, Laura V. Shaw, Miss L. B. Morrison, Mrs. Lavinia Jones, Mary Welsh, Nannie Owens, Ella Plummer, Ida S. Dove, Edith Hall, Mrs. Lila Goldsborough, Mrs. S. J. Clendenning, Mary Pitcher, Mary Travers, Minnie Yearly, Marie Talbott, Mrs. T. P. Hicks, Catherine Cowsill, Mrs. C. M. Brown, Edith Hogg, Miss L. T. Prettyman, Kate Scherer, Mrs. H. S. Magruder, Mrs. Bowie F. Waters, Miss L. Priest, Mrs. G. I. Banes, Dorothy Tschiffely, Mrs. M. A. Winslow, Mrs. M. E. MacGregor, Mrs. M. M. Alexander, Edith Hull, Mrs. J. P. Warthen, Mrs. Alexander Kilgour, Mrs. Randolph Dove, Minnie Anderson, Mrs. L. Birch.

Thomas E. Padgett, of near Seneca, died August 31$^{st}$.

September 17, 1915.
Mrs. Lizzie M. Gooding died suddenly last Saturday.

The residence of Hazlette Crawford, near Cedar Grove, was destroyed by fire last Friday. Nearly all of the furniture was also lost.

In furtherance of an effort to establish a volunteer fire department in Silver Spring, a committee has been formed to buy the necessary equipment. The names mentioned are Gist Blair, W. W. Jordan, F. M. Nally, B. R. Cannon, and J. H. Cissell.

Col. I. Mervin Maus, a native of Silver Spring, has recently retired from active service in the Army Medical Corps. He acquired international recognition when he eliminated bubonic plague and smallpox in the Phillipines.

The Executive Committee of the local W.C.T.U. met on Monday, in anticipation of the annual State convention which will be held in Rockville beginning on September 29$^{th}$. Those mentioned are Mrs. Anna Welsh, Mrs. Laura Higgins, Mrs. Ellen Waters, Mrs. Warren Choate, Mrs. Edwin Smith, Miss Ida Dove, Mrs. John B. Brewer, Mrs. H. J. Finley, Miss Lucile Welsh, Mrs. Emmett Dove, Mrs. Frank Allen, Mrs. Ellen Waters, Miss Margaret Higgins, and
Cont'd. on next page.

September 17, 1915, cont'd:
Mrs. O. C. Barnes.

Miss Elizabeth Laurence Hartshorne and Percy Garland Ligon were married last Saturday at 'Hillcrest', the home of the parents of the bride.

F. B. Nicholson, of Dickerson, commiteed suicide on Wednesday by jumping from a window of a hotel in Atlantic City.

Helen Bertha Howes, infant daughter of Elias Howes and Susie Howes, died August 17$^{th}$.

The results of the Democratic primary election show the following to have been nominated:

For Clerk of the Circuit Court, Preston B. Ray.

For State's Attorney, Albert M. Bouic.

For House of Delegates, Charles F. Brooke, John Gardner, Paul Y. Waters.

For Judges of the Orphan's Court, Winfield S. Magruder, Alfred C. Tolson, John E. West [Mr. West was the leading vote-getter of all candidates – later appointed chief judge]

For Register of Wills, Henry C. Allnutt

For County Commissioner, 3$^{rd}$. district, N. Hazel Metzger

For County Commissioner, 4$^{th}$. district, George C. Bradley Jr.

For Sheriff, W. Frank Gaither.

For members of the State Central Committee, Alexander G. Carlisle, Richard E. Darby, Robert G. Hilton, William H. Wade, Harry C. Williams.

September 24, 1915:

Miss Carrie V. Johnson, of Layhill, and Richard Whitehead, of Colesville, were married last Sunday in Rockville.

The home of Abraham Jones, near Rockville, burned on last Friday.

Miss Marie Maud Hewitt and Ralph Wellington Bohrer were married Wednesday.

Luther H. Young, a life-long resident of the Damascus district, died last week.

Miss Mary C. Davis, of Hyattstown, and Charles C. Rhodes, were married on Thursday of last week. The bride had been a teacher at the Rockville High School

Cont'd. on next page.

Sptember 24, 1915, cont'd:

Miss Frances Merle Magruder, of Montrose, and John A. Carlisle, of Cleveland, Ohio, were married on Wednesday of last week.

Miss Mary Randolph Janney, of Brookeville, and Jas. M. Shields, of Chicago, were married last Tuesday.

Miss Katherine Valeria Walling, of Poolesville, and Sidney Thompson, of Washington, were married Wednesday.

The *Sentinel* published a letter submitted by Alexander Kilgour, in which Mr. Kilgour congratulated Albert M. Bouic [Mr. Kilgour's opponent] on his success in the Democratic primary.

A challenge to the recent Democratic primary results has been filed by J. Furr White, who appears to have been defeated by 9 votes, and by J. Darby Bowman and Richard L. Saunders, who were apparently defeated by 47 votes and 164 votes respectively.

October 1, 1915.

The engagement of Miss Ruth Marjorie Haines and J. Ernest Hawkins was announced.

The engagement of Miss Carrie C. England and William D. Clark was announced.

Wm. F. Houser, a native of Montgomery County, died on Thursday of last week.

Daniel F. Feigley, a native of Frederick County but lately a resident in Montgomery County, died on Wednesday of last week.

Miss Margaret Kelly, of Forest Glen, and Harry Barrett, of Silver Spring, were married on Wednesday of last week.

The recount has been completed of votes cast in the recent Democratic primary, without changes in the results.

Bernard Bready, of Silver Spring, claims to have been the youngest drummer in the Union army during the Civil War. He says that he enlisted at the age of 9 years. At the end of the war, he re-enlisted, and was finally discharged July 12, 1873, at age 19.

The Prohibition party has put forward the following County ticket:

For Cerk of the Circuit Court: John T. Baker.

For House of Delegates: Samuel W. Beall, Geo. W. Easton, Joseph G. Watkins, Hezekiah Day.

For Judges of the Orphan's Court: Bradley Watkins, Daniel

Cont'd. on next page.

October 1, 1915, cont'd:
C. Ifert, Alburn H. Watkins.
    For Register of Wills: Vernon D. Watkins.
    For Sheriff: Ernest D. Beall
    John Wesley Linthicum, who died October 5, 1914, was remembered.

October 8, 1915.
    Miss Pauline Devine, of Germantown, and Vernon G. Bennett, of Gaithersburg, were married last week.
    Joseph Reading has been recommended for appointment as postmaster of Rockville.
    The engagement of Miss Carrie Crabb England and Wm. D. Clark was announced. The wedding will be held on October 20$^{th}$.
    The home of Jacob E. Nichols, near Boyd's, burned last Sunday.
    Wm. H. Hughes died last Friday at the home of his daughter, Mrs. Emma Stearn, near Potomac.
    J. Schaffer Brennerman, formerly of Washington, but who has recently been living in the Bethesda district with his daughter and son-in-law, Mr. & Mrs. Charles Parks, died last Sunday.
    Miss Helen Ridgely Banes, of Sandy Spring, sailed last Saturday for Puerto Rico, where she wll be the assistant superintendent of the Presbyterian Hospital. Miss Banes is the daughter of Mr. & Mrs. George I. Banes.
    The engagement of Miss Ruth Griffith and Charles Clifton Veirs was announced.
    The contention over the recount of the Democratic primary vote in the case of J. Furr White and Phillip D. Laird has continued with the filing by Mr. White of a petition in the Circuit Court seeking a further condsidertion of 4 disputed ballots.

October 15, 1915.
    Thomas Johnson died last Saturday at his home in Buck Lodge.
    Allen Peter, son of George Peter, of Kensington, died last Tuesday.
    James Clagett Holland died last Monday.

                                    Cont.d. on next page.

October 15, 1915, cont'd:
   Mr. & Mrs. J. Wm. Bogley announced the engagement of their daughter, Lelia Marie Bogley, to Jas. C. Dulin Jr. The wedding will take place October 20th.
   The marriage of Mrs. Mary Ray Dunlop and John B. Waters was announced.
   Miss Bertha Hamke, of Rockville, and W. C. Hoskinson, of Patterson, N. J., were married on Monday.
   The Circuit Court has dismissed the petition of J. Furr White seeking a reconsideration of 4 ballots cast in the past Democratic primary election.

October 22, 1915.
   The following have been drawn to serve as jurors during the November term of the Circuit Court:  Luther M. Duvall, William D. Bell, Henry R. Benson, Charles T. Kingsbury, Zaccheaus Warfield, Jas. H. Purdum, Arthur P. Fletchall, William W. Poole, Phillip F. Mossburg, Harvey J. White, Joseph H. Ward, Edmund A. Gloyd, Walter S. Thompson, Wm. Dorsey, Wm. L. Beall, Frank H. Karn, Morgan J. Boteler, Charles Hopkins, Emory F. C. Ray, Thomas L. Lechlider, Reginald Cross, Frank Esworthy, James Beall, Henry W. Offutt, Alexander A. Braddock, Robert Wilson, Robert P. Soper, Robert D. Isherwood, Joseph B. Janney, Charles R. Hartshorn, John A. Belt, Perry A. Gloyd, Samuel R. Pummer, Joseph M. Etchison, Joseph M. Harris, Thomas E. Bisset, James W. C. Higgins, R. Frank Gibson, Harvey J. Harriss, James P. Gott, J. Wellington Boyer, Willie B. Moxley, Thomas H. Pope, Joseph T. Hewitt, Joseph B. Glover, William H. Fidler, Wm. F. Matthews, James P. Raney.
   The contest between J. Furr White and Philip D. Laird over the votes cast in the last Democratic primary election was argued in the Maryland Courtr of Appeals on Wednesday.  The decision sustains the lower court, and thus the nomination goes to Mr. Laird.
   James R. Harvey, for many years a merchant at Sunshine, died on Thursday of last week.
   Mrs. Anna Windsor, widow of William R. Windsor of Clarksburg, died on Tuesday.of last week.
   Miss Carrie Crabb England and William Dorsey Clark were married on Wednesday, in Christ Episcopal Church, Rockville.
   Miss Eva Marie Austin and Earle S. Carlin were married on
                                        Cont'd. on next page.

October 22, 1915, cont'd:
Thursday of last week, in St. John's Church, Forest Glen. The Republican State Central Committee, composed of C. Scott Duvall, Galen L. Tait, Thomas Dawson, D. W. Baker, and Wm. H. Johnson, met last Saturday, and completed the ticket of Republican nominees to be entered in the coming general election, as follows:
For Clerk of the Circuit Court: Harry A. Dawson.
For Register of Wills: Ormsby McCammon.
For House of Delegates: William E. Brown, George D. Curran, Edward D. Lewis, Paul Sleman.
For State's Attorney: J. Dann Faber.
For Sheriff: Henry Latterner
For County Commissioner, 3$^{rd}$. district: Windsor W. Hodges.
For judges of the Orphan's Court: Henry C. Chaney, John R. Woodfield, Harrison G. Ward.

October 29, 1915.
Harrison G. Ward has withdrawn from the Republican ticket as a candidate for judge of the Orphan's Court.

John P. Lawson, a former merchant and farmer of Clarksburg, died on Thursday of last week.

Roger C. White and Miss Ruth A. Dooley were married on Wednesday of last week.

Wilbur S. Day has been named to the post of acting postmaster of Rockville.

Joseph Johnson, son of Walter A. Johnson of Washington, was killed last Friday in an automobile accident.

Leonard P. Bradshaw died on Thursday of last week at his home in Chevy Chase.

Mrs. Amanda E. Metzgar, widow of Wm. W. Metzgar, died last Monday at her home in Poolesville.

Miss Leila Marie Bogley and James C. Dulin were married on Wednesday of last week.

Miss Rita Dunbar and Hugh Mackay Davis were married on Wednesday of last week.

November 5, 1915.
Mrs. Mary J. Meem, widow of Cloreviere Meem, of
Cont'd. on next page:

November 5, 1915, cont'd:
Gaithersburg, died last Wednesday.

John T. Hawkins died on Thursday of last week at his home.

It was announced that Miss Sarah Frances Hamilton and Maurice Eugene Shoemaker were married October 28$^{th}$.

John Bonifant, son of the late George and Helen Bonifant, died on last Sunday at his home near Layhill.

Miss Julia S. Lewis, daughter of Mr. & Mrs. W. Motzer Lewis of Germantown, and Rev. John Wakeman Ayers were married on October 26$^{th}$.

The following jurors last drawn to serve in the coming term of the Circuit Court have been excused, namely, Harvey J. White, A. P. Fletchall, W. W. Poole, Phillip T. Mossburg, Frank H. Karn, John A. Belt, and Wm. H. Fidler. Their places will be taken by Walter M. Butler, John B. Byrd, Peter J. Stang, A. Dawson Trundle, Jacob R. Umstead, John C. Burns, and Alfred C. Warthen.

The foxhunters field trials, which had been set for last Friday and Saturday, could not be held, and have been postponed until November 16$^{th}$. The first bench show, held under the auspices of the Montgomery County Foxhunters' Association, was a success. The names mentioned in connection with the bench show are Cecil Allnutt, Jas. P. Gott, Artemus Griffith, Edmund C. Davis, Wm. V. Dawson, and Robert Aitcheson.

A fire last Monday at the farm of Howard Fawcett on River Road, near Potomac, burned a large barn and contents, including seven horses, a quantity of wheat, corn, machinery, etc.

Fire, possibly intentionally set, destroyed a barn on the farm of County Commissioner O. W. Robey last Friday.

A barn on the farm of George R. Rice, near Travilah, burned on Monday of last week.

The Rockville High School will present an Indian pageant at the Seco hall on Friday. The names mentioned are Chas. G. Myers, Elizabeth Prescott, Estelle Ricketts, Faith White, Helen Fisher, Mary Dawson, Rose Dawson, Edith Lamar, R. L. Watkins, W. E. Pumphrey, Theodore Ricketts, A. B. McFarland, Wm. L. Hartshorne, Wm. A. Baker, and Elizabeth Defandorf.

The results of the last general election show the following for Montgomery County: for members of the House of Delegates, elected, Charles F. Brooke, William E. Brown, John Gardner, Philip

Cont'd. on next page

November 5, 1915, cont'd:
D. Laird, and Paul Y. Waters: for Clerk of the Circuit Court, elected, Preston B. Ray: for State's Attorney, elected, Albert M. Bouic: for Judges of the Orphan's Court, elected, Winfield S. Magruder, Alfed C. Tolson, John E. West: for Register of Wills, elected, Henry C. Allnutt: for County Commissioner, elected, N. Hazel Metzger, George G. Bradley Jr., for Sheriff, elected, W. Frank Gaither: for Surveyor, elected, W. Ernest Offutt. Mr. Bradley was the top vote-getter.

November 12, 1915.
It was announced that Miss Ruth Griffith and Clifton Charles Veirs will be married November 17th. at the home of the bride, in Beallsville.

Mr. J. Forrest Gott has resigned as deputy clerk in the office of the Clerk of the Circuit Court, to be effective immediately.

Word has been received of the death of Mrs. Louise Waters Slifer, age 97. She was the wife of Thomas Slifer. Mr. and Mrs. Slifer were reputed to be the longest-married couple in the U. S., having celebrated their 76th wedding anniversary last March 24th. Mrs. Slifer was formerly Miss Mary Louise Waters, of Montgomery County.

November 19, 1915.
Mrs. Eleanor M. Steward, widow of Arthur P. Steward, died last Saturday at her home in Chevy Chase.

William S. Cooley has been appointed a deputy in the office of the Clerk of the Circuit Court.

Mrs. Alverda Griffith, wife of Harry Griffith, died Monday at her home near Laytonsville.

Miss Delma Etchison Souder and Leroy Harris were married last week in Laytonsville.

Members of the Montgomery County Fox Hunt Club renewed their field trials last Tuesday. The names mentioned are McCubbin Waters, James P. Gott, Edmund C. Davis, and Charles A. Clagett.

Wm. L. Purdum, age 14, son of Mr. & Mrs. Luther Purdum of Cedar Grove, was accidentally shot and killed last Saturday.

The marriage of Miss Ruth Griffith and Charles Clifton Veirs took place on Wednesday at the home of the father of the bride.

Cont'd. on next page

November 19, 1915, cont'd:
Dr. Charles G. Stone, a dentist in Rockville for a number of years, died November 11, at his home in Washington.

November 26, 1915.
The engagement of Mrs. Laura V. Shaw and Burton Stanley Bready was announced by Mrs. Mary Keys, mother of Mrs. Shaw. The wedding wil take place in December.

Judge John E. West has been designated Chief of the Judges of the Orphan's Court, replacing Judge Remus R. Darby in that position. Mr. Darby was not a candidate for re-election.

Edgar Franklin Oxley, a life-long resident of Montgomery County, died last Saturday.

Miss Lena Barbee Jones, of the Dawsonville vicinity, and Junius Page, of Aberdeen, N. C., were married Monday.

Mrs. Margaret Dove, wife of Joseph A. Dove, died last Saturday.

Miss Mary A. Manakee and Geo. L. Gardiner were married on Wednesday at the Cathedral in Baltimore.

Miss Rose Neel Henderson, of Rockville, and Everett F. Warrington, of New York City, were married last Saturday.

Henry P. Dwyer, who died November 25, 1914, was remembered.

December 3, 1915.
Wm. T. Minnis has been adjudged to be incometent, and has been committed to the Springfirld Hospital.

Stephen B. Blach, of near Seneca, and Miss Emma Grace Chaney, were married on November 3$^{rd}$, at Alexandria, Va.

Judson Wriley Jacobs and Mrs. Octavia Byrne Wood, of Gaithersburg, were married at Richmond, Va. on November 28$^{th}$.

The markmanaship skill of Miss Margaret Jones was noted She shot 3 partridges 'on the wing' and a rabbit 'running at full speed'.

Miss Beulah B. Barnsley and Lloyd Gassaway Linthicum were married on Wednesday of last week.

Newly-elected Commissioneers George G. Bradley and N. Hazel Metzgar took their seats on the Board on Tuesday. John R Lewis has been elected President, Berry E. Clark has been

Cont'd. on next page

Deember 3, 1915, cont'd:
re-elected clerk. Bowie F. Waters was named County Attorney Mr. Clark reappointed clerks E. W. Cissel, A. B. McFarland, and W. Welsh.

Wm. G. Soper, of Clarksburg, has been arrested and charged with the death of H. A. Latimer last Wednesday, when an auto operated by Soper hit and killed Mr. Latimer.

In news from the School Board, the resignations of Miss Deborah Iddings, Miss Eva Bready, and Miss Roberta Higgins were announced; and the appointment of Miss Edna H. Ladson, Miss Bruce Colton, Miss Edith Allnutt, and Miss Deborah Iddings [to a new assignment] was announced. Also, Douglas M. Blandford was appointed a trustee at the Burnt Mills school, replacing Geo. T. Windham, who has died.

December 10, 1915.

Miss Jennie Higgins, age 83, died last Tuesday at the home of her niece, Miss Josie Higgins, of Rockville.

Miss Elsie V. Jeffries and Charles H. Price, both of Dickerson, were married on last Saturday.

The engagement of Miss Jennie Lea, of Sandy Spring, and Dr. Gilbert Tyson Smith, of Connecticut, was announced.

Samuel Riggs died last Monday at his home in Catonsville. Excepting for a few months during which he lived in Catonsville, Mr. Riggs had lived all of his life in Montgomery County.

Charles H. Brooke died last Saturday at his home, 'Falling Green', near Olney. He was buried in the Friends' Cemetery.

A memorial service will be held on December 11th for Rev. J. T. Williams, pastor of Poolesville Methodist Church.

It was announced that Clerk of the Circuit Court Preston B. Ray will marry Miss Nancy Calvert Schuerman on December 18th.

President Wilson and Mrs. Norman Galt will be married December 18th, at Mrs. Galt's home in Washington.

December 17, 1915.

Mrs.Laura Canby Wilson died last Tuesday at her home.

Mrs Irene Bailey Brewer died last Sunday at the home of her daughter, in Washington.

Clyde Poss, of Rockville, and Miss Maude E. Kinsey, of Fort

Cont'd. on next page.

December 17, 1915, cont'd:
Wayne, Ind., were married last Wednesday, in Rockville.
Mrs. Nannie Willard, wife of C. Frank Willard, died last Sunday. She was the daughter of the late Andrew J. and Martha Hoskinson, of Montgomery County.
The newly-elected Sheriff, W. Frank Gaither, has appointed the following deputies, namely George W. Mullican, Thurston King, Preston L. Hewitt, Joseph R. Lillard, Millard E. Peake, Stanley Gingell, William P. Trail, Mareen Darby, Artemus Sullivan, and Dean Darby.
Miss Eva Katherine Bready, of Adamstown and Frank Carlin, of Boyd's, were married last Saturday.
The home of Judson C. Welliver on his farm near Derwood, was destroyed by fire on last Saturday. Much of the furniture and other contents were also lost. Mr. Welliver intends to rebuild, using bricks.

December 24, 1915.
Jerry N. Hobbs and W. Ernest Offutt have been added to the number of deputies in the sheriff's office.
President Wilson has sent the name of Joseph Reading to the Senate for confirmation as postmaster of Rockville.
Miss Vivian Myrtle Watkins and Uriah H. Lawson were married last Friday, in Rockville.
The following named have been appointed trustees of the Alms House, namely, Harry Riggs, Henson T. Miles, Samuel D. Byrd, W. T. Pratt, and Eleazar Ray.
Mrs. Nannie O. Poole, wife of J. Edward Poole, died last Tuesday, in Washington.
Upton Dorsey, a resident of Brookeville, died Tuesday, Dec 7th, while on a visit at the home of Mr. & Mrs. Hugh Harrison, near Ellicott City.
Mrs. Laura V. Shaw and Burton S. Bready were married December 18th, at the Emory M. E. Church, Oakdale.
Preston B. Ray and Miss Nancy Calvert Schuermann were married last Saturday, in Washington.

December 31, 1915.
Mrs. Mary I. Donaldson died last Tuesday.
Cont'd. on next page.

December 31, 1915, cont'd:
    Miss Clara Ellen Gloyd and Henry Slicer were married last Tuesday.
    Oliver H. P. Clark has been acquitted on the charge of embezzling funds while he was postmaster at Silveer Spring.
    Isabel J. Burgess and Geo. Trammell have been adjudged to be imcompetent, and have been committed to Springfield hospital.
    The County Commissioners have appointed Wm. H. Thompson, of the Clarksburg district, assistant County treasurer, succeeding Mrs. O. B. Wood, resigned; and have appointed George Fields of Rockvile to be Superintendent of assessments.
    The store at Barnesville, owned by Oscar K. Poole and occupied by Rosenburg Bros., burned last Friday.
    The School Commissioners have accepted the resignations of Misses Mary White and Ruth Pope as teachers at the schools in Clarksburg and Poolesville respectivel, and have appointed Miss Laura Frizzell to succeed Miss White at Clarksburg.
    Robert P. Stone died on Friday of last week at home near Potomac.
    Miss Bessie Vivian Beall and Maurice W. Magruder were married on Thursday of last week, in Rockvile.
    Miss Emma Hurlebaus, of the vicinity of Norbeck, and Louis E. Groot, of Philadelphia, were married of Thursday of last week.
    The marriage on Decembeer 27th, of Miss Elva Ellsworth Magruder, of Hunting Hill, and William I. Davis, of Indianapolis, Indiana, was announced.
    Mrs. Susan Watkins, wife of Charles Watkins, died on Friday of last week at her home at Boyds.
    Willliam L. Aud, of Poolesville district, and Mrs. Carrie V. Cubitt, also of Poolesville, were married on last Monday.
    Mrs. Hester Griffith died last Friday at her home in Laytonsville.
    Granville Farquhar, a prominent member of the Society of Friends, died on Thursday of last week at his home in Olney.
    Miss Elizabeth S. Hall, age 95, died last Saturday at her home in Brookeville.
    Dr. John Gardner, lately a member of the Board of School Commissioners, and recently elected to the House of Delegates, attended his last meeting of the School Board last Tuesday.
                                    Cont'd. on next apge.

December 31, 1915, cont'd:
   The engagement of Miss Clare Lipscomb and John James Higgins was announced, the wedding to take place in March. Also mentioned are Mr. Higgins' revolutionary ancestors Zadoc Magruder and Archibald Orme.
   Mrs. Sarah M. Hull, who died June 27, 1915, was remembered.

January 7, 1916.
   Sheriff Gaither has appointed Miel Linthicum a deputy for the Damascus district.
   Preston B. Ray, newly-elected Clerk of the Circuit Court, has appointed Clayton K. Watkins a deputy in his office, succeeding J. Hampton Jones.
   The dwelling of Frank L. Hewitt burned last Tuesday. Some of the contents were saved.
   Mrs. Sarah Virginia Hughes died on Wednesday, at her home in Rockville. See also January 28, 1916 and March 3, 1916
   Mrs. Marian Connell, widow of William Connell, died Wednesday.
   Miss Virginia Waters has been appointed principal of the public school at Hunting Hill, and Miss Helen Pumphrey has been appointed teacher of domestic science at the public school in Bethesda.
   Mrs. Grace E. Robey, wife of Commissioner Odorion W. Robey, died last Tuesday in a Washington Hospital. In another item in this issue, a resolution of regret for Mrs. Robey's death was adopted by the Board of County Commissioners.
   Miss Euphemia Small died last Sunday at the home of her nephew, Charles Small, at Cloppers.
   Thomas C. Young, formerly a resident of near Seneca, died December 28th, at his home in Georgetown, D.C.
   Mrs. Annie E. Jamison, widow of Alexander F. Jamison, of Barnesville, died last Tuesday. She was buried in the cemetery of the St. Mary's Catholic Church, Barnesville.

January 14, 1916.
   Henry W. Crismond, of Sligo, has been made a deputy sheriff.
   H. E. Rodgers has been appointed a notary public.
                              Cont'd. on next page.

January 14, 1916, cont'd:
    Miss Grace Elizabeth Larman and James E. Gartner were married on Wednesday of last week.
    Miss Jessie B. Gill, of the Ashton vicinity, and John L. Best, of the same area, were married on Thursday of last week.
    Mrs. Catherine Tolson, wife of Judge A. C. Tolson, died last Monday at her home near Colesville.
    Miss Carolyn Vera Nicholson and Henry Edward Craver were married last Saturday.
    Mrs. Adelaide S. Offutt, widow of John L. Offutt, died last November 25, in Offutts, Tenn. Both Mr. & Mrs. Offutt were formerly of Montgomery County.
    Louis E. Shoemaker died Thursday of last week at the home of Isaac E. Shoemaker, his son, in Chevy Chase.
    Directors as follows were elected by the stockholders of the Montgomery County National Bank of Rockville at the annual meeting held last Tuesday, namely: Wm. B. Mobley, James E. Williams, Lawrence Allnutt, Richard H. Stokes, Frederick P. Hays, Wm. T. Griffith, Perrie E. Waters, Lee Offutt, Thomas Vinson, Hattan A. Waters, J. H. Parsley, Robert B. Peter. Mr. Stokes was then elected president; Mr. Mobley was elected vice president; George M. Hunter was elected cashier; W. R. Brewer, assistant cashier; George P. Henderson, teller; J. G. Darby, discount clerk; Miss Leigh Athey, correspondent clerk, and Paul Brunett, clerk.
    The Montgomery County Agricultural Society met last Wednesday, and elected as directors the following, namely: Lee Offutt, Chas. Veirs, Chas. W. Fields, D. H. Warfield, J. W. Jones, C. F. Kirk, P. E. Waters, N. J. Ward, W. K. Jones, Wm. B. Trundle, J. B. Diamond Jr., and Wm. H. Fawcett.

January 21, 1916
    Charles E. Falin [ ? ][Eslin [?], of Silver Spring, age 51, died on Wednesday of last week.
    John C. Lydard, of Cedar Grove, died last Sunday.
    The board of directors of the Montgomery County Agricultural Society has re-elected Lee Offutt, president; Charles F. Fields, vice president; Jas. T. Bogley, secretary; and John J. Higgins, treasurer.
    The following named have been appointed to positions in the
Cont'd. on next page.

January 21, 1916, cont'd:
House of Delegates:   A. J. Fairall, Wm. T. Warfield, doorkeepers; Leonard Weer Jr., messenger to the Speaker.
    Charles H. Gibson, Wilson L. Townsend, and Lucius Q. C. Lamar are among the candidates who recently passed the Bar examination and who will be admitted to practice law.
    Mrs. Elmira D. Brown, wife of Edward O. Brown, died on Thursday of last week at her home near Laytonsville.
    Joseph Reading's nomination as postmaster of Rockville has been confirmed, and he will enter upon his duties at once.
    Mrs. Katherine Emily Lazell, wife of Herbert L. Lazell, died last week at her home in Grand Lodge, Mich. She was the daughter of Charles W. Oxley of Poolesville.
    Mrs. Anna McFarland Stabler, wife of Arthur Stabler of Sandy Spring, died last Saturday.
    The marriage on January $17^{th}$. of Miss Lucille Warren Gott and Ernest Chiswell Allnutt was announced.
    Mrs Sarah Agnes Fisher, widow of George Fisher, died on Thursday of last week.
    Mrs. Mary L. Johnson, wife of John T. Johnson, drowned herself last week.
    At the annual stockholders meeting of the First National Bank of Sandy Spring held recently, the following directors were elected, namely: Alban G. Thomas, Asa M. Stabler, Francis Thomas, Allan Farquhar, Josiah W. Jones, Charles F. Kirk, Geo. W. Bready, T. Lamar Jackson, Tarlton B. Stabler, Francis J. Downey, and Frederick L. Thomas. Alban J. Thomas was then re-elected president; Frederick L. Thomas was elected cashier; and Francis Miller was named assistant cashier.
    The First National Bank of Gaithersburg has elected the following board of directors, namely: I. T. Fulks, A. F. Meem, Z. M. Cooke, J. C. Higgins, J. B. Dianmond, J. S. Windsor, S. R. Plummer, E. C.Etchison, C. H. Hoskinson, C. C. Waters, Nathan Cooke, J. W. Walker, H. M. Talbott, and F. B. Severance.  The following officers were then elected:   J. B. Diamond, president; C. H. Hoskinson, vice president; Frank B. Severance, cashier; and J. B. Stover, assistant cashier.
    Mrs. Margaret Smith, widow of Joseph R. Smith, died last Friday. She was formerly a Miss Gardner, of Montgomery County.
                                  Cont'd. on next page.

January 21, 1916, cont'd:
Gov. Goldsborough has pardoned Susan B. Thompson, George S. Mills, Thos. Thomas, and Beverly Smith. All had been previously convicted in Montgomery County and sentenced to serve terms in the State penitentiary.

At the annual stockholder's meeting of the Bethesda Hall and Library Association, the following officers were elected: H. Latane Lewis, president; Emory H. Bogley, secretary; Evan Condon, Treasurer. The Board of Directors consists of the officers just named together with John R. Cox, Jed Gittings, A. L. Flint, C. H. Becker, and W. B. Kilpatrick.

Francis Eugene Welsh, son of Frank and Virgie Welsh, age 2 years, died December 18, 1915.h

January 28, 1916.
Frank P. Smith, of Forest Glen, has been named a deputy sheriff.

George Mullican, of Rockville, has been appointed assistant to postmaster Joseph Reading, in the Rockville office.

The residence of John W. Shipley, at Browningsville, was destroyed by fire last week.

Dr. Thomas Sollers Waters, a native of Montgomery County, died last Monday, at University Hospital, in Baltimore.

Enoch G. Johnson, of Alta Vista, won eighteen prizes at the poultry show in Wasington last week. Among the awards was the Prudhomme cup for the best display of Silver Campines, which he now is entitled to keep because he has won it twice before.

Charles O. Mills, of Washington, and Miss Mary E. Heffner, of Dickerson, were married January 15th.

Lewis Watson, principal of the Rockville Acadamy, won first prize in the spelling bee sponsored by the Woman's Club of Rockville. He divided the prize – a cake – with Miss Mary Almoney, runner-up.

The Ridgely Brown Camp of Sons of the Confederacy met in Rockville last Wednesday to celebrate the birthdate of Gen. Robert E. Lee. Names mentioned are Capt. Samuel Riggs, Daniel Shreve, Miss F. May Sellman, John P. Sellman, and John Holland.

Gov. Harrington will make appointments to the Board of Election Supervisors, School Commissioners, and police justices
Cont'd. on next page.

January 28, 1916, cont'd:
within the next few weeks. The names being mentioned for election supervisors are Julian Griffith, Richard L. Stanley, Joseph N. Darby, Warren V. Magrudeer, and Charles J. Lyddane, democrats; and Thomas Vinson, Maurice M. Browning, A. Clinton Brown, Wilber S. Day, and Wm. W. Dronenburg, republicans. For the appointments as school commissioners, the names mentioned are John Gardner, Roger B. Farquhar, Zadoc M. Cooke; and for police justice, the names mentioned are H. Maurice Talbott, J. Alby Henderson, and Wm. Griffith of D. P.

An article describing the origin of the Savings Institution of Sandy Spring was published.

Committees have been named to prepare for the next annual Fair. The names mentioned are Charles Veirs, Charles W. Fields, David H. Warfield, N. J. Ward, Lee Offutt, Josiah W. Jones, John B. Diamond Jr., Perrie E. Waters, Wm. K. Jones, Wm. H. Fawcett, John J. Higgins, Chas. F. Kirk, and Wm. B. Trundle.

Helen Bertha Howes, child of Elias and Susie Howes, who died August 17, 1915, was remembered.

February 4, 1916.
Wm. H. Roach, Mayor of Glen Echo, died suddenly last Tuesday.

Miss Leona Floyd Oland and Leonard C. Burns Jr., were married last Saturday.

The engagement of Miss Lydia Chichester and Phillip D. Laird of Wilmington, Del., was announced.

Messrs. Randolph Hall, of Poolesville and Thomas E. Lechlider have announced that they are candidates for appointment as police justices.

Henry Reisinger, who has been conductring a baking business in Rockville for the past 21 years, has made an assignment for the benefit of creditors.

Dr. Charles Farquhar died last Tuesday at his home in Olney.

Mrs. Mary E. Nichols, widow of Charles W. Nichols, died on Thursday of last week

Miss Hilda Elizabeth Bready, of Forest Glen, and Wallace Cashell, of Olney, were married on Wednesday of last week.

Mrs. Helen Lee Ricketts, age 19, wife of E. Clayton Ricketts
Cont'd. on next page.

February 4, 1916, cont'd:
was killed on Wednesday of last week when she was thrown from the horse that she was riding, and broke her neck. She was the daughter of John W. Peters, of the Kensington area. See also February 18.
James Henry Bolton died on Wednesday of last week.
Washington D. Waters, a lifelong resident of Montgomery County, died last Monday at his home in Rockville.

February 11, 1916.
Miss Dora Staley, age 28, daughter of Mr. & Mrs. Fleet Staley, died last Monday of ptomaine poisoning, attributed to some clams she ate.
It was announced that Miss Edith Clugston and William L. Schaeffer were married on February $2^{nd}$, in Philadelphia.
Mrs. Mary E. Fisher, widow of Geary Fisher, died last Monday at her home in Darnestown.
It was annnounced that Miss Clare Marie Lipscomb, of Washington, and John J. Higgins Jr., of Rockville, were married last Saturday, in Baltimore.
Dr. Montgomery Earle Higgins, son of James L. Higgins of Boyds, has been assigned to duty at the Naval Hospital in Norfolk.
About two years ago, Messrs. Thomas Dawson, of Rockville, and Howard Allnutt of Frederick County, bought the 'Gold Mine' property near Potomac for $5000. Mr Allnutt died several months ago, and the property was sold last week by Mr. Dawson for $50,000.
Mrs. Georgia A. Williams, widow of Jonathan C. Williams, for many years a merchant in Olney, was buried last Saturday in the cemetery at Olney. Date of death is not stated.
Articles of Incororation of 'White's Ferry Company' have been filed in the Clerk's office in Rockville The incorporators are Hugh H. Hanger, Albert S. Hanger and McCarthy Hanger.
Dr. Elisha C. Etchison, of Gaithersburg, died last Sunday in a hospital in Washington. Despite his failing health for the last several years, he had been able to attend to his large practice until recently.

February 18, 1916.
Raymond B. Linkins, formerly of Wheaton, and Miss Edna L. Whispell, of Washington, were married on last Sunday, in Rockville.
Sarah Edwards, of Dickerson, died last Sunday.

Cont'd. on next page.

February 18, 1916, cont'd:

Otho F. James was chosen Mayor of Glen Echo, to serve until the May election, succeeding former mayor Capt. Wm. H. Roach, who died suddenly. [on January 25th. ?]

February 25, 1916.

Mrs. Jessie M. Moore, wife of Samuel Moore, of the vicinity of Norwood, died last Sunday.

John B. Pumphrey has been selected by the judges of the Circuit Court in Montgomery County to be the Court crier. He will succeed Washington D. Waters, who died March 31.

Miss Mary Mills, age 75, died last Saturday, in Kensington.

Col. L. Marvin Maus, a native of Montgomery County, has been directed to be placed on the retired list of the U. S. Army Medical Corps, with the rank of Brigadier General.

Mrs. Ella Virginia Waters, wife of Perrie E. Waters, died last Monday at her home in Germantown. See also March 3, 1916.

Margaret A. Thompson was remembered by her granddaughter, Mattie.

Mrs. Mary C. Boswell, who died February 15, 1909, was remembered.

Mrs. Lucinda Bean, who died February 24, 1915, was remembered

March 3, 1916.

The County Commissioners have appointed Robert L. Saunders, of Potomac, road-roller engineer, at a salary of $75 per month. See also March 10th.

Miss Ada Virginia Small and John T. Higdon were married on last Tuesday, in Rockville.

Miss Belle Esther Coar, of Burtonsville, and William E. Disney of Highland, Howard County, were married last week.

Jesse A. Higgins, son of Mr. & Mrs. John J. Higgins of Rockville, has gone to work in the gun cotton section of the DuPont powder works in Hopewell, Va.

Mrs. Josephine E. Cleaver died last week at the home of her son-in-law and daughter, Rev. and Mrs. O. A. Gillingham, at Darnestown.

Cont'd. on next page.

March 3, 1916, cont'd:

The home of David R. Hershey, at Comus, was destroyed by fire on last Sunday. Very little was saved.

The dwelling house occupied by Charles R. Stone at Potomac, owned by John L. Bell, burned last Saturday. All of the contents were also lost.

John J. Higgins and Miss Claire Lipscomb were married about two weeks ago.

The following named have been drawn to serve as jurors during the coming term of the Circuit Court, namely; Downey M. Williams, Otho B. Williams, Thaddeus T. Bussard, Robert B. Price, Chas. W. Gibson, Eldridge Z. Bowman, Daniel S. Ramsburg, Benoni D. Allnutt, John A. Jones, Dewalt L. Willard, Nelson H. Robertson, Henry C. Crown, Samuel T. Butt, Charles W. Sage, Leonidas W. Adamson, Thos. M. Hoyle, Jos. D. Miller, Lawrence E. Harding, Basil W. Nicholson, Frederick W. Kruhm, Horace D. Waters, Jacob. C. Snyder, Wm. M. Lewis, Cyrus Keiser, Lewis P. Oldfield, John H. Harper, Wm. L. Purvis, Francis H. Cashell, Clarence L. Gilpin, Seth W. Griffith, Rufus W. Devilbiss, Wm. S. Caulfield, Bennie O. Woodward, McKendree Walker, John G. Stone, John T. Hill, Mason Havener Sr., George F. Cooley, Wm. E. Robertson, Wm. M. Williams, William H. Darby, Claude H. Burdette, Chas. Lee Watkins, Geo. G. Getty, Robert L. Tolson, Clayton Rabbitt, Benjamin C. Stein, James Halpin.

The Governor has made the following appointments for Montgomery County:

School commissioners: Dr. Warren E. Price, Dr. James E. Deets, Zadoc M. Cooke. Drs. Price and Deets succeed Roger B. Farquhar and Dr. John Gardner - Mr. Cooke succeeds himself.

Supervisors of elections: Lawreson B. Riggs, Henry W. Offutt, Mauricc M. Browning. The old board was composed of Julian Griffith, Thomas Vinson, and Maurice M. Browning.

Notaries public: William A. Anderson, Edward Story, Samuel D. Byrd, F. Bache Abert, George P. Henderson, Lydia F. Prettyman, Henry W. Chesley, John Jones, J. Janney Shoemaker, Frank D. Leizear, Louis C. Beall, Forrest E. Walker, James E. Trundle, Hatton D. Brown, Russell E. Duvall, Ralph M. Hendricks, Frank L. Hewitt, H. Edson Rogers, William O. Culver, Rebecca Hall.

Justices of the peace: Police justices: J. Alby Henderson,
Cont'd. on next page.

March 3, 1916, cont'd:
Edward O. Brown, George E. Hughes, Jesse P. Wolfe, Robert L. Hickerson, Thos. R. Hall, Edward O. Edmonston, John McCeney, E. P. B. Margerum, John A. Hall, Alfred Wilson, James E. Keliher, Chas. M. Iddings, Alfred F. Fairall, James E. Garrett, Rosell Woodward, Arthur Myers, Perry L. Pyles, James D. Young, Robert E. Lee, John H. L. Sawyer.

George H. Culver died suddenly on February 21, 1916.

March 10, 1916.
Thomas Coleman, a lifelong resident of Montgomery County, died last week in a Washington hospital.

Mrs. Annie Howard Veitch, widow of Col. John W. Veitch who was a resident of Rockville for several years, died last Sunday.

The County Commissioners have appointed local assessors as follows: first district, Z. M. Waters Jr; second district, E. D. Warfield; third, W. W. Pyles; fourth, Alfred Ray; fifth, P. H. Ray; sixth, A. J. Cissell; seventh, J. F. Whalen; eighth, Leonard Weer Jr; ninth, J. E. Clagett; tenth, Millard C. Fisher; eleventh, Melvin M. Poole; twelfth, Noah Watkins; thirteenth, Frank B. Stubbs.

Miss Lena A. Collins, of Washington, and Edwin S. Hege, of Rockville, were married last Tuesday.

The County Commissioners have designated the following constables to also act as dog-tax collectors: Laytonsville, Camden Windham; Clarksburg, Thurston L. King; Poolesville, Randolp Luhn; Rockville, Ollie Shaw; Colesville, Claude Hobbs; Darnestown, Wm. H. McCrossin; Bethesda, Millard E. Peake; Olney, Ober W. Dailey; Gaithersburg, Thomas Small; Potomac, John T. McGaha; Damascus, Franklin Darby.

At a recent meeting of the stockholders of the Montgomery Mutual Building and Loan Association of Kensington, the following men were re-elected to serve as directors until their successors shall have been elected, namely: Alfred S. Dalton, Albert S. Gatley, Eugene Jones, Will D. Nichols, H. O. Trowbridge, Parker L. Weller, B. H. Warner Jr., Herbert Wright. Benjamin W. Kumler was also elected to fill the vacancy caused by the death of Francis M. Webster.

March 17, 1916.
J. Howard Ward has been appointed a constable and dog-tax
Cont'd. on next page

March 17, 1916, cont:
collector for the Rockville district.

Edward T. Ricketts died last Saturday at his home near Potomac.
The following named have been excused from jury duty, viz, Robert V. Price, Basil W. Nicholson, Horace D. Waters, George F. Cooley. Their places will be taken by George A. Merson, James F. Turner, Bernard W. McCrossin, and Edward L. Chiswell.
Miss Lucile Welsh, daughter of Warner W. Welsh, and Rev. Frank M. Richardson were married on last Tuesday.
Miss Virgie Eleanor Day, daughter of Dorsey W. Day, of Browningsville, and William Carl Purdum, of Frederick County were married on Wednesday of last week.
Mrs. Addie B. Johnson, daughter of Rev. and Mrs. Isaiah Parker, and Charles E. Gates, both of the Rockville area, were married last Monday.
Gordon Strong, of Chicago, has offered to build a school near Dickerson on a parcel of 100 acres of land, and to turn it over to Frederick County and Montgomery County authorities for the education of children living in the Sugar Loaf area. The proposal is to be considered at a meeting of the Frederick County Board of School Commissioners at which Montgomery County will be represented. Mr. Strong has already built one school in the area.
Some students of Maryland Agricultural College living in Montgomery Count, have formed a club to be known as 'The Montgomery County Club of M. A. C.' The names mentioned are W. J. Aitcheson, H. R. Shoemaker, F. D. Day, D. J. Howard, L. R. Smoot, L. D. Oberlin, L. Aitcheson, A. H. Sellman, T. Riggs, H. A. Reisinger, H. B. Derrick, E. J. Renkin, M. D. Engle, and C. H. Bacon.
Mrs. Mry Ellen Kisner died March 7th, 1916.

March 24, 1916.
The engagement of Miss Marcia Katherine Wright, of Forest Glen, and Lewis A. Wright of Kensington was announced.
Miss Anna M. Smith, of Rockville, and Artis H. Waters of Washington, were married on Wednesday of last week.
The M. E. Church South, at Poolesville, burned last Sunday. All the contents, including a new pipe organ, were lost.

cont'd. on next page.

March 24, 1916, cont'd:

While driving on the road leading from Rockville to Potomac, Sweetie Williams, who conducts a store at Snake Den, was attacked and robbed. Upon information from Mr. Williams, the sheriff has arrested Milton Stewart and James Stewart, who live near Potomac, and charged them with the crime.

The following named have won prizes for selling Red Cross seals: Mildred Zither, Raymond Bolton, George Ray, Allen Magruder, Frank Dudley, Alice Darby, Millard Griffith, Marian Schwartz, Catharyn Griggsby, Lester Welsh, Clements Gloyd, William Troxall, Gorman Love, Myrtle Henderson, Gladys Williams, Esther Luhn, Roger Cecil, Wightman Smith, John Yeabower, Walter French, Pearl Musgrove, Roscoe Garrett, Mildred Baker, Linda V. King, Richard Janney, Lucy Thom, Wilson Stabler, Martha Barnesley, Francis Kirk, Fred Gilpin, Virginia Carrell, Kenneth Barnsley, Claire Hutton, Sallie Fenwick, Delas [?] Adams, Byron Cook, John Hay, Herman Day, Wm. Armstrong, Dorothy Milstead, Maud Thompson, Horatio Allison, Guy Camp, Filmore Camp, Alexander Britton, Ennis Robertson, Hamlin Hodge, Harry Woolford, James Cummings, Mary Ellen Bruner, Elizabeth Wilson Jones, Mary Dowell, Aubrey Sisson, Edna Ray, Thomas Anderson, Josephine Esputa, Julia Knight, Elizabeth Larcombe, Braxton Mannar, Charles Fisher, Hilton Darby, Upton Beall.

Mr. & Mrs. Asa M. Stabler, of Sandy Spring, celebrated their golden wedding anniversary on Wednesday of last week

March 31, 1916.

Mrs. Andrew James Caldwell, of Washington, announced the engagement of her daughter, Rosalind Deering Caldwell, to John Brewer, of Rockville. See also June 9, 1916.

James W. Barrett died last week at the home of his son-in-law and daughter, Mr. & Mrs. J. W. Hough, near Poolesville.

Alexander Carter, age 37, died on Thursday of last week at his home in Gaithersburg.

Mr. & Mrs. John W. Keys, who live near Rockville, celebrated their golden wedding anniversary on last Wednesday.

Mrs. Helen Grather, age 22 years, daughter of Mr. & Mrs. James Sutton, formerly of Montgomery County, died recently.

Cont'd. on next page.

March 31, 1916, cont'd:
Mrs. Sarah J. Riggs, widow of Remus Riggs, died on Thursday of last week at the home of her daughter, Mrs. Robert H. Pumphrey.
T. L. Richards, of Germantown, a senior at Wooster College, has become one of the best mile-runners in Ohio.
Miss Geneva E. Peake and Clyde H. Cronise were married on last Saturday.

April 7, 1916.
Joseph Smith died suddenly last Monday, in front of the postoffice in Rockville, of a heart attack.
Rev. Chas. G. Cady, presently pastor of the Presbyterian Church at Sparrows Point, will become pastor of the Warner Memorial Presbyterian Church, Kensington.
Thomas B. Butt died last Wednesday at his home near Rockville.
John Jones died last Monday at his home near Poolesville. See also April 14, 1916 and April 28, 1916.
Phillip T. Stabler died on Thursday of last week.
Miss Ethel M. Grubb and Howard W. Spurrier were married on Mrch 28th, in Washington.
Dr. Otho Magruder Muncaster died last Saturday. [8th.]

April 14, 1916.
Charles L. Purdum, of Darnestown, and Miss Ella M. Stone, of Washington, were married on Thursday of last week.
Welby H. Mills, age 31, died on last Wednesday in a Washington hospital.
Mrs. Martha Josephine Eccleston, widow of Col. Charles A. Eccleston, died last Saturday at her home near Forest Glen.
Edwin S. Hege has recently moved to Washington, and has tendered his resignation as a member of the Rockville town council.
The Baltimore conference of the M. E. Church South has made the following appointments for Montgomery County: to Gaithersburg, L. M. Bennett; to Kensington, C. T. Weeds; to Laytonsville, J. F. Fort; and to Spencerville, R. H. K. Gill.
Miss Bessie Priscilla Bussard, of Redland, and Crittenden H. Walker Jr. were married on Wednesday of last week

Cont'd. on next page.

April 14, 1916, cont'd:

The home of Dorsey Gloyd, in Gaithersburg, and the nearby garage of Garnet Etchison, were destroyed by fire last Tuesday.

Winfield Offutt died on Thursday of last week at his home in Travilah.

It was announced that Miss Mary Courtlandt Wallace and M. Campbell Oliphant will be married April 24th.

A resolution in memory of Barak T. Graves was adopted by the members of the Men's Bible class, Grace M. E. South Church, Gaithersburg.

April 21, 1916.

J. Gibbons Conroy, son of Michael Conroy, was among the recent graduates of the Untited States College of Veterinary Surgeons.

James F. Braddock died on Wednesday.

It was announced that Miss Ellen Coleman DuPont and Hollyday A. Meeds Jr., of Chevy Chase will be married April 29th.

H. Dorsey Etchison, of Frederick County, announced that he is again a Democratic candidate for U. S. Congress from the 6th. district, and asked for the support of the voters in Montgomery County.

April 28, 1916.

Mrs. Margaret Wells, of Washington, and John E. Ward, of Gaithersburg, were married last Saturday, in Rockville.

G. W. Etchison has been nominated to be postmaster of Gaithersburg.

Jesse Higgins, son of Mr. & Mrs. John J. Higgins, of Rockville, has gone to Topeka, Kansas, to work for the engineering department of the Santa Fe Railway Co.

Norman Peter, son of Mr. & Mrs. George Peter of Kensington, has been awarded a scholarship to Yale University.

Rufus Kent King died last Saturday at his home in Damascus.

Miss Elizabeth Darnell Jones, of near Poolesville, and William Sothoron Smoot, of Raccoon Ford, Va., were married April 26th, at 'Blenheim'.

At the annual election of the Cropley Presbyterian Church, the following were elected: Trustees; L. Hill, W. H. Bolton, E. Redden, O. Lynch, C. F. Bodine, A. F. Hill, G. E. Ricketts, M. V. Lynch; Treasurer, C. F. Bodine; Organists, Misses Anna Lippert and Susie

Cont'd. on next page.

April 28, 1916, cont'd:
Lynch; Deaconesses, Mrs. S. R. Pennifill, Mrs. J. R. Redden, Miss Dora V. Redden, Mrs. W. H. Bolton; Mite Society President, Mrs. W. H. Bolton; Secretary, Mrs. O. Hill; Treasurer, Mrs. A. F. Hill; Ushers, F. G. Hill, R. K. Bissett, and W. Schley.

At the annual election at the Hermon Presbyterian Church, the following were elected; Trustees, F. P. Stone, J. M. Harrison, W. E. Hamilton, W. B. Myers, L. W. Moore; Treasurer, F. P. Stone; Deaconesses; Miss M. V. Harrison, Mrs. A. Myers, Mrs. J. H. Stearn, Mrs. F. Embrey, Mrs. J. H. Harper, Mrs. F. P. Stone, Mrs. E. E. Crockett, Mrs. A. Hinner, Mrs. R. W. Stone, Mrs. C. S. Davidson; ushers, Dunbar Stone, Lester Kinney, Earl Stearn.

Mary Courtlandt Wallace and M. Campbell Oliphant were married last Monday.

The town election in Rockville will be held May 1$^{st}$. The following are nominees for Mayor and Council: For Mayor, Lee Offutt, Willis B. Burdette; for Council, Joseph Clagett, William E. Viett, Louis Watson, Otis M. Linthicum, Otho H. W. Talbott, Winfield Scott Magruder, Martin Heim.

John Harrison. Surratt, last survivor of the alleged conspirators to assassinate President Lincolm, died last Friday at his home in Baltimore. He had been tried on the conspiracy charge, and acquitted.

May 5, 1916.
Dr. W. T. Pratt has been appointed health officer for Montgomery County.

Harry J. Lambert and Mrs. Minnie M. Hammond, both of Cropley, were married last Saturday.

Harold G. Waters, vice consul at Berlin, is visiting at the home of his father, Perrie E. Waters, in Germantown.

Mrs. Mary E. Harding died on April 30 at the home of her son, Louis W. Harding.

Miss Rose F. Williams died last Tuesday at her home in Rockville.

At the recent town election, Willis B. Burdett was elected Mayor of Rockville, and Joseph H. Clagett, Martim Heim, Otho H. W. Talbott, and O. M. Linthicum were elected councilmen.

Miss Ellen Coleman DuPont and Hollyday S. Meeds Jr. were married last Saturday, in Trinity Episcopal Church, Wilmington, Del.

Cont'd. on next page.

May 5, 1916, cont'd:
The results of the primary election show:
For U. S. Senate, Democratic race: Blair Lee was the winner
For U. S. House of Representatives, Democrat: H. Dorsey Etchison was the winner.
For U. S. House, Republican, Gist Blair, Frederick N. Zihlman were the winners

.May 12, 1916.
The Governor has appointed Clifford H. Robertson and Wm. E. Morgan to be notaries for the Rockville district, and Wm. R. Kroll to be a notary for the Wheaton district.

Wm. H. Griffith has been appointed a member of the Board of Supervisors of Elections, succeeding Henry W. Offutt.

Capt. John L. Husband, a prominent Republican politician of Montgomery County, was found dead last Tuesday on an island in the Potomac river, opposite Chain Bridge. An inquest will be held to determine the cause of death.

Miss Annie E. Tolson and George F. Bonifant, both of Colesville, were married last Saturday.

Miss Marie Viola Gibson, of Barnesville, and Wm. J. Lewis, of Indianapolis, Ind., were married Monday.

Eugene A. Veirs has received an honorable discharge from the U. S. Marine Corps. at the expiration of his term of enlistment, and has returned to his parent's home near Rockville.

The third educational day exercises were held in Rockville last Friday. There were drills, tableaux, team sports, and individual competition in athletic events. The names mentioned are Earle Baker, Clarence Becraft, Samuel Berry, Gordon Burroughs, Lawrence Butt, Edward Cashell, Lawrence Darby, Lindsay Edmonds, Edward Gandy, Marbury Gates, Harold Gilpin, Darby Ward, William O. Young, Charles Adams, Fred Barber, Lester Barber, Talbott Barnesly, Ralph Benson, Arthur Bell, Louis W. Berry, Byron Cook, Sterling Cooley, Theodore Crawford, Dalton Erwin, Leslie Etchison, Edwin Fry, Huber Garrett, Wm. Garrett, Craig Glascott, Clements Gloyd, Clayton Gray, Win Green, George Hamilton, James Holland, Robert Howes, Edward Noyes, Alexander Offutt, Herbert Peddicord, Sylvester Phoebus, Edward Popkins, William Prescott, John Pumphrey, Warren Rabbitt, Hugh Reading, Edwin Ronsaville, William
Cont'd. on next page.

May 12, 1916, cont'd:
Shoemaker, Russell Sibley, Phillip Smith, Anthony Walstrum, Carroll Waters, Wilbur Watkins, Allan Welliver, Edward Welliver, John Welsh, Anna Bancroft, Naomi Aman, Eleanor Barnesly, Angeline Berry, Pearl Bohrer, Myrtle Burgdorf, Evelyn R. Butt, Catherine Cook, Alma Gloyd, Anna Henry, Mary Miller, Helen Moulden, Caroline Muncaster, Ivy Rabbitt, Hannah Schwartz, Jean Coulter, Dora Disney, Mary Downey, Katherine Engle, Alma English, Josephine Esputa, Ethel Fletcher, Mildred Griffith, Eugenia Harris, Gladys Hilton, Ethel Inscoe, Annie Lee Jones, Elizabeth Leizear, Elizabeth Wilson, and Lottie Wilson.

In School Board news: The members of the Board of School Commissioners recently re-organized themselves by re-electing Judge Stanton J. Peele to be president, and appointed Edwin W. Broome assistant superintendent of schools. Robert G. Hilton has been appointed auditor. The superintendent of schools has not been agreed upon, with the result that Willis B. Burdette will continue to act: an attorney has not been agreed upon, so there is none. In further school board news, the following named teachers have been selected to attend summer school for five weeks in the coming summer, namely Carrie M. Fulks, Laura Frizzell, Effie H. Shreve, Sarah Griffith, Helen Pumphrey, Mary Brewer, Virginia Waters, Frances Ricketts, Landella Etchison, Lula White, Maude England, Isabel B. Jones, Esther Scott, Agnes Frizzell, Irene Brown, Ruth E. Beall, Gertrude Lane, Minnie Carlisle, Mabel King, Daisy Higgins, Ruby A. Robertson, Katie Frizzell, Daisy Cecil, Edith Lindig, Mabel Gott, Lillian Sage, Edna E. Hawke, Grace Beall, Edna Baltzell, Mary Green, Blanche Creamer, Corrine Duff, Stella Thomas, Charles G. Myers, Wilson S. Ward, Jas. W. White, and Bruce Colton.

James Upton Beall, age 14, died April 29.

May 19, 1916.
Franklin T. Boswell has been appointed a deputy sheriff.
Maurice A. Lochte, age 40, died on Wednesday of last week, at Garrett Park, survived by a widow and four children.
Blanche Nicholson, granddaughter of Mr. & Mrs. Leonard L. Nicholson, of Rockville, died on May 11th.
The Governor has appointed Phillip D. Laird a member of the Service Commission. He replaces W. Laird Henry.

Cont'd. on next page.

May 19, 1916, cont'd:
  Miss Nellie A. Proctor and Frank L. Hewitt were married on Thursday of last week.
  Brainard H. Warner died on Tuesday at his home in Chevy Chase. He was credited with founding the town of Kensington.
  John Byrd was killed on last Monday in an accident involving a runaway team of horses.

May 26, 1916.
  The Governor has appointed George M. Wolfe and I. Thomas Wilson notaries, and Edmund P. E. Margerum a justice of the peace.
  Miss Frances Scott Veirs will graduate from Academy of the Visitation, Georgetown, on June $5^{th}$. See also June $9^{th}$, 1916.
  Mrs. Ietta E. Welsh died last Friday at her home near Rockville.
  Marion H. Keys, age 63, a cousin of John W. Keys of Rockville, died last Saturday.
  Mrs. Eliza Matilda Soper, age 87, wife of Isaac Soper, died Tuesday at her home at Quince Orchard.
  The coming marriage of Miss Lydia Chichester and Phillip Dandridge Laird was announced. The wedding will take place on June $7^{th}$. See also June $9^{th}$, 1916.
  The coming marriage of Dr. Bates Etchison, of Gaithersburg, and Miss Helen S. Myers was announced, the wedding to take place June $3^{rd}$.
  Charles H. Vincent died last Friday at his home in Darnestown.
  The coming marriage of Miss Grace Elizabeth Birgfeld and Robert Murphy was announced. See also June 9, 1916.
  The Governor has appointed J. Dawson Williams a regent of the Maryland State University. The position is honorary and carries no salary.
  The Board of Elections, consisting of William H. Griffith, Laurason B. Riggs, and Thomas Vinson, met last Saturday, and elected Mr. Griffith president, Wm. H. Wade, clerk, and Alex. Kilgour, attorney. Carey Kingdon, clerk for the past four years, will continue as deputy clerk.
  W. B. Burdette, recently elected Mayor of Rockville, has declined to serve. He will continue as superintendent of schools.
                              Cont'd. on next page.

May 26, 1916, cont'd:
The graduates this year from the various County high schools will be: Rockville; Rose Kiger Dawson, Catharine Reed, Louise McCeney, Anna Lyles Offutt, Mary Peter Dawson, Margaret E. Duvall, Margaret E. Hughes, Marguerite J. Kohlhoss, Marjorie I. Clum, Mary Lappin, Edward H. Cashell, Earle O. Baker, Graham E. Getty, Joseph G. Reading; from Gaithersburg, Ellen Britt Ricketts, Lillian Belle Hoyle, Ida Ellen Kemp, Anna Louise Williams, Alverda Griffith Cooke, Barry Ella Ward, Anna Mary Bottlemay, Lillian L. Day, George F. Pollock, William C. Gloyd, Oscar T. Gaither; from Germantown, Julia M. Barber, Mariel Virginia Gott, Eleanor H. Houck, Fanny Thelma King, Mary Waters, William O. Young, Walter A. Neel; from Brookeville, Helen C. Howard, Anna Lee Higgins, Helen Louise Higgins, Mary E. Peddicord, Bertha Virginia Brown; from Poolesville, Lulu Mae Chiswell, Jessie M. Bodmer, Edith Blanche White, Barbara J. Trundle, Leona White Soper; from Darnestown, Gertrude Estelle Offutt, Howard C. Sauerwein; from Chevy Chase, Helen Elizabeth Hodges, Charles Shoemaker, Thomas D. Servis; from Sandy Spring, Anna Lee Jones, Elizabeth B. Jones, Katherine H. Townsend, Mildred Anne Powell, James Janney Shoemaker, George F. Nesbit Jr. See also June 9th, 1916.

The School Commissioners have appointed trustees for the various public schools as follows: Laytonsville district, Jos. T. Allnutt, Wm. D. Bell, T. Cramner Griffith, Clifford L. Howard, W. J. Royer, C. N. Zeitler, Mrs. Joshua Burns, Wm. L. Griffith, William Jackson, A. B. Arnold, Z. M. Waters, Wm. Warfield, Hanson G. Cashell, Thaddeus T. Bussard, Lawrence Gingell, Samuel R. Plummer, John Snouffer, Walter Plummer; Clarksburg district, John O. T. Watkins, L. D. Watkins, E. M. Beall, Webster V. Burdette, Luther Burdette, Samuel P. Miles, Randolph Windsor, Cassidy Linthicum, John Gardner, Edward D. Lewis, James E. Maughlin, Clarence L. Ayton, John W. Carlin, Wm. Knott, Geo. C. Pearre, E. C. King, G. W. Watkins, Melvin Beall, Charles T. Day, Geo. Merson, Washington Burdette, R. C. Beall, Tobias C. Watkins, E. C. King; Rockville district, Washington Hicks, Mrs. George H. Lamar, Robert E. L. Smith, George F. Garrett, Thomas C. Keys, Alexander Garrett, John Ertter, A. B. Claxton, Geary Fisher, Samuel S. Welsh, George M. Kephart, Thomas Barnesley, T. Maynard Hoyle, Mrs. Jessie R. Thompson, Joseph G. Gurly, Charles F. Chisholm; Colesville district, Cont'd. on next page.

May 26, 1916, cont'd:
Phillip H. Ray, Benton G. Ray, Jas. E. Thompson, Wm. H. McCeney, William R. Wheeler, Geo. C. Windham, Charles Duvall, Geo. W. Athey, Frederick W. Kruhm, Asa M. Stabler, Robert H. Miller, Chas. E. Bond, Wilson G. Johnson, Thomas J. Robey, Howard Marlowe; Darnestown district, Millard Rice, Charles H. Nourse, James S. Windsor, Clifton R. Nicholson, Charles Stearn, Preston L. Snyder, Frank Schaffer, Jacob Snyder, John Hargett, Reginald Cross, Ernest O. Ricketts, Harry West, Jas. Small, Edgar Clagett, Linwood Howard, Charles Allnutt, Elmer Herspberger, Joseph Darby; Bethesda district, Vernon E. Hodges, Mrs. Clarence E. Dawson, John Imirie, Ninian Perry, William B. Horn, Mrs. Anna H. Roach, John A. Fleming; Olney district, Mrs. Marianna M. Miller, Newton Stabler, Dr. J. W. Bird, Harry C. Williams, Lewis Barnsley, Joseph Finneyfrock, R. P. Soper, Leonard C. Burns, William E. Brown, Arthur Brown, Joseph Janney; Gaithersburg district, Israel G. Warfield, Thomas I. Fulks, Dr. Horace C. Haddox, Perrie E. Waters, C. H. Browning, Upton Bowman, Robert L. Hickerson, Worthington Griffith, Lewis Bussard, Charles E. Becraft, Arthur Gloyd, William F. Hill; Potomac district, Howard C. Fawcett, Dr. William T. Pratt, Chester Clagett, George D. Moyer, Francis S. Kilgour, Scott Collins; Barnesville district, Octavius O. Baker, Charles T. Brosius, C. C. Hilton, David R. Hershey, George Cooley, George Holland, J. A. Padgett, D. T. Shreve, Louis B. Scholl, John Jones, Lawrence A. Chiswell, W. E. Wade, Oliver Johnston, Reginald D. Poole, Damascus district, James D. Young, Dr. George E. Boyer, F. E. Burdette, W. B. Moxley, W. E. Watkins, John H. Burdette, T. D. King, Robey F. Brown, Jesse B. Smith, James M. Kemp, John J. Burdette, F. M. King, Downey M. Williams, Emory Mullinix, A. M. Bowman, Franklin E. Gue, Samuel Kemp, Harry J. King, J. O. Barnes, A. J. Greene, Samuel V. Broadhurst; Wheaton district, William P. Hay, Mrs. Anna C. Rhinehart, Frank L. Hewitt, Mrs. Herbert S. Parson, Osgood Dowell, J. P. Sullivan, Arthur Eckloff, Mrs. B. F. Harvey, Ashton Coburn, William T. Gray, Upton B. Mackall, Edward P. Rabbitt, Louis B. G. Graeves, Charles Dwyer, Kirk Alderton, Edward Beall, Hazel W. Cashell, Mrs. L. M. Moore, Homer Guerry, Geo. G. Davis.

    Mrs. Donald McLean, former President-general of the D. A. R., died May 19[th.]

.    Mrs. Helen Lee Peters Ricketts, wife of E. Clayton Ricketts, who died January 27, 1916, was remembered.

June 2, 1916.

Clara Demuth has resigned as principal of the school at Layhill.

Richard Gray has been appointed constable and collector of dog taxes for the Barnesville district.

Leonard Weer has been appointed a justice of the peace for the Olney district.

Dr. Eugene Jones has been named health officer for Kensington. He succeeds Dr. W. L. Lewis, resigned.

James M. Matthews died on Monday at his home in the Bethesda district.

Dr. Leonard Hays has sailed for Falmouth, to visit London and Paris. He will do general hospital work.

Miss Mollie Fugitt, of the Rockville vicinity, and Ralph Edwards, of Beane, were married on Thursday of last week.

Hezekiah Garner, a resident in the home of his sister, Mrs. John H. Kelchner in Rockville, died last Sundsay as a result of injuries sustained when he was struck by an automobile about three weeks ago.

Mrs. Sarah Roberts Hammond died May 27th, at Germantown. She was the widow of William Edgar Hammond.

June 9, 1916.

Dr. S. B. Milford has resumed the practice of dentistry at Poolesville.

The Governor has announced the appointment of W. W. Skinner, of Kensington, as a member of the board of governors of Maryland Agricultural College.

Among the graduates this year from the State Normal School are Misses Isabelle S. Bissatt, Elizabeth Dawson, and Glenna Dawson.

Miss Rebecca Lamar will graduate from Woman's College, Lynchburg, Va.

The marriage on May 20th, of Miss Deboarh Jane Burdette and Lawrence Price was announced.

The dairymen of the Gaithersburg and Germantown area have completed the organization of a cow-testing association. The names mentioned are F. J. VanHoesen, J. B. Diamond Jr., F. G. Boland, G. L. Gardiner, J. F. Hargett, and McKendree Walker.

Cont'd. on next page.

June 9, 1916, cont'd:

Miss Helen Starr Myers and Dr. Bates Etchison were married last Saturday, in Washington.

Miss Ethel Lytton Spates and Roger Hawkins were married on Thursday of last week.

The fourth annual commencement of Briarley Hall Military Academy was held last Friday. The only graduate was Franklin Carlisle, of Gaithersburg. Others mentioned are Clayton Clark, S. Webster Tull, Wilson McDonald, and Thomas Somerville.

Charles Grimes, a native of Brookeville, died recently in Pasadena, California. He had made a considerable fortune in gold mining.

June 16, 1916.

Rev. Millard F. Minneck, who has been the rector of the Episcopal Church at St. Mary's City for the past 25 years, will become rector of Christ Episcopal Church, Rockville.

Mrs. Florence Noyes VanVleck, of Linden, died on Thursday of last week.

Miss Frances Catherine Mainhart and Windsor Scott Day were married on Wednesday of last week.

Miss Mary Louise Hurley and Prof. Guy Lee Carter were married on June 6th.

Mr. & Mrs. Thomas Hoskinson, of Poolesville, celebrated their 40th. wedding anniversary on the 31st. of last month.

Mr. J. Hilleary Bogley died on last Tuesday.

June 23, 1916.

Miss Ethel Waters, of Gaithersburg, has been appointed stenographer in the office of the School Board Commissioners.

Mrs. Martha E. Ricketts, wife of Henry T. Ricketts, died at her home in Gaithersburg on last Monday.

The graduates of the Rockville Academy are Miss Leona B. Rabbitt aand Lewis Watson. John McDonald was awarded a medal for higher mathematics.

Miss Ethel Virginia Windham and William Joseph Murphy were married on Wednesday of last week.

Mrs. Zora S. Darby, wife of J. Gardiner Darby, of Rockville, died last Sunday, following an operation for appendicitis.

Cont'd. on next page.

June 23, 1916, cont'd:

Miss Grace Amelia Mackintosh and John Emory Pollock were married last Saturday at the home of the mother of the bride in Washington.

Wm. Jenkins, colored, is being sought in the killing of James Martin, also colored. Both men were residents of the Seneca neighborhood.

The June meeting of the Janet Montgomery chapter of the D.A.R. was held at 'Milton', near Bethesda, the home of Mrs. James H. Loughborough The oldest part of the home was built in 1700.

The following is a complete roster of Company K, 1st. Infantry, Maryland National Guard. It is presently at camp at Laurel, Md., and has been ordered by President Wilson to prepare for duty on the Mexican border. The officers are: Captain, R. B. Clayton; $1^{st}$. Lt., E. Brooke Lee; $2^{nd}$. Lt., Frank L. Hewitt; $1^{st}$. Sgt, George Landon; Q.M. Sgt., J. E. Burdette; Sgts; O.H.P. Clark, Chas. Cooley, Ernest Eslin, Frank P. Clark; Cpls., Leon P. Shoemaker, Ernest VanHorn, Burt Cowell, John Stevens, John Gladmon, William Howes; Pvts., Carl Shaifer, Clarence E. Dawson, Wm. G. Links, Geo. Price, Daniel Allen, Raymond H. Andrews, Jack Arnold, Charles V. Arnold, Wm. C. Barnes, Vernon Bennett, Terence Bready, Jas. M. Buffin, Mack H. Carlisle, Wm. B. Carr, Carroll Cissell, Herbert C. Claude, John B. Cross, Paul H. Curran, Harry J. Curtis, E. Daymude, Herman D. Devine, Louis L. Donaldson, Clarence F. Duvall, Louis H. Ely, Henry Eslin, Geo. Fallin, Wm. Fallin, Neal D. Franklin, Jos. A. Gibson, Russell Gill, Wm. T. Harvey, Oscar Hilton, Thomas Holt, Cliff Howes, Lenox Howes, Paul. H—[Hill ?] Arch Johnson, Jas. B. Jones, Dorsey Jones, Geo. A. M. Kelchner, Wm. W. Lewis, L. W. Lindner, Wm. Lusby, John K. Magee, Nathan T. Mills, Frank Murray, Chas. R. Parks, Wm. S. Poss, Chas. Purdum, Jas. P. Raney Jr., Wm. J. Rankin, Arthur Sabin, Frank Savage, Joseph Savage, John W. Saxon, Jas. Simmons, Wm. H. Small, Harry Sparks, Chas. Shoemaker, Carl B. Springirth, Wm. S. Tyler, Hugh O. Thompson, Walter Thompson, Claude Waddill, Harry A. Welsh, Frank W. Wick, Geo. A. Wilburn, Geo. VanHorn.

The County Commissioners have appointed William T. S. Curtis, of Chevy Case to be a commissioner of 'The Washington Suburban Sanitary Commission'; and the Governor has appointed J. William Bogely, of Betheda district to membership on the Commission. A third Commissioner is yet to be appointed.

June 30, 1916.

Mrs. Charlotte F. Neff died on Sunday at the home of her daughter, Mrs. Allan Rutherford, near Gaithersburg.

Twin daughters were born last Wednesday to Mr. & Mrs Harrison G. England, of Rockville.

It was announced that Miss Ellen Thomas and Frederick Haller will be married 'in the near future'.

Miss Annie Cecelia Raney and Lewis Christopher Kengla, both of the Kensington vicinity, were married last Wednesday.

Harry Robertson has died – no date stated – as a result of injuries suffered when he jumped from a window of Casualty Hospital, Washington about two weeks ago. His funeral was held last Sunday. He was a grandson of Jacob Poss of Rockville.

A grange was organized on June 17$^{th}$, at Germantown. The names mentioned are James D. King, F. G. Boland, John W. Henderson, R. L. Hickerson, Kirtley Jones, Mrs. Frank Schaeffer, R. K. Waters, E. D. Gloyd, Mrs. Geo. L. Gardiner, Mrs. James D. King, Mrs. J. T. Neel, Mrs. R. L. Waters, J. T. Neel, R. L. Waters, and Calvin Bready.

The School Commissioners have announced the appointment of the following teachers for the public schools:  Laytonsville, Mary E. Oliphant, Lena Ricketts, Mary White;  Unity, Lulu White; Etchison, Viola Gillis;  Goshen, Effie K. Ternent;  Redland, Lina D. Watts;  Snouffers, VitginiaWaters; Cedar Grove;  Margaret Watkins;  Hyattstown, Isabel Bissett, W. O. Rhodes;  Clarksburg, Katherine Hughes, Margaret Lindsay;  Boyds, D. W. Shork;  Slidell; Edith Allnutt;  Kingsley, Anice C. Murphy;  Burdette, Effie H. Shreve; Lewisdale, Sarah Griffith, Deborah J. Iddings;  Poolesville, Robert W. Stout, Katie Frizzell, Clarine Fletchall, Elizabeth Griffith, Margaret Williams;  Sugarland, Ida C. Jarboe;  Elmer, Jane Williams; Martinsburg, Ida M. Hickman;  Rockville, C. G. Myers, Edith L. Ford, Alice E. Hepburn, Elizabeth Defandorf, Elberta T. Rice, Virginia F. Brewer, Lillian A. Bennett, Estelle Ricketts, Mary Brewer, Francis L. Horner, Wison Ward, Theodore Bailey;  Baileys, Carrie M. Fulks;  Montrose, Francis Ricketts, M. Landella Etchison;  Avery, Mary Thompson;  Derwood, Maria Spates;  Garrett Park, Agnes Frizzell;  Colesville, Grace Townsend;  White Oak, Jesta Warthen, Glenna Fisher;  Burtonsville, Estelle Batson, Elsie M. Soper;  Ednor, Isabel B. Jones, Esther Scott;  Fairland, Eleanor Reed;  Darnestown,

Cont'd. on next page.

June 30, 1916, cont'd:
Jas .W. White, Margaret Darby, Evelyn McAtee, Mary Rice; Travilah, Leta Riggs, Nellie Grock; Old Germantown, Esther Pumphrey; Seneca, Claudia Hall; Quince Orchard, Bessie Woodward; Oakley, Eleanor Darby; Bethesda, Ruth V. Pope, Bruce Colton, Irene Brown, Ruth E. Beall; Chevy Chase, Florence M. Barksdale, Gertrude Lane, Lillian Morgan, Emma Washington, Mary Tracey, Effie Barnsley, Edgar Thompson; Friendship, Mary Easton; Sandy Spring, W. K. Klingaman, Sally P. Brooke, Ruth Shoemaker, Minnie Carlisle; Oakdale, Katherine Moore; Brookeville, Rexford Hartle, Hattie J. Montgomery, Hilda M. Benson, Mary Reed; Olney, Lillian B. Price; Brighton, Daisy Higgins; Gaithersburg, Thomas W. Troxall, Caroline Henderson, Anna C. Pace, Ruby Robertson, Henriette Rich, Lucy Brewer, Corinne Duff, Maude V. Broome; Germantown, Robert L. Tolson, Maude England, Marian True, Mabel King; Middlebrook, Nellie Duvall; Washington Grove, Laura Frizzell; Potomac, Clark F. Brown, Carrie Bodmer, Elizabeth Lauxmann, Ida L. Isherwood; Barnesville, A. Grace Baker, Daisy Cecil; Comus, Lois Holland, Irene Sibley; Poole's Tract, Edith A. Lindig; Dickerson, Alice Spates; Buck Lodge, Mabel Gott; Damascus, John T. Baker, Griffith Chiswell; Clagettsville, Ola Lawson; Kings Valley, Blanche Walker; Woodfield, Belle P. Watkins; Mount Lebanon, Albert E. Warthen; Cedar Heights, Violette Murphy; Browningsville, F. S. Gladhill, Maude Ashton; Kensington, Dorothy Clum, Lillian Sage, Edna E. Hawke, Helen Schwartz, Mrs. Lanahan; Woodside, J. Edwin Lodge, Helen Neel, Katherine M. Houghtalling, Marie Boardman, Geneva Walters, Amanda Griffith, Blair, Blanche E. Creamer, Sue A. Collins; Dwyers, Grace Beall; Layhill, Frank W. Watkins; Takoma Park, Stella A. Thomas, Josephine Chaney, Edna M. Baltzell.

The Supervisors of Elections have named the following registrars, judges and clerks. The first named in each precinct is a democrat – the others republicans: Laytonsville; registrars, Z. M. Waters Jr., T. Cramner Griffith; judges, Ledoux E. Riggs, Henry H. Griffith; clerks, Lloyd C. Colliflower, Garry W. Bell: Clarksburg, registrars, Charles W. Gibson, William W. Dronenburg; judges, Delaney King, J. William Johnson; clerks, Robert L. Hickerson, Robert S. Windsor: Poolesville; registrars, Joseph N. Darby, Charles V. Willard; judges, Walter W. Pyles, Usher Charlton; clerks,

Cont'd. on next page

June 30, 1916, cont'd:
Benjamin T. Gott, William T. Compher; Rockville, first precinct, registrars, William T. Griffith, J. Gardiner Darby; judges, George A. M. Kelchner, John L. Dawson; clerks, Charles B. Dowden, John A. England; Rockville, second precinct; registrars, Robert L. Warfield, John M. Heagy; judges, Thomas N. Bailey, J. Somervell Dawson; clerks, Clifford H. Robertson, Urban N. Wagner: Colesville; registrars, Wilson G. Johnson, Henry C. Chaney; judges, Frank L. Wilson, Samuel S. Bond; clerks, Lawrence E. Harding, Charles E. Bond: Darnestown; registrars, Thomas D. Darby, Preston L. Snyder; judges, John N. Richter, Ernest H. Darby; clerks, Clyde Harriss, Reuben F. Martin. Bethesda, first precinct; registrars, H. Latane Lewis, Lewis Keiser; judges, William M. Renshaw, A. A. Braddock; clerks, Leroy Lochte, Edward E. Crockett. Bethesda, second precinct; registrars, Eugene H. McLachlan, Vernon B. Hodges; judges, William J. Callaghan, Thomas E. Robertson; clerks, John E. Stout, Roscoe E. Ridgeway. Olney, first precinct: registrars, George E. White, George H. Jones; judges, Nicholas R. Griffith, Tarlton B. Stabler; clerks, Frank Cashell, Frederick Stabler Jr; Olney, second precinct, registrars; Arthur W. Brown, Charles R. Hartshorne; judges, Allen B. Craver, Lafayette M. Dwyer; clerks, James W. Brown, Francis Miller. Gaithersburg, first precinct, registrars; Perry A. Gloyd, John W. Case; judges, Charles F. Hogan, E. D. Kingsley; clerks, John T. Martin, C. Scott Duvall. Gaithersburg, second precinct, registrars, Charles E. Becraft, J. William Garrett; judges, Samuel B. Briggs, Harold S. Kingsley; clerks, George A. Gloyd, Emory H. Crawford. Potomac; registrars, Clarence H. Creamer, John L. Ball; judges, Thomas E. Jackson, Charles R. Stone, clerks, Harrison Myers, Edward C. Ricketts. Barnesville; registrars, R Frank Gibson, W. Windsor Hodges, judges, William L. Hoyle, A. Clinton Brown; clerks, John J. Umstead, Charles O. Robinson. Damascus; registrars, Richard H. Stanley, William H. Burdette; judges, Hiram G. King, Samuel V. Broadhurst; clerks, Elgie D. Hawkins, John W. Hager. Wheaton, first precinct; registrars, Lewis B. F. Graeves, Upton B.Mackall, judges, Frank D. Stubbs, Alfred C. Warthen; clerks, William A. Fidler, Clarence V. Sayer. Wheaton second precinct: Registrars, Ollie J. Hughes, Edward W. Birgfeld; judges, Abner H. Hardesty, William T. Lusby; clerks, Archer L. Haycock, Marshall Faber.

July 7, 1916.
Louis W. Maxon died last Sunday at Johns Hopkins hospital.
A second branch of the Camp Fire Girls has been organized in Sandy Spring. The names mentioned are Elizabeth Gilpin, Isabel Lee, Caroline Stabler, Elizabeth Wilson, Anna Gilpin, Claire Hutton, and Cornelia Chichester.
Mrs Jane D. Watkins, wife of Lorenzo Watkins, died last Tuesday at her home near Cedar Grove. See also August 4, 1916.
Miss Ianthe May Monred and William Wilson Briggs, both of the Gaithersburg area, were married on Wednesday of last week.
Mrs. Ella Jane Fawcett died last Monday at the home of her daughter, Mrs. C. E. Nicholls, in Washington.

July 14, 1916.
Dade Griffith has been appointed to a clerkship at the Montgomery County National Bank of Rockville.
Grace Carrell Diamond, third child of Herbert L. Diamond and Marie J. Diamond, died July 11th.
Miss Olive Rebecca Selby and Geo. W. Linthicum were married on Wednesday of last week.
Leonard D. Sale, widely known in this county, died on Tuesday.
Miss Alice Gertrude Morand and Robert Clifford Lyddane were married last Saturday, in Woodside.
Rev. Oscar W. Henderson has resigned as pastor of Rockville Baptist Church in order that he may accept a call to the pastorate of the East Baptist Church, Baltimore.
Remus R. Darby died last Monday at his home near Buck Lodge. He had been a judge of the Orphan's Court for 12 years, and a member of the Board of County Commissioneers for 4 years. He was a son of the late John W. Darby, and was a life-long resident of this county.
Miss Nicie Tabitha Yingling, of Adamstown, and Morgan Lee Trail, of Clopper, were married on Thursday of last week.
In School Board news: the following teachers have been appointed: Grace L. Ryan, Mariel Gott, Edith Allnutt, Isabel Bissett, Elizabeth Dawson, Julian Griffith, Ruby Robertson, Lillian Chaney, Rebecca Lamar, and Willie Baker. Mary Magruder was appointed attendance officer.

July 21, 1916.

James F. Burroughs died last Sunday at his home in Rockville.

Mrs. Virginia McAtee, wife of William McAtee, died last Friday.

E. Bruce Flack, formerly of Wheaton, died July 13th, at his home in Los Angeles, Calif.

George B. F. Walter died last Friday at his home in Dickerson.

During a severe storm on Thursday of last week, lightning struck the barn of L. A. Renneberger near Comus, and it burned completely.

Miss Ethel Mae Fawsett and Dr. Robert Perkins were married last Saturday.

President Wilson has appointed Andrew J. Cummings, of Chevy Chase, to the Excise Commission of the District of Columbia. The appointment must be confirmed by the Senate District Committee. See also August 4, 1916 and August 11th.

The following named have subscribed to the Chautauqua for next year by agreeing to buy tickets, namely : Norman Bouic, W. W. Welsh, George M. Hunter, Harry A. Dawson, J. F. Collins, Dr. R. C. Warfield, Hon. E. C. Peter, Dr. C. H. Mannar, W. C. Bean, R. W. Vinson, W. B. Burdette, Frank Higgins, Miss R. L. Wagner, Alexander Kilgour, Thomas Vinson, W. H. Beard, C. W. Prettyman, Dr. Geo. E. Lewis, O. H. Talbott, J. C. Welliver, J. J. Higgins, H. C. Allnutt, Berry E. Clark, E. W. Broome, Preston B. Ray, J. W. McFarland, W. S. Magruder, W. Hicks, A. J. Almoney, F. M. Hallowell, J. J. Hutton, C. F. Kirk, Dr. J. W. Bird, Dr. O. M. Linthicum, Mrs. Henry Howard, David Bissett, Thomas Dawson, J. W. Jones, R. G. Hilton, W. R. Brewer, Albert Bouic, Alexander Garrett, William T. Griffith, Wm. H. Talbott, George M. Anderson, James T. Bogley, H. C. Hickerson, R. E. L. Smith, George H. Lamar, Joseph Reading, Bowie F. Waters, Wm. H. Baden.

July 28, 1916.

Miss Alice Jane McCauley and William E. Duvall were married last Saturday.

Miss Deborah E. Bowman and William C. Harding were married last Saturday.

The engagement of Ruth Marie Spates, or Gaithersburg, and Maston T. Carlisle, of Cooksville, Tenn. was announced.

Cont'd. on next page.

July 28, 1916, cont'd:

The engagement of Miss Rosa May Lewis and Herbert D. Barnes was announced. The wedding will take place on July 29th.

Mrs. Emma C. Marlow, wife of Elias P. Marlow of Colesville, died suddenly on Wednesday of last week.

The *Sentinel* referred to an article in the *Philadelphia Press*, which it quoted, sketching the life of General Richard Montgomery.

The County Commissioners have appointed tax assessors as follows: for the first district, Z. M. Waters Jr; for the second district, E. Dorsey King; for the third, Harry M. Williams; for the fourth, Alfred Ray; for the fifth, Philip H. Ray; for the sixth, George R. Rice; for the seventh, Joseph F. Whalen; for the eigthth, Louis W. Barnsley; for the ninth, John E. Clagett; for the tenth, George Edington Bell; for the eleventh, Charles G. Griffith; for the twelfth, Claud H. Burdette; for the thirteenth, Vernon Beall. For the town of Kensington, John A. Cannon; for Takoma Park, H. Edson Rogers; for Gaithersburg, John W. Walker; and for Rockville, Martin F. Heim.

Phillip T. Stabler, who died March 30, 1916, was remembered by resolution of the Board of Directors of the Savings Institution of Sandy Spring.

August 4, 1916.

Mrs. Helen Howard, widow of Dr. Florodoardo Howard, died on Thursday of last week.

Homer M. West, 19 year old son of Eraasmus West, of Hunting Hill, died last Monday.

Miss Rosa May Lewis and Herbert D. Barnes were married last Saturday.

Charles Corby, of near Garrett Park, has given a yearling Holstein bull to the Montgomery County Agricultural Scoiety, to be raffled during the coming Fair.

Miss Bertha Adele Scheaffer, of Seneca, and Edward Rawlings Brosius, of Barnesville, were married on Wednesday.

Miss Emma B. Ward, daughter of Edward Ward and Emma B. Ward, died on Saturday a week ago.

August 11, 1916.

The engagement of Miss Cynthia Noyes VanVleck, of Linden, and Maurice J. Stabler, of Sandy Spring, was announced.

Cont'd. on next page.

August 11, 1916, cont'd:

The marriage on August 10th, of Clintie Irene DeVilbiss, of Gaithersburg, and Lorenzo H. Yancy, of Clarksburg, was announced.

Mrs. Savilla Simmons, widow of Samuel T. Simmons, died on Wednesday of last week at her home in Clarksburg.

Miss Susie Creamer committed suicide on Wednesday of last week.

Miss Sarah M. Musser, age 75, died last Sunday.

Mrs. Sarah T. Byrd, widow of John B. Byrd, died last Sunday at her home near Dawsonville.

Miss Priscilla Dawson Gibbons and Lucius Q. C. Lamar were married Tuesday, in Belair.

Mrs. Bertha M. Jackson, until recently a resident of Rockville, has been arrested and charged with having forged the name of Arthur R. Parsley on a note.

Randolph Talbott, of Rockville, has been appointed to prepare the plans for the new school buildings to be built at Chevy Chase and Kensington.

John William Keys died on Friday of last week at his home near Rockville.

The death of McKinley West was remembered by the Hunting Hill Epworth League. See also August 18th, 1916.

Bertha Adell Schaeffer and Edward Rollins Brosius were married August 2nd, at the home of the father of the bride, in Seneca.

Mary Emma Offutt, age 18 months, daughter of Raphael T. Offutt and Florence Conroy Offutt, died July 19th.

August 18, 1916.

Julian F. Walters has been appointed assistant cashier at the national bank in Silver Spring, succeeding Ira C. Whitacre, resigned.

The funeral of Mrs. Nellie Jackson, wife of Arthur Jackson of Potomac, took place on Wednesday. No date of death stated.

It has been announced that Miss Pearl May Burroughs and Rufus Smith were married April 24, in Elkton.

Fire on Thursday of last week destroyed the barn on the farm owned jointly by Dr. Wm. H. Trail and George G. Bradley.

The wedding of Miss Ruth Marie Spates, of Gaitheresburg, and Prof. Masten T. Carlisle, of Cooksville, Tenn. took place on Tuesday, in Grace Methodist Church, Gaithersburg.

Cont'd. on next page

August 18, 1916, cont'd:
Mrs. Nellie L. Hartshorne has died as a result of injuries suffered when the porch of the Brookeville High School, on which she had sought refuge during a storm, collapsed.

In school board news: Miss Rose T. Coursey, of Centerville, Md., has been appointed Supervisor of primary schools of Montgomery County. Also, it was announced that the following teachers have been appointed, namely, Grace Buxton, Leta Riggs, Elizabeth A. Lauxman, Carrie Fulks, Maude V. Broome, Helen Pumphrey, Wilson S. Ward, Edgar Thompson. It was also announced that William D. Warfield, of Damascus, has been awarded a scholarship at Charlotte Hall Academy.

At the annual meeting of the Montgomary County Anti-Saloon League, officers as follows were elected: President, Rev. O. C. Barnes; vice-president at large, Thomas J. Owen; secretary, E. Wilson Walker; treasurer, Walter M. Margruder; district vice presidents, Rev. John E. Fort, John W. Boyer, Howard W. Spurrier, Edward G. Ward, Reuben T. Baker, Brooke Vincent, Lewis Keiser, R. Bentley Thomas, E. Wilson Walker, Edington Bell, Dr. Geo. M. Boyer, and Alfred C. Warthen. Others mentioned are Rev. M. H. Keen, Rev. Frank M. Richardson, Major Samuel H. Walker, Rev. Henry P. Hamill, Mrs. John B. Brewer, Miss Ida S. Dove, Mrs. Henry J. Finley, Stanley Gingell, and Rev. Oscar W. Henderson.

Montgomery Countians owning horses which have been entered in races in the coming Fair are: Javin Bros., E. C. Allnutt, Wm. H. Fawcett, H. F. Weissner, W. J. Umstead, Mrs. C. A. Beard, A. F. Prescott, W. V. Dawson, Wm. J. Selby, H. C. Fawcett.

August 25, 1916.
Charles G. DuFief, age 61, a lifelong resident of Montgomery County, died last Sunday at his home near Travilah.

Mrs. Catherine Gaither Bowie, wife of George Washington Bowie, died last Saturday

The Montgomery County Library Association has been organized in Rcovkille, with the following temporary officers: Chairman, Isabel Kingdon; secretary, Mrs. Robert E. L. Smith; treasurer, Mrs H. C. Allnutt. The Association has been given permission to use 'the little building on the high school grounds'. Others mentioned are Mrs. Otis M. Linthicum, Mrs. Wm. H. Holmes,
Cont'd. on next page.

August 25, cont'd:
Mrs. Wm. H. Talbott, Mrs. Robert N. Baylis, Mrs. Lewis R. Watson, Mrs. Alexander Kilgour, Mrs. Frank A. Spencer, Misses Lucy R. Simpson and Rose Henderson.

The Board of Directors of Monocacy Cemetery Association adopted a resolution of respect in memory of Remus R. Darby, former President of the Association.

The executive committee of the Social Service League met in Rockville on August $15^{th}$. The following are mentioned: Dr. J. W. Bird, Rev. P. P. Flournoy, Mrs. H. L. Wells, Eugene E. Stevens, Mrs. H. J. Finley, Mrs. O. H. Tibbott, Dr. John L. Lewis, Dr. Frederick Henderson, Cannon Austin, Mrs. L. A. Allnutt, Mrs. John B. Brewer, Rev. O. C. Barnes, Miss Canby Ray, Dr. D. C. Chambers, Dr. James E. Deets, Mrs. E. L. Darby, W. E. Emory, E. W. Walker., Rev. H. H. Marsden, Joseph T. Janney, C. Norman Bouic, Rev. E. L. Bennett, Mrs. Wm. B. Mobley, Mrs. George H. McGrew, George R. Rice, Mrs. Archibald Hopkins, Asa M. Stabler, A. G. Thomas, Mrs. J. D. Defandorf, Mrs. J. Frank Wilson, and Richard White.

The Supervisors of Elections have appointed the following doorkeepers, to act at the various polling places at the coming November election: Benjamin F. Allnutt, Charles H. Trout, Eli G. Cooley, A. B. Thompson, Wm. T. Hoskinson, Roy L. Wright, Ulysses M. Ricketts, Wm. Skillman, Edward C. Robey, Michael Conroy, Francis E. Valdenar, Newton Stabler, Charles W. Pennifield, Lenox Howes, John E. Lynch, Joshua E. Broadhurst, Frank E. Brown, Chas. P. Marlow, Louis M. Leizear, Wm. E. Dill, Walter M. Howes, Geo. W. Nicholson, Gideon D. Briggs, Jacob T. Gartner, Clarence Sparrow, Howard Crawford, Charles F. Bodine, George W. Burroughs, Jas. B. Holland, Charles C. Orme, Nicholas E. Burns, Darius F. Watkins, Wm. Gray, N. M. Howes, John E. Thompson, Adam Seek.

September 1, 1916.
Mrs. Mary V. Swain died last Saturday.

Messrs. Harry Kengla and Charles Kengla have rented a stall in the P. street market, and will begin business there on September $15^{th}$.

Miss Mary Cruit and Clarence M. Kiefer, both of Takoma Park, were married September $15^{th}$.

Cont'd on next page.

September 1, 1916, cont'd:
J. Mahlon Sullivan died on Monday at his home in Rockvlle.
It was announced that Anna Offutt Miller and Dr. William L. Millea were married on August 26$^{th}$, in Baltimore.
Mrs. P. Flack Hannan, a former resident of Montrose, died on Wednesday of last week at her home in Kansas City, Kansas.
Senator Blair Lee has appointed James I. Diggs, D. M. Page, and J. M. Plaskett to the Naval Academy.
Wm. Glaze, of the Damascus district, shot himself on Sunday. He had previously been committed to Springfield Hospital, but had walked away and returned to his home on Saturday.
Mrs. Elberta Tschiffely Rice died last Monday at her home near Travilah.
Miss Pearl Elizabeth Ray and Forrest King were married on last Wednesday at the home of the parents of the bride, Mr. & Mrs. George F. Ray, of Germantown.
Fire, started by lightning, last Sunday destroyed the new barn of the farm of Wm. Thompson near Olney.
The following is a list of the prizes awarded at the 1916 Fair. Where a person won more than one prize in a single category and is therefore entered twice or more, the duplication is not copied here.
Cattle: R. G. Ray, Kahlert & Ray.
Holstein Friesians: J. B. Diamond Jr. Davis Bros., Javin Bros.
Jerseys: Lee Ricketts.
Guernseys: H. C. Hurley, W. H. Beard.
Grade Holsteins: Davis Bros., Chas. Veirs, James P. Veirs,
Grade Jerseys: J. B. Pumphrey, Chas. Veirs.
Angus: A. T. Powell.
Hogs: Davis Bros., J. R. Lechlider, J. S. Gillis, Phillip Case.
Sheep: John E. Muncaster Jr.
Works of art: Mrs. B. P. Wilson, Rose Wagner, J. G. Hall, Wilson Offutt Jr., Mrs. Fred Keplinger, M. E. Moran, F. A. Snyder, Mrs. E. C. Taylor Smith, Frank Snowden, Florence A. Snyder, S. Peter Wagner, Hughes Monday, Miss S. A. Pumphrey, Lewis Reed, Mrs. C. M. Grubb, Beulah Dove, Edmonia Gardiner, Lutie Griffith, Louise C. Bready, Fred VanHosen, Lily Shorts, Mrs. Lawrence Darby, Mrs. J. G. Hall.
Garden products: R. P. Hines, T. A. Barnesley, Alice Cashell, Mrs. W. S. Thompson, E. E. Burton, Seth Warfield, J. W. Graff,
Cont'd. on next page.

September 1, 1916, cont'd:
Ellen Farquhar, Charles F. Henshew, R. P. Hines Jr., Mildred Powell, F. Stabler, Margaret Welsh, Kenneth Barnesley, Dorothy Magruder, Emmett Dove, W. A. Ricketts, Melvin L. Ridgley, Rebecca Lamar, J. R. Lechlider, Hattie Granger, J. B. Diamond Jr.

Fruits: R. P. Hines, W. S. Thompson, Melvin Ridgley, Mrs. Alfred Ray, Rebecca Lamar, Samuel Thompson, Ben Davis, Mrs. U. Bowman, Urban Wagner, Lillian Robertson, Margaret Welsh, Seth Warfield, T. A. Barnesley, J. H. Hale, Edward Mount.

Culinary: Mrs. W. E. Ricketts, Josie Higgins, Mildred Powell, Mrs. S. B. Hege, Mrs. George Henderson, Rose Wagner, Mrs. S. C. Wimsatt, Mrs. M. Brown, Edith Hull, Adele Maus, Ada Warfield, Mrs. U. Bowman, Mrs. Lawrence Flack, Mrs. Martim Heim, Mrs. C. T. Johnson, Mrs. Wallace Ricketts, Margaret Shorts, Lillian Robertson, Mrs. J. H. Ward, Edmonia Gardiner, Mrs. G. W. Bready, Mrs. Artemus Sullivan, Mrs. Bernard Poss, Alice Cashell, Mrs. W. B. Carr, Mrs. G. W. Davis.

Miscellaneous culinary: Mrs. A. C. Warthan, Ada Warfield, Mary M. Stabler, Mrs. Roger Shaw, Mrs. W. E. Ricketts, Mrs. T. A. Barnesley, Mrs. G. W. Bready, T. A. Barnesley, Edgar Higgins, Mary M. Stabler, Urban Wagner, A. T. Powell Jr.

Children's garden products: Henry Warfield, C. F. Hines, Arthur Shorts, Mildred Morrison, John E. Muncaster Jr., Jennie Beckwith, Courtland Trundle, Clarence Burton, Roland Stabler.

Children's handicraft: Lily Shorts, Nettie Shorts, Catherine Hall, Myrtle Rabbitt, Fannie Oldfield, Catherine England, Mildred Morrison, Hilmer Morris, Fannie Phillips, L. G. Hall, Stonestreet Lamar, Gladys Hilton, Gertrude Hines, Elizabeth Bowman, Annie M. Shorts, Mildred Powell, Catherine Hines.

Farm products: Albert Stabler, D. H. Horner, J. R. Lechlider, George Shaw, Lillian Fields, R. P. Hines, C. M. Brown, Seth W. Warfield, C. T. Johnson, Alice Cashell.

Horses / mules / ponies: J. C. Otwell, James W. Barnesley, A. T. Powell, T. A. Barnesley, W. E. Ricketts, Canby Ray, Javins Bros., Chas. A. Beard, O. T. Stonestreet, Laura McNair, B. C. Hoskinson, Clay Edwards, John Lethbridge, C. S. Holland, Willis L. Moore, John Rabbitt, C. W. Craver, W. V. Beall, Oscar Gaither, A. T. Powell, P. F. Tippett, J. B. Welsh, Richard White, Tyler Case, Imogene Schwartz, John Kalfbus, John Dawson, Rhoda Welsh.

Cont'd on next page.

September 1, 1916, cont'd:
Process flour made in Montgomery County: Hickerson Bros. Dairy products: J. R. Lechlider, M. B. Nichols. Honey: Mrs. C. S. Weber. Culinary, bread, cake, &c: Margaret Dawson, Rose Wagner, Adele Maus, Mrs. U. Bowman, Carrie Barnesley, Ellen Farquhar, Mary M. Stabler, Mrs. A. R. Speare, L. B. Morrison, Jennie Beckwith, Mrs. W. E. Ricketts, Dora Ward, Mabel Ward, Mrs. T. F. Pierce, Jane Offutt, Edith Hull, Lavinia Wagner, Mrs. T. C. McGaha, Claudia Robinson, Mrs. J. H. Starkey.

Domestic manufactures: Mrs. B. M. Wissner, Marian Shorts, Mrs. C. O. Bean, Miss M. A. Winslow, M. L. Thompson, Mrs. George Henderson, Estelle Hicks, Beulah Dove, Mrs. Harry Dickerson, Mrs. Emmet Dove, Mrs. L. A. Brewer, Mary P. Dawson, Irma Fisher, Elsie England, Catherine Poole, Mrs. S. C. Wimsatt, Elizabeth Dawson, Miss S. D. Bradley, Mrs. J. S. Gruver, Estelle Smith, Mrs. Lawrence Darby, Laura M. Higgins, L. V. Morrison, Mrs. W. B. Trundle, J. D. Brown, Mary Welsh, Mrs. M. E. Hughes, Maria Hodges, Jane Offutt, Hattie Granger, Vera Travers, Jester Warthen, Mrs. A. R. Speare, Martha Poole, Mrs. Lawrence Flack, Mrs. E. C. Taylor Smith, Mrs. Bowie F. Waters, Mrs. H. S. Darby, Mrs. William Gittings, Mrs. H. Trail, Mrs. Charles G. Holland, Catherine Reed, Mrs. Lucy M. Dove, C. M. Brown.

Poultry: F. A. Kerr, J. F. McNeilly, Mrs. L. L. Nicholson, R. P. Hines Jr., J. H. Shorts, D. P. Edmonston, A. E. Burroughs, G. C. Gorsuch, R. C. D. Hunt, Harry Hunt, J. F. Defandorf, L. R. Watson, Edward Monday, A. E. Burriss, C. W. Rippey, B. C. Hutchinson, D. P. Smith, C. N. Hight, Artemus Sullivan, Edward J. Hickey, Gladys Kefauver, Corrinne C. Anderson, Lillian Fields, Myrtle Gilliss, J. F. Riffet.

Miss Lillian Fields and Theodore Ricketts won prizes for having the best decorated cars in the automobile parade at the Fair. Miss Fields also won a driving contest, in which Clinton Waters took second place and Mr. Ricketts placed third.

Thomas Edgar Padgett, who died August 31, 1915, was remembered.

Mrs. Sallie Byrd was remembered by resolution of the Dawsonville Reading Club

September 8, 1916.

Miss Nellie Hester Beall and Thomas H. Athey were married on Thursday of last week.

Owing to an error in the published list of Fair prizes, the name of Miss B. A. Dove was incorrectly listed as a prizewinner in the Domestic Arts section. Miss Dove had no entries there; and the name of Miss B. Daishe should be substituted in that list.

Miss Margaret Amelia Burton and Keefer Linwood Thompson were married on Thursday of last week.

Miss Susie Dutrow and Dr. Robert C. Warfield were married on Thursday of last week.

In school board news: Julian F. Walters has been named principal of the Hyattstown public school; Miss Elizabeth Lauxmann has been appointed principal of the Bailey school; Miss Eleanor Darby has been appointed principal at the Potomac school; Miss Nellie Gorck [Grock] has been named assistant at the Travilah school; and Miss Mary Easton has been named assistant at the Takoma Park school

September 15, 1916

Miss Mary Matilda Hyatt and Edward Prescott Abbe were married on last Wednesday.

Dade Griffith and Dr. Charles Pyles, brothers-in-law, have purchased the business of P. E. Waters, in Germantown.

Fire destroyed the barn, silo, and carriage house on the farm of Tarlton B. Stabler, near Sandy Spring. No date stated.

Prizes have been awarded for the best dancing at Fountain Grove Park, Seneca, to C. V. Belt & Miss W. E. Winslow; to Ike Cubitt & Mrs. Chas. Willard; to Ellis Willard & Miss Ruth Beall; and to John Young & Miss Nettie Miles.

Rev. Edward Callender has submitted his resignation as rector of the Christ Episcopal Church of Kensington, to take effect October 15th.

September 22, 1916.

Martha A. Holland died last Monfay at her home near Norwood.

W. T. Gray has been appointed deputy game warden at large.

Cont'd. on next page.

September 22, 1916, cont'd:
Miss Mary Emily Ray died last Sunday at the home of her niece, Mrs. John B. Waters.
Robert S. Suddath died last Sunday at his home near Travilah.
Harry L. Nicholson died on Thursday of last week at his home near Cedar Grove.
Franklin Mace died last Sunday at his home near Montrose.
Miss Rosie May Johnson and Charles Lee Watkins Jr. were married on Thursday of last week.
Miss Gladys Wilmer Wheeler, daughter of Mrs. Frederick M. Wheeler, and Douglas Byrne Diamond, of Gaithersburg, were married on Saturday at Basket Neck Farm, Long Island, the summer home of the mother of the bride.
There are now 4 cases of polio in Montgomery County, and Dr. Pratt, the health officer for the County, has recommended that the opening of the public schools be delayed until September 25$^{th}$.
Ella L. Hartshorne was remembered by resolution of the Brighton Grange. See also August 18, 1916.

September 29, 1916.
Joseph W. Esworthy, age 88 years, died last Tuesday at his home near Seneca.
J. Hampton Jones and Wm. T. Umstead have been appointed to reassess property in the towns of Garrett Park and Kensington, as a part of the general reassessment of real estate recently ordered.
Miss Nellie C. Kemp and Amos Dewey Burdette were married on Wednesday of last week.
Stephen M. Bailey, a native of Rockville, is visiting friends and family after an absence of about 38 years.
The Democratic State Central Committee has named the following men to arrange meetings and to assist in registration of voters in preparation for the coming election. The names mentioned are: Laytonsville district, Alex G. Carlisle, Richard E. Darby, Robert G. Hilton; Laytonsville district, J. Ernest Hawkins, J. C. Christopher, Samuel Riggs Jr., B. R. Codwise, W. H. Griffith, C. L. Howard, J. C. Dorsey, Calvin Mullinix, Charles H. Griffith, L. E. Riggs; Clarksburg district, W. T. Warfield, B. F. Waters, E. D. King, J. M. Purdum, P. E. Waters, R. L. Waters, C. C. Waters, John W. Henderson, C. M. Griffith, J. B. Maughlin, C. T. Kingsbury, A. B. Reid, C. R. Israel,
Cont'd. on next page.

September 29, 1916, cont'd:
John Gardner, J. H. Price, E. B. Wood; Poolesville district, J. Furr White, W. L. Aud, T. N. Gott, H. N. Williams, W. J. Offutt, H. W. Spurrier, T. R. Hall, N. H. Metzger, C. S. Fields, John A. Jones, Norman Wootton,W. T. Griffith, Howard Griffith; Rockville district, Thomas C. Keys, Alex. Garrett, R. B. Peter, J. L. Clagett, J. T. Bogley, John Ertter, Ben Lenowitz, H. C. Allnutt, W. F. Ricketts, J. L. Welsh, W. W. Mobley, J. Alby Henderson, C. H. Robertson, O. H. W. Talbott, Geo. G. Earp, W. C. Veirs, J. W. Rabbitt, C. A. Clagett; Colesville district, D. M. Blandford, B. G. Ray, G. Rust Canby, Edw. C. Brown, Lewis Hobbs, G. B. McCeney, W. Z. Tolson, O. W. Roberts, W. T. Wheeler, Geo. Bonifant, H. L. Bradford, W. G. Johnson, E. L. Fawsett; Darnestown district, John A. Mall, H. C. West, E. P. Ricketts, H. D. Waters, J. D. King, E. A. Vinson,T. C. Darby, Samuel Atwood, C. M. Thrift, Wm. Fawsett, C. C. Harriss, Clyde Griffith; Bethesda district, Henry J. Hunt, E. H. Bogley, B. P. Whalen, H. W. Offutt, W. V. Magruder, N. M. Perry, M. E. Peake, Alfred Wilson, M. W. Offutt, Dr. John L. Lewis, James L. Morrison, John W. Bogley, S. D. Caldwell Jr., W. C. Balderson, Richard Evans, B. A. Leavell, W. Lyles Offutt, John H. Stout, Jesse W. Nicholson, E. H. McLachlin, W. Golden Carter, R. E. L. Gillott, Dr. Wilber Evans; Olney district, A. T. Marlow, W. B. Chichester, H. C. Williiams, L. W. Barnesly, Frank Cashell, E. D. Leizear; John Jones, L. Wear Jr., J. J. Hutton, W. P. Jones, A. W. Brown, J. W. Jones, G. W. Cashell, Henry Howard, J. H. Parsley; Gaithersburg district, E. D. Gloyd, Lewis Bussard, G. L. Gardiner, W. H. Wade, H. G. Thompson, J. E. Clagett, Robert A. Young, Dr. Carlton Etchison, Porter Musser, J. Clark Galliher, Forest Walker, G. W. Etchison, Dr. E. H. Etchison, W. F. Gaither, Richard Offutt, Beverly Mills, W. O. Dosh; Potomac district, Dr. W. T. Pratt, S. K. Bready, John Magaha, John G. Stone, Chester Clagett, Fountain Peters, W. A. Ricketts, Jesse Magruder, Carter Clagett, Geo. G. Bradley Jr., C. E. Benson; Barnesville district, C. C.. Hilton, Charles R. Darby, Leonard Hays of F., Lloyd Jones, W. S.Cooley, D. R. Hershey, Henry Kennedy, C. G. Griffith, J. F. Lewis, W. L. Chambers; Damascus district, A. W. Souder, Arthur Burns, Clayton Watkins, John R. Lewis, R. H. Stanley, John W. Burdette, Miel Linthicum, Sherwood Duvall, W. H. Darby; Wheaton district, Dr. Eugene Jones, P. B. Ray, J. D. Williams, G. W. Hyatt, Dan Clark, H. M. Martin, I. H. Beall, J. T. Cashell, W. H. Cashell, H.

Cont'd. on next page

September 29, 1916, cont'd:
Stearman, R. C. Windham, C. T. Cooley, E. C. Stubbs, A. Kelley, E. C. Keys, Samuel Grubb, Frank Ray, C. A. Frazier, H. F. O'Donnell, O. J. Hughes, James H. Cissell, W. E. Anderson, Thomas Hunter, Arthur Eckloff, F. M. Wolfe, J. Bond Smith.
End p. 215
October 6, 1916.

Mrs. Carrie V. Ray, formerly of Montgomery County, died on September 23$^{rd}$, in Baltimore city.

George R. Rice has resigned as tax aassessor for the Darnestown district.

Miss Ethel Linthicum and Ivan Thompson Lawton were married on Wednesday of last week.

Mrs. Ella Merryman Gatch Ray, mother of Preston B. Ray, the present Clerk of the Circuit Court, died on Thursday.

Fire of unknown origin burned a large barn on the farm of Charles Veirs, located about 2 ½ miles west of Rockville. The contents, including some animals, were also lost.

J. Brooke Jones has declined the offered appointment as tax assessor for the Darnestown district to succeed Geo. R. Rice, resigned.

On October 8$^{th}$, the Janet Montgomery chapter of the D. A. R. will place a marker at the site of the first Presbyterian church in Montgomery County, dating to 1716, located at Potomac and formerly known as 'Captain John's Church' and also as 'Presbyterian Meeting House'. See also October 13$^{th}$.
End p. 219
October 13, 1916

Horton G. Thompson and Walter W. Plummer have been appointed tax assessors for the ninth election district.

Wm. J. Umstead has resigned as tax assessor for the town of Kensington. Mr. Umstead had been appointed to replace . John A. Canon, who had resigned.

The engagement of Miss Sarah Julia Reich, of Brunswick, and Garner Campbell Ball, of Akron, Ohio, was announced,

Miss Pearl Musgrove and Dorsey Pugh were married on Wednesday of last week.

It was announced that Earl Lintthicum and Miss Ada Marie Ogle were married recently - no date stated

Cont'd. on next page.

October 13, 1916, cont'd:

Miss Margaret A. Shine, of San Aantonio, Texas, and Porter Garrett Ward were married on September 28$^{th}$., in Baltimore..

Mrs. Lucy Dove, widow of Thomas Dove, died on Saturday of last week.

Fire, believed to have been set deliberately, destroyed the office building at the coal yard of Charles F. Miller & Co., Bethesda on last Tuesday

October 20, 1916.

Mrs. Elizabeth Bohrer died on Thursday of last week at the home of Mrs, Martha Shoemaker, her daughter, in Washington.

The marriage of Miss Louise Higgins and Earl Bruner, on October 19$^{th}$, was announced.

William H. Winchell, for many years a teacher in the public schools of Frederick and Montgomery counties, died last Monday.

Mr. & Mrs.A. Sonnenburg have leased the Montgomery House, in Rockville, and took charge of it on the 15$^{th}$.

The Rockville Baptiat Church has invited Rev. A. T. Howard, of Clarks, La., to accept the pastorate here. It is understood that he will accept, and move to Rockville within the next 2 months.

Miss Dolly Tschiffely and Charles G. Myers were married last Saturday in Baltimore.

Wm. E. Gingell died on Thursday of last week.

Neal Mckay, age 4, was struck by an automobile last Sunday, afternoon, and died about 30 minutes later. He was the son of Mr. & Mrs. Benjamin McKay of Silver Spring.

Robert S. Suddath, who died September 17$^{th}$, was remembered by his daughter, Mrs. Agner Hunter.

End p. 227***

October 27, 1916.

John Thomas, of Ednor, died Tuesday.

The engagement of Miss Carrie Wheeler Wiliams and Edwin R. Allnutt Jr. was announced. The wedding will take place on November 9$^{th}$.

To fill vacancies, the supervisors of elections have announced the following appointments: George C. Earp, Democratoic judge for the 1$^{st}$ precinct of the Rockville district; Wm. F. Prettyman, Democratic clerk for the 2$^{nd}$. precinct off the Rockville district; L.

Cont'd. on next page.

October 27, 1916, cont'd:
Curtis Mortimer, Democratic clerk for the Clarksburg district; Frank D. Day, Republican clerk for the Clarksburg district; and John J. Dolan, Republican judge for the $2^{nd}$. precinct of the Wheaton district.

It was announced that Miss Florence May Jackson and William Ashton Garrett were married on Thursday of last week.

Mrs. Anna S. McCeney, widow of Henry McCeney, died last Monday at her home in Burnt Mills.

The engagement of Miss Lillyan Pierce, daughter of Mr. & Mrs. Charles B. Pierce of Georgetown, and Lieut. Harold Clifford Pierce U. S. M. C., of Lexington, Mass., was announced.

William L. Dunlop, a native and lifelong resident of Georgetown but well known in Montgomery County, died last Monday.

November 3, 1916.
Enos C. Keys has been appointed to reassess all the real estate in the Wheaton district.

Richard T. Harding, age 25, only son of Samuel T. and Martha Harding of Burtonsville, died on October 24.

Miss Emmalee Catherine Hines and Harry Z. Musgrove were married last Saturday.

Dr. John P. Caulfield died last Sunday at his home near Cloppers. He had come to Montgomery County from Ireland.

Miss Sallie Blanche Watkins and Carson Edward Nicholson were married on Wednesday of last week.

Edward Peirce, one of the oldest resident of the Sandy Spring area, and one of the last 'Forty-Niners' of Marylanad, died on October 22, age 97 years.

November 10, 1916.
Mrs. Elizabeth Jones, widow of Nida Jones, of Dickerson, died last Tuesday.

Miss Mamie K. Hughes, formerly of Kensington, and James Lumsden, were married last Friday.

John A. Heisler, of the Redland area, died last Friday. He was a native of Germany, and had lived here about 10 years.

Mrs. Harriet Anna Carter, wife of Franklin Carter, died on Wednesday of last week at her home near Germantown.

Cont'd. on next page.

November 10, 1916, cont'd:

Reuben C. Creamer, of the Potomac district, died last week at the home of his daughter and son-in-law, Mr. & Mrs. Porter Butt, in Tenleytown.

Miss Ethel V. Day and Eugene W. Walker, both of the Browningsville area, were married on Saturday.

Mrs. Sarah H. Clagett, widow of Z. Thos. Clagett, died last Friday at the home of her daughter, Mrs. Charles Allnutt, near Laytonsville.

Mrs. Mary M. Page, widow of Nathan Page, died last Saturday at her home near Germantown.

The following named, having been previously drawn to serve as jurors, have been excused, namely, Frank L. Mortimer, Elmer C. Hersperger, Chas. E. Bond, Walter T. Burton, H. Latane Lewis, James O. Taylor, Louis C. Kengla, John W. Lucas. Their places will be taken by James W. Johnson, Seneca V. Aud, Frank P. Chaney, J. Lacey Shaw, Henry Latterner, Chesterfield Clagett, Jos. Childs, and Hazel W. Cashell.

Woodville W. Moore, a resident of Montgomery County for about 17 years, died on Wednesday of last week

Company K, of the National Guard, having been stationed for the past two weeks on the Mexican border, returned last Saturday, and were welcomed by a feast, at which Capt. Samuel Riggs was presented with a gold watch by the members of his company.

Miss Emmalee Catherine Hines, and Harry Z. Musgrove were married October 28th, at 'Oak Grove' farm, the home of the parents of the bride, Olney.

Frances Rosalie Briggs died on October 28th.

November 17, 1916.

Miss Sarah Reich and Garnett Campbell Ball were married on Tuesday of last week at 'Rock Hall', the home of the bride's uncle, McGill Belt, in Dickerson.

Miss Carrie Wheeler Williams and Edwin R. Allnutt Jr. were married on Thursday of last week at the home of the parents of the bride, in Poolesville.

Miss Grace Parsley, of Brookeville, and Jas. Guy Thompson, of Annapolis, were married on Thursday of last week at the home of the parents of the bride.

Cont'd. on next page

November 17, 1916, cont'd:
Richard T. Harding, only son of S. T. and Martha R. Harding, died October 24th, at Burtonsville.

November 24, 1916.
State Game Warden LeCompte has appointed the following deputies for Montgomery County, namely, J. Stanley Gingell, Joseph Waters Bowie, F. Mason Miller, and Lucian G. Swindells.

A daughter was born last week to Mr. & Mrs. Preston B. Ray.

Charles W. Oxley and Miss Catherine A. Waesche were married on Wednesday of last week, in Washington.

Miss Frances T. Butler and James Spencer Fisher were married on Wednesday, in Rockville.

Philip Reed, of Rockville, has been appointed bailiff of the Circuit Court, succeeding Thomas C. Keys who has retired after having filled that job for about 15 years.

George B. Remsburg and Clyde Harriss have been appointed tax assessors for the Poolesville and Darnestown districts, respectively. They take the place of Harry Williams and Harry C. West, who declined to serve

Tthe engagement of Miss Frances Adelaide Archer, of Bel Air, and Thomas Earl White, of Washington Grove, was announced. The wedding will take place in the near future.

Mrs. Sarah Louise Cashell, widow of John George Cashell, died last Saturday at her home near Layhill.

Charles E. Riley, age 29, died last Sunday.

Miss Bertus Eugenia Barr, of Gaithersburg, and Harry Allen Boyles, of Winchester, Va., were married on Tuesday of last week.

Miss Myrtle Irene Riley and Charles Henry Steinbraker were married on Wednesday of last week, in Washington.

December 1, 1916.
Eugene Bissett died last Monday.

Miss Sarah Louisa Brunett died last Monday at her home near Silver Spring.

The engagement of James Anderson Jr., son of Capt. & Mrs. James Anderson of Rockville, and Miss Ella Watson, of New Orleans, La. has been announced. The wedding will take place on December 4th, in New Orleans.

Cont'd. on next page

December 1, 1916, cont'd:
E. Lloyd Fawcett has resigned as a tax assessor. The following have been suggested to the State Tax Commission as possible tax assessors: Ignatius Ward, Perrie E. Waters, Harry M. Williams, Wm. T. Griffith, and Robert H. Miller.

Fire last Friday destroyed the home of S. Duncan Bradley in the western part of Rockville.

Mr. & Mrs. Elgar L. Tschifffely celebrated their $50^{th}$. wedding anniversary last week.

Miss Martha Dorsey Lansdale, of Unity, and Bernard Hodges Williams, of Davidsonville, were married last Saturday.

December 8, 1916.
Mrs. Ellen E. Howe, age 82 years, died last Saturday.

The straw-baling establishment of Chas. T. Johnson, at Germantown, burned last Monday.

The dwelling on the farm of James W. Nicol burned on Wednesday. Several outbuildings and about 20 cords of wood also were lost.

Miss Nellie Louise Hawkins and Albert Edward Warthen were married on Wednesday of last week.

Following is a list of the forest wardens for Montgomery County: A. M. Thomas, E. M. Waters, C. Brashears, J. M. Etchison, Benjamin C. Hughes, Frank L. Hewitt, John N. Kelly, R. H. Davis, L. E. Riggs.

A basketball team has been organized in Rockville, with the following names mentioned: V. Valentine Wilson, John McDonald, Brownell Riggs, Ernest Thompson, Melvin Hutchinson, and Lindsay Edmonds.

Edward O. Edmonston died on Wednesday at his home in Rockville.

Wm. H. Connolly died last Monday at his home in Bradley Hills.

Miss Mary Frances Heffner and Milton Brooks Austin, both of the Bethesda vicinity, were married on Thursday of last week.

Wm. J. P. Clarke died last Sunday at his home in Woodside.

Willis B. Burdette has been re-elected the superintendent of schools. Edwin W. Broome will continue as assistant superintendent.

John W. Clagett died last Friday.

Cont'd. on next page

December 8, 1916, cont'd:
    Miss Harriet Griffith, of Barnesville, and Alvin N. Bastable, of Baltimore, were married last Monday, in Washington.
    Mrs. Emily Ann Holland, wife of John W. Holland, of Dickerson, died on Thanksgiving.

December 15, 1916.
    John H. Lynch, of Barnesville, died last Sunday.
    Miss Ethel O. Andrews and Walter Trail were married on December $2^{nd}$, at Cloppers.
    The State Tax Commission has announced the appointment of Perrie E. Waters as tax assessor, succeeding Lloyd Fawcett, resigned. Mr. Waters has entered upon his duties.
    Miss Mabel Magdeline Hilton, daughter of Mrs. John H. Hilton, of Rockville, and John Edward Hughes of San Francisco, were married last Saturday.
    Charles Edward Rice, a resident of Kensington for the past 14 years, died last Sunday.
    Mr. & Mrs. Jas. W. Nicol wrote a letter expressing their thanks to the people who helped during their recent house fire.

December 22, 1916.
    The County Commissioners have appointed Oliver Smith tax assessor for Chevy Chase.
    Mrs. Rachel A. Gardner, widow of E. Grafton Gardner, died on Tuesday. She was the mother of Dr. John Gardner, of Clarksburg.
    A volunteer fire department has been organized in Rockville. The names mentioned are F. Bache Abert, Wilson Ward, W. Bradley Carr, Frank Higgins, and Edgar Thompson.
    The engagement of Miss Annie Lucille Higgins and Wallace J. Clark was announced. The wedding will take place on December $30^{th}$.
    Miss Louise Vaille Camp, of Chevy Chase, and Elwood K. Pierce, of New Jersey, were married last Monday at the home of the bride.
    Alexander C. Scheirer died at his residence [in Rockville ?] on December $13^{th}$. He was a native of Pennsylvania, but had lived in Maryland about 45 years.

                        Cont'd. on next page.

December 22, 1916, cont'd:

At the regular monthly meeting of the Janet Montgomery chapter of the D. A. R., Miss Marie Talbott reported the death of Mrs. Laura V. Dulin, and the resignation from the chapter of Mrs. Charles Dickens.

Decemer 29, 1916.

Thawley T. Harmon died last Monday. He is the son of John E. Harmon, of Rockville.

Smith L. Putman has been appointed a notary public.

J. Roy Thomas, of Woodside, died last Sunday.

James A. Linkins, of the Wheaton district, died last Monday.

The barn on the farm of John Carlin burned last Tuesday. A large quantity of hay, straw, feed, etc., was lost, along with several horses.

Miss Irma King, age 18 years, daughter of Mr. & Mrs.Charles E. King of Boyds, died on Wednesday of last week.

Mrs. Martha Ann Selby, age 90 years, widow of Eden Selby, died – no date stated. Funeral took place on Friday - again no date.

Elliott Robertson, age 19 years, son of Charles A. H. Robertson of Travilah, accidentally shot himself. He died on Wednesday of last week of blood poisoning which developed from the injury.

Mr. & Andrew J. Thompson, of near Ednor, celebrated their golden wedding anniversary on Wednesday of last week with a dinner party at the home of their son-in-law and daughter, Mr. & Mrs. George H. Richardson.

End

Abbe
  Edward P., 166
  Lillian J., 79
Abel
  John R. 55
Abert
  Bache, 14,17
  F. B., F. Bache., 35,
    44,46,55,63,139,175
  Maria Bache, 96
Adams
  Barry, 105
  Charles, 146
  Delas, 142
  E. D., 21
  James H., 23
  Jas. Mrs., 93
  R. R., 105
  Warren, 50
Adamson
  Leonidas W., 139
Ailes
  Milton E., 6,53
Aitcheson
  J. L., 72
  L., 141
  Robert, 43,44,126
  W. J., 141
Alderton
  Kirk, 150
Alexander
  Emma Louise, 41
  M. M. Mrs., 120
Allen
  Daniel, 113,153
  Frank, Mrs., 120
  Jas. F., 1
  William A., 42
Allison
  Horatio, 142
  Louis, 80
  Mildred Esther, 65
Allnutt
  Aden, 9,11
  Allnutt cont'd. next column

Allnutt cont'd.
  Alice, 13
  Anna Maria, 40
  Aubrey D., 11
  B. W., Mrs., 37
  Benjamin, 69,93,84,162
  Benoni D., 139
  Bessie May, 45
  Cecil, 78, 87,113,126
  Charles, 2, 21,35,150
  Charles, Mrs., 87
  Clinton, 19,71
  Clyde, 21
  E. C., E. Cecil, 22,161
  Edith, 129,154,157
  Edward R., 8, 170,172
  Ellen, 13
  Emily, 13
  Ernest C., 134
  Florence, 24
  Fred, Mrs., 31
  Frederick A., 32, 37,112,113
  H. C., 109,158,168
  H. C. Mrs., 39,94,161
  H. Clinton, Mrs., 25
  Henry, 1, 21, 42,121,127
  Howard, 137
  James Mears, 39
  Jos. T., 149
  L. A., L. P , 103
  L. A. Mrs., 162
  Lawrence, 3, 50, 90,133
  M. E. C., 119
  Natalie, 13
  Russell, 13
  Smith, 57, 58
  W. Mrs., 36
  William, 21
Almoney
  A. J., 158
  Albert, 14
  Lydia, 24, 52, 92
  Mary, 14, 76, 135
Altdorfer
  Wm. D., 34

Aman
 Naomi, 147
Amiss
 Edmund L., 29, 52, 54
Anders
 Clarence, 13, 47, 113
Anderson
 Corrinne C., 165
 Earle, 2
Anderson
 Edward, 45, 87
 Ella, 33, 64
 Florence, 41
 G. Minor, 1
 G. Minor, Mrs., 7
 George M., 158
 James, 4, 18, 43, 51, 65, 66, 91, 173
 Julia, 76
 Minnie, 120
 Paul, 2, 18, 24, 118
 Tavie, 70
 Thomas, 83, 142
 W. E., 169
 Warren, Mrs., 36
 William, 26, 139
Andrews
 Carrie V., 20
 Edwin Julius, 110
 Ethel O., 175
 Raymond H., 153
 Sarah, 7
Andrus
 H. C., 55
Annesly
 Ravenel, 107
Appleby
 A. O., 73
Archer
 Frances Adelaide, 173
Armstrong
 William, 142
Arnold
 A. B., 149
 Arnold cont'd. next column

Arnold cont'd.
 Charles V., 153
 Jack, 153
 Marguerite, 80
Ash
 George M., 116
Ashbridge
 Margaret C., 68
Ashby
 Orpah, 69, 105
Ashton
 Maude, 155
Ashworth
 Geo. Mrs., 19
Athey
 Geo. W., 150
 Lea., Lee., Leigh, 2, 30, 49, 50, 133
 Thomas H., 166
Atkin
 Mary R. R., 110
Atkinson
 George W., 23, 54
Atwood
 Edward P., 69, 82, 83
 Ida, Ida C., 10, 57
 James T., 55
 Samuel, 168
 W. E., 14
 Wm., 10
Aud
 Mary, 95
 Seneca V., 172
 T. Edward, 80
 Trujean, 73
 W. L., William L. 32, 82, 105, 131, 168
Austin
 Cannon, 162
 Ethel, 52
 Eva Marie, 124
 J. Thomas, 105
 M. Rawlings, 51
 Mahlon H., 115
 Austin cont'd. next page

Austin cont'd.
  Mary I., 41
  Milton Brooks, 174
  Automobile vs. horse, 1914, 53
Ayers
  John W., 126
Ayton
  Clarence L., 149
Aytono
  Edward, 72
Bacon
  C. H., 141
Bacon-Foster
  Cora, 27
Baden
  Wm. H., 158
Bai Nola, 84
Bailey
  John F., Mrs., 117
  Stephen M., 167
  Theodore, 154
  Thomas N., 29,156
Baker
  A. Grace, 112,155
  D. W., 48,111,125
  D. W. Mrs., 93
  D. William, 32
  Earle, 146,149
  Harold L., 21
  Harry Franklin, 89, 91
  James H., 94
  John Jacob, 7
  John T., 39, 43, 122, 155
  Jonathan J., 65
  Katherine, 94
  Mildred, 142
  Octavius, 43,44,150
  Reuben T., 56,72,114,161
  Willie, 157
  Wm. A., 126
Balderson
  W. C., 168
Baldwin
  Thomas P., 106
  Wm. D., 96
Ball
  Alton C., 55
  Arthur L., 84
  Garner Campbell, 169,172
  John L., 156
  Stella E., 108
Ballenger
  Lula C., 5
Baltzell
  Edna, 147,155
Bancroft
  Anna, 147
  John T., 18
Banes
  G. I. Mrs., 120
  George I. Mr. & Mrs., 123
  George L., Mrs., 76
  Helen R., 123
  Lafayette, 104,107,109
Barber
  Albert, 103
  Fred, 146
  James H., 69
  Julian M., 149
  Lester, 146
Barden
  William J., 27
Bardroff
  Lillian F., 68
Barker
  Samuel N., Mrs., 27
Barksdale
  Florence, 16,112,155
Barnes
  Daniel W., 82
  Helen L., 67
  Herbert D., 159
  J. O., 150
  J. William, 8
  Margaret E., 8, 16
  Mildred, 109
  O. C.,  O. W., 71, 92, 161,162
  O. C., Mrs., 121
  Wm C., 153

Barnesley, Barnsley
  Beulah, 35,36,117,128
  Carrie, 165
  C. W., 116,117
  Chas. W., 99
  Effie, 112,155
  Eleanor, 147
  George, 5,81
  J. I., J. N., J. W., 35,77, 115,116
  J. N. Mrs., J. W. Mrs., 36,76
  James, 104,164
  Jonathan D., 82
  Kenneth, 116,142, 164
  Lewis, Louis, 150,159
  L. W., 35, 168
  Martha, 142
  T. A., 75, 1116, 117,163,164
  T. Alex, 34
  Talbott, 146
  Thomas, 73,149
  T. T. Mrs., 116,117
  William, 54, 56
Barnesville
  election 1913, 17
  election 1914, 63
Barr
  Bertus Eugenia, 173
  Ellwood E., 41
Barrett
  Harry, 122
  James W., 142
Bartgis
  Della P., 52
Bartlett
  George W. B., 12
Barton
  Clara, 69, 90
Barwick
  Lena, 19
Bastable
  Alvin N., 175
Batson
  Estelle, 154
  Batson cont'd next column

Batson cont'd.
  J. R., 91
  John R., 101
  Josephine, 89
Baxton
  W. H., 30
Baylis
  Robert N., Mrs., 162
Beall
  A. E., 117
  A. P. Mrs., 76
  Albert B. Mrs., 76
  Albert P., 35,110
  Albert P. Mrs., 35,36,75,77
  Alton, 77
  Bessie V., 131
  E. M., 149
  Edward, 74, 98, 115, 116, 150
  Elbridge, Mr. & Mrs., 89
  Ellen Louise, 89, 91
  Elmer Vincent, 89
  Emily M. C., 10
  Ernest D., 123
  Frank, 101
  Grace, 147,155
  H. S., 1
  Harry, 2,21,34
  I. H., 168
  James, James Upton, 124,147,
  John W., 10
  Lemuel Thomas, 79
  Louis C., 91,139
  Marion F., 83
  Mary Elizabeth, 70
  Maurice, 30
  Melvin, 149
  Nellie Hester, 166
  Nora M., 87
  Palmer, 77
  R. B., R. C., 85,149
  Reverdy B., 8,101
  Richard C., 39
  Ruth, 98,115,147,155,166
  S. W., 6
  Beall cont'd. next page

Beall cont'd.
Samuel W., Samuel O. W.,
 39,43,122
Upton, 142
Vernon, 159
W. V., 164
William, Wm., 45,53,95,124
Bean, Beane
A. Henson,61
Agnes, 36
Alton, 78
Amos W., 90
C. O. Mrs., 36,76,119,165
Charles O., 94
Cornelia, 25
Cornelius, 94
Dorsey R., 22
Elijah T., 43,113
Eugene, 44
Geo. H., 82
Henry S., 82
J. C., 75
J. C. Mrs., J. T. Mrs., 37,75
James W., 6
Lucinda, 94, 96, 138
Mary Elizabeth, 24
Sarah E., 93
Spencer J., 82
W. C., 40,158
William C., 40
William Henry, 101
Beard
C. A., Mrs., 161
Charles, Chas., 119,164
H. Mrs., 77
Harry, 35,75
Martha A., 58
W. H., 158,163
W. Harry, 116
William H., 55
Wm. H., Mrs., 40
Beck
C. W., Mrs., 2
Beck cont'd. next column

Beck cont'd.
W. C., Mrs., 7, 15, 39
William C. Jr., 2
Becker
C. H., 135
Charles H., 107
Wm. S., 77
Beckwith
Jennie, 36,164,165
John, 4
Jos., 5
Sarah L., 4, 5
Becraft
Charles E., 83,108,150,156
Clarence, 146
Bell
A. P., Mrs., 37
Arthur, 146
Charles, 6, 45, 53
Edington, 114,161
Emma R., 104
Frank L., 5
Garrison, 28,155
George E., 159
John L., 139
Miss, 39
Silas A., 104
William D., 124,149
Belt
Alfred C., 96
C. V., 166
John A., 124,126
Julia, 108,118
Millard W., 82
Stacy, 34
Virginia, 118
Walter, 5, 9
Watson, 104
Benedict
J. E., 71
James F., 29
Bennett
E. L., 162
Bennett cont'd. next apge

Bennett cont'd.
  George H. Mr. & Mrs., 106
  Herbert, 58
  L. M., 143
  Lillian, 67,154
  E. L., 135
  George H. Mr. & Mrs., 106
  Herbert, 58
  L. M., 143
  Lillian, 67,154
  Titus, 58
  Vernon, 123,153
Benson
  C. E., 168
  Henry, 88,124
  Hilda M. 155
  J., 35
  Ralph, 146
Bentley
  Jack, 78
  John C., 2,21,48,52
  Mildred Hallowell, 106
Benton
  James N., 43
Berry
  Angeline, 147
  Louis W., 146
  Mary Canby, 41
  Mr., 87
  Samuel, 81,146
  W. E., 115
  Winfred, Winifred, 19,28, 53, 56
  Winfred E., Mrs., 40
  Winfred, Mr. & Mrs., 71
Best
  John L., 133
  Simon D., 11
Bevans
  Ralph, 118
Biggs
  A. Edgar, 6
Birch
  L. Mrs., 120

Bird
  Anna B., 104
  J. W., 19, 91,150,158,162
Birgfeld, Birgfield
  Edward W., 26, 156
  Edwin W., 94
  Frank, 23, 71
  Grace, 112,148
  Wm. K., 11
Bishop
  W. W. Mrs., 15,95
Bissatt
  Isabelle, 151
Bissett
  Beulah, 19
  David, 78,158
  Eugene, 173
  Isabel, 78,151,154,157
  R. K., 145
  T. Mrs., 19,59
  Thomas E., 124
Blach
  Stephen B., 128
Black
  Harry, 101
  Henry, 31
Blair
  Gist, 4, 8,15,111,120, 146
  Montgomery, 30, 72
  Woodbury, 6, 53,71
Blandford
  D. M., 168
  Douglas, Douglass, 8,32, 33, 71, 72, 129
Blenheim, 22
Bliss
  R. G., 73
Blizzard
  Bertram, 41
  Edna, 41
Blodgett
  E. E., 17
Blunden
  Frank, 71
Blundon cont'd. next page

Blunden cont'd.
  Charles F., 96
  Elizabeth Ann, 96
  Robert E., 53
Boadman, Boardman
  Marie, 14, 65,255
Board of Elections 1914, 63
Bobbinger
  William H., 12
Boblets
  Luther, 13
Bodine
  C. F., 19, 59, 144
  C. F. Mrs., 19
  Charles F., 162
  Ida H., 62
  Jos. H., 94
Bodmer
  Carrie, 155
  Jacob, 21
  Jessie M., 149
  Minnie, 24
Bogley
  E. H., 168
  Emory H., 135
  Erma Helen, 88
  J. Hilleary, 152
  J. T., 168
  J. W. Mr. & Mrs., 124
  J. William, 153
  James, 40, 51, 60, 101, 133, 158
  James, Mrs., 119
  John W., 82,168
  Lelia Marie, 124,125
  William A., 8, 98
Bohrer
  Alice, 96
  Anna H., 62
  Charles C., 43, 44
  Elizabeth, 170
  H. B., 96
  Milton, 96
  Pearl, 147
  Ralph W., 121

Boland
  F. G., 151,154
  H. M. Mrs., 93
  Harry M., 88,100
  Josephine, 93
  Wm. F., 112
Bolton
  Ida, 35
  J. S., 78,116
  James S., 82
  John Henry, 137
  Raymond, 142
  W. H., 19, 59, 144
  W. H. Mrs., 59,145
Bond
  Belle, 67
  Charles E., 150,156,172
  Jos., 55,56
  Samuel S., 29,156
Bonifant
  Geo; George, 37, 71,73, 146,168
  George, Mr. & Mrs., 126
  John, 43, 46, 126
  Margaret C., 107
  Marie C., 106
Borland
  William P., 27
Bosley
  Lillia May, 43
  Lillie, 24
Boswell
  Edward C., 82
  Franklin, 86, 99, 147
  John R., 69
  Mary, 54, 92, 138
Boteler
  Morgan J., 124
Bottlemay
  Anna, Annie, 61,80,81,149
Bouic
  Albert M., 16, 63, 71, 106, 121,127,158
  Eulalie, 14
Bouic cont'd. next page.

Bouic cont'd.
  Norman, 19,40,71,77,158,162
  Norman, Mrs., 77
Bourdeau
  Augustin J. S., 110
Bowie
  Allen, 66
  Catherine Gaither, 161
  Donald, 31, 35
  Donald, Mrs., 36,76,117,119
  George Washington, 161
  John M. S., 23
  Joseph Waters, 173
Bowman
  Darby, 19, 28
  Deborah E., 158
  Eldridge Z., 139
  Elizabeth, 118,164
  J. Darby, 7, 76,102,119
  J. Darby, Mrs., 76
  L. R., Mrs., 76
  Rebecca Beatrice, 59
  Richard, 56
  U. Mrs., 36,164,165
  Upton, 21,150
  W. E. Mrs., 76
  W. U. Mrs., 75, 116,117
  William C., 64
Boyd
  Graff, 73
  Marian Estella, 73
Boyer
  Charles, 90
  George E., Geo. M., 91 150,161
  J. Wellington, 124
  J. Wesley, 72,114
  John F., 39,43,161
  Lyndall L., 20
  Nellie Irene, 9
Boykin
  Basil, 71
  Erma, 4
Boyles
  Harry Allen, 173

Boynton
  L. P. Mrs., 95
Braddock
  A. A., 156
  Alexander A., 29,124
  Edward, Gen., 27
  George, Geo., 10,23,30,49
  James F., 144
  Mary G., 10
  Tabitha Austin, 87,89
  William M., 156
Bradford
  H. L., 168
Bradley
  George G., 71, 86, 121, 127, 128,160,168
  George G. Jr., Mrs., 86
  Henry, 33,67
  Joseph H. 60, 73
  Mary R., 73
  S. Duncan, 174
  S. Duncan, Mrs., 40
Bradshaw
  Leonard P., 125
Brady [see also Bready]
  S. D., Miss, 165
  Terence, 113
Brake
  Bessie, 18, 64, 118
  Eleanor, 118
  G. S. Mr. & Mrs., 118
  Jos., 118
  W. H. Mr. & Mrs., 118
Brandenburg
  Pearl, 39
Brashears
  C., 174
  Columbus, 17, 82, 99
Bready
  Annie L., 20
  Bernard, 122
  Burton S., 128,130
  Calvin, 6, 88, 154
Bready cont'd next page.

Bready cont'd.
　David T., 43
　Eli, 73
　Eva, 129,130
　G. W., 164
　G. W. Mrs., 117, 164
　Geo. W., 92,134
　Hilda E., 136
　Ivy, 61
　John T. Mrs., 107
　Louise C., 163
　S. K., 168
　Samuel K., 33,43,95
　Terence, 153
　Virginia, 9
Brennerman
　J. Schaffer, 123
Brewer
　Ellen, 76
　George, 2
　Guy Conrad, 111
　Irene B., 129
　John B. Jr. Mrs., 24
　John B. Mrs. 39, 72, 92,
　　120,161,162
　John, 28,142
　L. A., Mrs., 165
　Lillian, 108
　Lloyd, Mrs., 37, 76, 120
　Lucy, 2, 37, 155
　Maria Tallard, 6
　Mary, 1, 2, 19, 21, 91, 92,
　　147,154
　Milton W., 108
　Nicholas, 92
　Russell, 50,76,90,99
　Virgie A., 22
　Virginia, 2, 91, 154
　W. R., 133,158
　W. Russell, 1
　Wm. G., 82
Brian
　Isabel E., 65
　Putnam F., 44

Briarley Hall Academy
　1913, 25
　1915, 107
　1916, 152
Briggs
　Charlotte, 103
　Garnett H., 109
　Gideon, 69, 162
　Herman, Hermon, 1,46,100,
　　103,108
　James M. W., 78
　John W., 55
　Lottie Ward, 64,100
　Manor, ]place], 46
　Samuel, 29,43,156
　Samuel T., Mr. & Mrs., 88,
　William Wilson, 157
Brigham
　Reuben, 106
Britton
　Alexander, 142
Broadhurst
　Joshua E., 69, 162
　Samuel V., 29,150,156
Brock
　Walter B., 103
Brockway
　B. H., 23
Brooke
　A. D., 19
　Alban, 55
　Allen F. 86, 104
　C. F. Mrs., 35, 75
　C. M., 35, 36, 37
　Charles, 2, 32, 121, 126, 129
　Dorothy, 36,76, 89
　L. T., 15
　Mary B., 19
　Richard, 66, 90
　Sallie P., 155
　W. A., 14
　Wm. A., 48
Brookeville
　High School 1913, 20
　Brookeville cont'd next page.

Brookeville cont'd.
  High School, 1914, 65
  High School, 1915, 104
  High School, 1916, 149
Brooks
  Beulah, 24
  Thos. B., 56
Broome
  E. W., 158
  Edwin, 2, 14, 24, 50,
    62, 147
  Maude V., 14
Brosius
  Charles T., 100,150
  Edward, 31,159,160
Brown, Browne
  A. Clinton, 29, 136, 156
  A. W., 35,116,168
  A. W. Mrs., 36
  Allan R. 94
  Arthur, 112,150,156
  Bertha V., 65,149
  C., C. M., 59,165
  C. M. Mrs., 120
  Carl T., 69
  Carroll T., 74
  Chancellor, 69
  Clark, 69, 155
  E. W., 19
  Edward., Edw., 38,55,105,
    134,140,168
  Ella B., 57
  Elmira, D., 134
  Evans, 29
  Frank E., 162
  Hatton, 31,139
  Helen Mae, 20
  Herbert M., 34
  Irene, 147,155
  J. D., 165
  James P. Mrs., 76
  James W., 156
  Jesse A., 82
  Brown cont'd. next column.

Brown cont'd.
  Jim, 106
  John William, 14
  M., 76
  M. Mrs., 164
  Malcolm R., 104
  Marie Helena, 40, 42, 43
  Martha, 29
  Pearl A., 118
  Raymond G., 46
  Robey F., 150
  Ruby, 112
  S. Thomas, 8
  Sophie, 22
  Thomas J., 98
  W. T., 34,116
  W. T. Mrs., 71
  William, Wm., 55,73,111,
    112,125,126,150
Browning
  C. H., 150
  Maurice M., 26,55,63,
    136,139
Bruner
  Earl, 170
  Mary Ellen, 142
Brunett
  Adrian, 2, 89
  Helen, 2, 24,105
  John L., 88, 91
  Mary J., 13
  Paul, 53,133
  Sarah Louisa, 173
  Victor E., 8, 9
Buck
  George R., 58
  H. H., 71
  J. N. Mrs., 39
  J. W. Mrs., 19
  Joseph W., 86
  Joseph W. Mrs., 25
Buckingham
  Abraham, 44
Buffin
  Jas. M., 153

Bullard
  E. L. Mrs., 21, 27, 37, 90, 93
  Ernest L., 62
Burch
  L. Mrs., 37, 76
Burdette
  Amos Dewey, 167
  Annie, 88
  Aubrey W., 99
  Carlton, 69
  Claude H., 139,159
  Cora, 11
  Deborah Jane, 151
  Edward Lewis, 1
  F. E., 8,150
  George, 113
  Herbert P., 103
  J. E., J. W., 21, 55, 153
  James, Jas., 29,88,113
  John, 69, 150, 168
  Jos. A., 38
  Luther, 149
  Nathan J., 88
  W. B., 1
  W. B., 65, 148, 158
  Washington, 149
  Webster V., 26,149
  William H., 156
  Willis B., 19, 62, 63, 73, 91,
    105,145,147,174
  Wm. H., 26, 89
Burford
  William E., 46
Burgdorf
  Myrtle, 147
Burgee
  W. K., 16, 28
Burgess
  Isabel J., 131
Burn, Burns
  Arthur, 55,168
  C. A., 71
  George E. L., 36
Burn, Burns cont'd. next column.

Burn, Burns cont'd.
  Jesse H., 83
  John C., 126
  Joshua, Mrs., 149
  Leonard C., 136,150
  Mildred I., 104
  Nicholas E., 70,162
Burr
  Joseph, Mrs., 40
Burriss
  A. E. & Sons, 77
  A. E., 75, 119, 165
  A. E. Mrs., 117
  Annie A., 4
  Eva, 36, 76, 110
  Hazel, 35,118
  Jennie, 108
  John, 51, 70, 108
  Reuben A., 58
Burroughs
  A. E., 165
  George W. 162
  Gordon, 146
  Hazel C., 77
  Isabel, 64
  James F., 158
  Pearl May, 160
Burton
  Clarence, 164
  E. E., 163
  Margaret Amelia, 166
  Walter T., 172
Bushee
  R. J. Mrs., 33
Bussard
  Bessie Priscilla, 143
  Henry, 95
  Lewis, 150,168
  Thaddeus, 139,149
Bussart
  J. J., Mrs., 120
Butler
  Frances T., 173
Butler cont'd next page.

Butler cont'd.
  Harry L., 81
  John A., 32
  Joseph Gorman, 49
  Julia May, 111
  W. R., 33
  Walter M., 126
  Wm. G., 114
Butt
  Evelyn R., 147
  Lawrence, 146
  Neoma, 87
  Samuel T., 139
  Thomas, Thos., 104,107,143
  William Edward, 41
Buxton
  Grace, 12, 20, 161
  Miss, 80
Byrd
  Henson T., 130
  John, 126,148,160
  Sallie, 165
  Samuel D., 47, 84, 139
  Sarah T., 160
Byrn
  E. W., 71
Cady
  Charles G., 143
Caldwell
  Andrew James, Mrs., 142
  Rosalind Deering, 142
  S. D. Jr., 168
Callaghan
  William J., 156
Callahan
  William J., 29
Callender
  Edward, 166
Camp
  Filmore, 142
  Guy, 142
  Louise Vaille, 175
Campbell
  Robert H., Dr., 11,13
  William D., 89

Canby
  Anna R., 21
  Benjamin, 21
  G. Rust, 32,168
  Medford, 103
  Rust, 71
  William, 103,112
Cannon, Canon
  B. R., 120
  John A., Jno A., 94,95,96, 159,169
  Robert A., , 96
Captain John's Church, 169
Carey
  John T., 52
Carlin
  Clydia Marie, 100
  Earle S., 124
  Frances R., 114
  Frank, 130
  James S., 2
  John, 114,149,176
  Pansy Cecelia, 25
Carlisle
  A. G., 34
  Alex, Alexander, 21,32,34, 37,71,73,83,121,167
  Franklin, 152
  John, 25, 107, 122
  Mack H., 153
  Masten, Maston T., 160
  Maude, 69
  Minnie, 15, 16, 20, 112, 147, 155
  Miss, 59
  Richard C., 94
Carr
  Mabel, 12
  W. B. Mrs., 164
  William B., 17, 32, 153
Carrel
  Virginia, 142
Carroll
  Clarence B. F., 29,66
  Daniel, 66

Carter
  Alexander, 142
  Franklin, 171
  Guy Lee, 152
  Harriet Anna, 171
  W. Golden, 168
  William A., 62
Case
  John W., 156
  Minnie, 116
  Phillip, 45,163
  Samuel T., 43, 44
  Samuel, Mrs., 86
  Tyler, 116,164
Cashell
  Alice, 72,104,107,163,164
  Edgar H., 84
  Edward, 146, 149
  F. H., 37, 75, 78
  F. Hazel, 28
  Francis H., 139
  Frank, 75,156,168
  G. W., 168
  H. H., 34
  Hanson G., 149
  Harriet A., 97
  Hazel A., Hazel W., 8,32,56, 97,150,172
  Irving M., 67
  J. T., 168
  John George, 173
  Joseph W., 8
  Montgomery W., 55
  Sarah Louise, 173
  W. H., W. L., 92, 168
  Wallace, 77, 78, 136
  William Lycurgus, 104,109
Cass
  Newton R., 11
Cator
  Margaret S., 90
Caulfield
  John P., 171
  Wm. S., 139
Caywood
  Edward V., 3
Cecil
  Daisy, 89,47,155
  Mary, 108
  Roger, 142
Chambers
  D. C., 162
  Mr., 87
  W. L., 168
Chance
  Merritt, 9, 23, 65, 115
Chandler
  Elizabeth, 95
  George, Mrs., 71
Chaney
  Emma G., 128
  Frank P., 172
  Henry C., 8, 26, 111, 125, 156
  Josephine, 26,112,155
  Lillian, 23,157
Chapin
  Mary Agnes, 118
Chapman
  F. B. Mrs., 19
  Mary A., 25
Chappell
  Ralph H., 65
Charlton
  Usher, 28,155
Chesley
  Henry W., 139
  James B., 100
  Mrs., 25
Chevy Chase
  High School 1916, 149
Chichester
  Cornelia, 157
  Lydia, 18,136,148
  Sarah, 104
  W. B., 168
  Washington, 2,43,106,
Chick
  Henry H., 68

Childs
  Joseph, Jos., 15,71,172
  Sarah Eleanor, 15
  Thomas S., 58
  Virginia L., 18
Chisholm
  Charles F., 149
Chiswell
  Edgar B., 28
  Edward L., 141
  Eloise, 16,20,22,
  Griffith, 155
  Lawrence A., 32,150
  Lulu, 24,149
  Marie, 24
  Thomas F. Mrs., 81
Chitty
  William, 21
  William, Mrs., 21
Choate
  Warren, 71,97
  Warren, Mrs., 120
Christ Episcopal Church,
  Kensington, 1913, 23
Christopher
  J. C., 18, 67
Cissel
  E. W., 129
  T. R., 85
  A. J., 140
  Carroll, 113,153
  Delos, 115
  E. W. 77
  Eugene H., 41, 47
  Hardy S., 70
  J. Floyd, 40
  J. H., 71,120
  James H., 30,169
  John C., 10
  Maurice, 3,34,48,73
  Merle, 24
Clagett
  C. A., 168
  Clagett cont'd next column.

Clagett cont'd.
  Carter, 25, 26, 168
  Carter, Mrs., 86
  Charles A., 87, 113, 127
  Chester, 150,168
  Chesterfield, 101,172
  Darius, 86
  Edgar, 150
  Edna C., 57
  Henry M., 42, 44
  J. E., J. L., 140,168
  Jennie E., 18
  John, 18,43,56,159,174
  Joseph, Jos., 63,145
  Morris J., 46
  S. A. Mrs., 76,77,117
  Sarah H., 172
  Z. Thos., 172
Clark, Clarke
  B. F., 71
  Berry E. Mrs., 14, 19, 40
  Berry E., 1,14,19,22,47,65,68,
    85,103,128,158,
  Charles, 113
  Clayton, 152
  D. W., 34, 78
  Dan, 168
  Dorothy, 83
  Frank, 21,113,153
  Mary E., 26
  Minnie G., 92
  O. B., Oliver B., 82,115,
  Oliver H. P., 4, 29, 47, 60, 113,
    115,131,153
  Paul, 71
  Rose, 97
  Thomas, 100,102
  Wallace J., 175
  William D., 122,123,124,
Claude
  Herbert C., 153
Clausen
  Bertha C., 47

Claxton
  A. B., 149
Clay
  Henry L., 83
Clayton
  R. B., 153
  Richard B., 113
Cleaver
  Josephine E., 138
Clements
  Clarence E., 113
  William, 31
  Wm. Mrs., 31
Clendenning
  S. J. Mrs., 120
Clephane
  Walter C., 19
Clifton Park Stock Farm, 114
Cloverly, 48
Clugston
  Edith, 137
Clum
  C. W., 23, 71
  Cornelius W., 65
  Dorothy, 112, 155
  Marjorie I., 149
Co. K., First Infantry, Maryland
  National Guard, 113, 153,
Coar
  Belle Esther, 138
Coburn
  Ashton, 150
Cochran
  S. J., 73
Codwise
  B. R., 167
Coleman
  Basil B., 107
  Thomas, 140
Collier
  Walter L., 5
Colliflower
  Lloyd C., 28, 155
Collins
  J. F., 158
  John F., 1, 40
  Lena A., 140
  Margaret A., 11
  Scott, 150
  Sue A., 155
Colton
  Bruce, 147, 155
  Bruce, Miss, 115, 129
Columbus
  M. F., 72
Company D, Maryland Nat.l.
  Guard, roster 1914, 58
Compher
  William, 28, 156
Conaway
  Emma Elizabeth, 49
Condict
  Causin, 29
Condon
  Evan, 135
  Fannie, 112
  James M., 36
  Ruth, 35
Confederate monument
  Rockville, 14, 20
Connell
  John, 69
  Marian, 132
  William 132
Connelly
  John W., 109
  Walter, 7
  Wm. H., 174
Conrad
  Thomas K., 62
Conroy
  Florence, 24
  J. Gibbons, 144
  Mary Florence, 49
  Michael, 69, 144, 162
Conter
  Zelpha L., 51

Cook, Cooke
 Byron, 142,146,
 Catherine, 147
 James B. Mrs., 95
 Nathan, 4, 51 ,91,134
 Paul, Mrs., 19
 Z. M., 134
 Zadoc M., 4, 51, 91, 136, 139
Coolahan
 J. T., 27
 John, 19
Cooley
 C. T., 169
 Charles, Chas., 82,113,153
 Eli G., 162
 Garrett, 53, 69
 George F., 139,141,150
 Sterling, 146
 W. S., 168
 William S., 127
Corbett
 S. Munson, 50
Corby
 Charles, 159
 R. L., 21
 W. S., 19
Cordell
 Margaret Bell, 46
Cornelison
 Anna Jane, 1
Cornell
 Bedia F., 45
Corrick
 Harry K. Mr. & Mrs., 97
 Ruth B., 84
 Wm. J., 70, 97
Corry
 A. J., 71
Corson
 Florence V., 67
Costello
 Eleanor M. L., 99
Cottage, 25

Coulter
 Emily, 21
 Jean, 147
Counselman
 Frank, 1
 William G., 71
Coursey
 Rose T., 161
Cowell
 Bert, Burt, 113,153
 Frank B., 13
Cowsill
 Catherine, 116.120
Cox
 John R., 135
Coxey
 Jacob, Gen., 64
Crabb
 Jeremiah, 66
Craver
 Allen B., 156
 C. W., 164
 David S., 55
 Henry Edward, 133
Crawford
 Eliza, Mrs., 71
 Emory H., 156
 Geo. L., 103
 Hazlette, 120
 Howard, 162
 Nicholas, 109
 Osborne, 94
 Theodore, 146
 Wm. C., 82
Creamer
 Blanche, 147,155
 Charles H., 43, 59
 Clarence H., 156
 Reuben C., 172
 Susie, 160
Crigler
 Emma Lucile, 29
Crismond
 Henry, 52, 113, 132

Crockett
  E. E. Mrs., 59,145
  Edward E., 29,156
Cromwell
  Arthur, 21
Cronise
  Clyde H., 143
  George W., 55
Cropley Presbyterian Church
  1913, 19
  1914, 59
  1916, 144
Cross
  John, 68, 79, 153
  Reginald, 124,150
Crouse
  George V., 57
Crowl
  Gladys Alice, 14
Crown
  Benjamin, 84
  Henry C. 139
  Joshua R., 28
  Zadoc T., 114
Croxall
  M. L. Mrs., 25,27
  Mrs., 27
Cruit, Cruitt
  L. R., 63
  Mary, 162
Cubit, Cubitt
  Carrie V., 131
  Ike, 166
  James, Jas., 8, 9, 66
Cuff
  John H., 62,140
Culver
  William O., 139
Cummings
  A. J., 59, 72, 87
  Andrew, 31,37,40,42,44,
    86,158
  Charles J., 5
  Cummings cont'd. next column.

Cummings cont'd.
  James, Jas., 48, 84, 142
Cunningham
  Elma, 36
  Elsie, 58, 61
  J. H. Mrs., 19
Curran
  George D., 111,125
  Paul H., 153
  Robert, 87
Curtin
  Mary, 46
  Thomas, 46
Curtis
  Emma V., 62
  Fannie B., 12
  George V., 12
  Harry J., 153
  W., 71
  William T. S., 32,111,153
Cutts
  Madison, 2
Dade
  Joe, Mrs., 27
  Robert, 39
  Townsend, 66
Dahl
  John Casamir, 27
Dailey
  Beatrice Helen, 38, 39
  H. H., 3
  Ober W., 140
Daishe
  B. Miss, 166
Dalton
  A. S., 56
  Alfred S., 140
Daniel, Daniels
  D. Leslie, 89
  Deatherage Leslie, 87
  James, 34,73
  William A., 99
Darby
  A. Somers, 8
  Darby cont'd. next page.

Darby cont'd.
 Alice, 142
 Charles R., 63, 94, 108, 168
 Dean, 48,130
 E. L. Mrs., 162
 E., 36
 Edward, 42
 Eleanor, 16, 39, 81, 104, 107, 109,155,166
 Elizabeth, 13, 77
 Ernest H., 156
 Franklin, Frank, 95,140
 Gardner, 90
 George E., 60
 H. S., Mrs., 165
 Hilton, 83,142
 J. G., 133
 J. Gardiner, 50, 29, 152, 156
 Jacob Meriam, 100
 James, Mrs., 81
 John W., 54
 Joseph, 26,136,150,155
 L. A. Jr. Mrs., 37, 60
 Lawrence A., 25, 85, 103, 146
 Lawrence, Mrs., 163,165
 Mareen, 48,130
 Margaret, 13, 49, 87,155
 Mary, 71
 R. R., 103
 Reginald, Mrs., 118
 Remus R., 52,157,162
 Richard E., 32, 37, 121, 167
 Sallie A., 25
 Samuel, 100
 T. C., 168
 Thomas D., 29,156
 Valeria, 13
 Virginia L., 54
 W. H., 168
 William, Wm., 16,63,139
 Zora S., 152
Darnall
 T. W., 103
Darne
 William, 113

Darnell
 Mr. & Mrs., 87
 T. W., 74, 87
Darnestown
 High School 1916, 149
Dasher
 Bessie A., 54
Davidson
 C. S., Mrs., 145
Davis
 Arie, 36
 Ben, 10, 35, 164
 E. C., 87
 Edmund C., 29,126,127
 Frank, Mrs., 108
 G. W., 164
 G. W. Mrs., 76
 Geo. G., 150
 Harry, 76
 Horace, 108
 Hugh M., 125
 Joshua, 92
 Margaret K., 110
 Mary, 2, 16, 113, 115, 121
 Minnie, 17
 R. H., 174
 Rufus, 95,101
 Thomas, 66
 William, Wm., 87,131
Davis Bros., 163
Dawson
 Annie Elizabeth, 65
 Clarence E., 26, 32, 43, 55,103, 113,150,153
 E. S., 119
 Edward S., 28
 Elizabeth, 69, 120, 151,127,165
 Geo. C. Mrs., 7
 Glenna, 151
 H. A., 116
 Hal, 75
 Harry, 53, 80, 83, 88, 111, 125, 158
 J. Somervell, 28,156
Dawson cont'd next page.

Dawson cont'd.
  J. Somervell, Mrs., 92
  James M., 27
  John, 14, 83, 156, 164
  Joseph, Jos., 39, 77
  Lavinia G., 78
  Margaret, 117,165
  Mary, 27,149,165
  Priscilla, 14, 48, 49
  Robert Doyne, 66
  Rose, 126,149
  Somervell, Mrs., 14
  Thomas, 32,55,62,63,74,
    89,111,125,137,158
  W. V., Wm. V., 126,161
  Wm. B. Mrs., 112
Day
  Bradley, 12
  Charles T., 43, 55, 149
  Columbus, 55,71,73,111,114
  Elsie, 50
  Emma J., 6
  Ethel V., 172
  F. D., 141
  Franklin, Frank, 65,69,171
  George W., 43
  Herman, 142
  Hezekiah, 43,122
  James E., 6,118
  Lillian, 80,149
  Sarah A., 88
  Sterling Elwood, 45
  T. H., 20
  Titus W., 66
  Virgie Eleanor, 141
  Wilber S., 26,125,136
  Windsor Scott, 152
Daymude
  Clarence, 13
  E., 153
  James, 6
  Thomas, 115
  Wm., 6, 38

Decker
  Ann, 13
Deets
  James E., Jas. E., 16, 25, 63,
    91, 103, 139, 162
  Samuel R., 105
Defandorf
  Elizabeth, 67, 126, 154
  H., 119
  J. D. Mrs., 162
  J., J. F., 18, 77, 119,165
Delaney
  John C., 101
Democrat
  Primary winners 1913, 37
  Nominees 1913, 42
  Primary ticket 1913, 31
Demuth
  Clara, 3,151
  R. J., 3
Derrick
  H. B., 141
Devereaux
  Dr., 34,106
  John Ryan, 22
  Joseph, 34
  Ryan, 34, 62
Devilbiss
  Clifton M., 15
  Clintie Irene, 160
  Corrie V. 30, 80
  Rufus W., 139
Devine
  Herman D., 153
  Pauline, 123
Diamond
  D. B., 77
  Douglas B., 167
  Grace Carrel, 157
  H. L., 34,37,75,78
  H. L. Mrs., 114
  Herbert L., 9, 33
  J. B., 37, 75, 133, 134, 151,
    163, 164
  Diamond cont'd. next page.

Diamond cont'd.
  John B., 4, 31, 51, 60, 52, 78,
    90, 91, 94, 136
Dickens
  Charles, Mrs., 176
Dickerson
  Harry, Mrs., 165
Diehl
  Raymond S., 110
Diggs
  James I., 163
Dill
  Flora M., 66
  Wm. E., 162
Dishner
  E. Mrs., 37
Disney
  Dora, 147
  William E., 138
Dobe
  B. A., Miss, 166
Dobson
  A. N., 17
Dodd
  Jennings, 103
Dodge
  J. Heath, 45
  L. L. Miss, 76
Dolan
  John J. 171
Donaldson, Donalson
  Amanda, 21
  Charles Washington, 42
  Louis L., 153
  Mary I., 130
Dooley
  Ruth A., 125
Doolittle
  Myrick Hascall, 27
Dorcas
  Milton, 13
Dorrence
  Herbert, 107

Dorsey
  Clinton, Mrs., 45
  George S., 94
  J. C., 34, 60, 167
  J. Clinton, 21
  Lloyd, 39
  Minnie, 15, 20
  Upton, 130
  Wm., 2, 34, 124
Dosh
  W. O., 114,168
Dove
  B., B. A., 116, 119
  Beulah, 163,165
  Emmet, 35,116,119,164
  Emmett, Mrs., 35,119,120,165
  Ida, 27,72,76,120,161
  Margaret, 128
  Mary, 33
  Randolph, Mrs., 120
  Wm. B., 117
Dowden
  Charles B., 156
  Ruth B., 3
Dowdens Ordinary, 103
Dowell
  Mary, 142
  Osgood, 97,150
Downey
  Francis, 21,134
  John J., 18
  Mary, 147
Dronenburg
  William W., 26,136,155
Drum-Hunt
  R. C., 77
  Richard C., 8, 32, 142
Duff
  Corinne, 115,147,155
  Frank S., 70
DuFief
  Alpha Omega, 33
  Charles G., 29,161

Duley
  John W., 55
Dulin
  James C., 124,125
  Laura, 176
Dunbar
  Rita, 125
Dunlop
  Mary Ray, Mrs., 124
  William L., 171
DuPont
  Ellen C., 144,145
Dutrow
  Aschah, 49
  Bradley H., 111
  Philip, 49
  Susie, 166
Duvall
  Ada, 20, 53
  Benjamin D., 94
  C. S., Mrs., 36, 76
  C. Scott, 32,111,125,156
  C. Scott, Mrs., 117
  Carroll F., 58
  Charles, 150
  Clarence F., 153
  Ernest D., 55
  Harry U., 47
  J. W., 23
  Luther M., 26,124
  Margaret E., 149
  Nellie, 104,107,112,155
  Oliver M., 64
  Russell E., 45,139
  Sherwood, 168
  William E., 158
Dwyer
  Charles, 26, 150
  Cuyler D., 45
  Frank, 4
  Goldie, 49
  Henry, 86, 94, 128
  Lafayette M., 29,156
Dynes
  J. L. Mrs., 21
Dyson
  Paul, 94,95
  Vernon H., 91
  William, 39
Eaden
  Robert, Mr. & Mrs., 10
  Virginia, 10
Earp
  Alfred, 16,17,31,83
  George, Geo., 168,170
  John W., 45
East
  S. E. Mrs., 120
Eastburn
  Samuel E., 28
Easterbrook
  W. T., 33
Easton
  Geo. W., 122
  Harry, 60
  John L., 28
  Mary, 4, 91,155,166
  Milton, 34
  Roland B., 65
Eccleston
  Charles A., 143
  Martha J., 143
Eckloff
  Arthur, 150,169
Edmonds
  Lindsay, 146,174
Edmonston
  D. P., 165
  Edward O., 140,174
Edmunds
  Lethia, 119
Edson
  John J., 14, 16, 63
Education Day
  1914, 65
  1916, 146

Edwards
  Bertie, Mrs., 82
  Clay, 87,164
  David S., 22
  Douglass, 53, 87
  George, 9, 87
  Letha, 76
  Ralph, 151
  Sarah, 137
Elder
  James, 8, 10
Election
  Officials, 1913, 28, 116, 155
  Results 1913, 44
Elgin
  Charles F., 55, 59
Elliott
  Etherl A., 106
Ellis
  Gertrude, 72
  Laura Ellison, 8
Ely
  J. B., 71
  Louis H., 113,153
  R. L., 35
Embrey
  F. Mrs., 19,145
  Frank, Mrs., 59
  M. J. Mrs., 19
  Milton F., 82
  Rosa P., 1
  Wm. H., 8
  Isaac N., 29
Emory
  W. E., 162
England
  C. H., 117
  Carrie C., 122,123,124
  Catherine, 164
  Elsie, 2,165
  Harrison, Mr. & Mrs., 154
  Harrison, 6,113
  England cont'd. next column.

England cont'd.
  J. G., 2
  John, 9,101,107,156
  Lillian, 2
  Mary R., 18
  Maud, 2,30,115,147,155
  Nannie, 2
Engle
  Elizabeth, 95
  Katherine, 147
  M. D., 141
English
  Alma, 147
  Blanche, 80
  Frances, 91,113,115,118
  Samuel L., 55
Ensey
  Perry, 3,48,55
Ertter
  John, 102, 149,168
Erwin
  Dalton, 146
Eslin
  Charles E., 133
  Ernest, 113,153
  Henry, 113,153
Esputa
  Josephine, 78,116,142,147
Esworthy
  Frank, 124
  Joseph W., 167
Etchison
  Bates, 148,152
  C. N., 77
  Carlton, 168
  E. C., E.H., 51, 34, 68
  Elisha C., 4,91,137
  G. W., 144,168
  Garnet, 144
  H. Dorsey, 144,146
  J. M., 35,75,95,174
  J. Melvin, 47,93,98,105
  Joseph M., 124
  Etchison cont'd. next page.

Etchison cont'd.
  L. Bates, 110
  Landella, 26,67,112,147
  Leslie, 146
  Lysander, 7
  M. Landella, 23,154
  Martha Jane, 93
  Ralph, 17,24,38
  Robert, 12
  Roy Osborne, 96
Eury
  Grace, 17,38,39
Evans
  Richard, 168
  Wilber, 168
Evely
  Jesse J., 5, 9
Exley
  Alice I., 62
Faber
  J. Dann, 125
  Marshall, 156
Faher
  F. Doan, 55
Fair
  Judges
    1913, 31
    1914, 71
    1915, 112
  Prizes
    1913, 34
    1914, 74
    1915, 115
    1916, 163
Fairall
  A. J., 134
  Alfred F., 55
Fairfax
  C. W., 72
Falin, Fallin
  Charles E., 133
  Geo., 153
  Wm., 153
Falling Green, 129

Farmer
  R. Watt, 48, 49
  Watt, 68
Farmer's Banking & Trust Co.,
  1913, 16
  1914, 62
Farquhar
  A. B., 21
  Allan, Allen, 46 71,91,134
  Charles, 19,136
  Charlotte H., 46
  Ellen, 35,36,75,77,116,
    119,164,165
  Granville, 131
  Granville, Mrs., 56
  Roger B., 136
  Sarah, 14
Farr
  Mary, 94
Fawcett, Fawsett
  A. G., 35
  Blanche, 70, 88
  E. L., 168
  E. Lloyd, 70,174
  Ella Jane, 157
  Ethel Mae, 158
  Gertrude, 89
  H. C., 114,161
  Howard, 69,106,126,150
  W. H., 5,90
  Walter, 34,43,44,60
  William, 6,51,60,133,136,161,
    168
Fearon
  Julia, 52
Feigley
  Daniel F., 122
Felka
  Marian, 79
Fell
  Georgia, Mrs., 6
  Randolph M., 6
Fenwick
  Agnes, 27
  Sallie, 142

Ferran
 S. E., 77
Fidler
 Frank, 71
 W. H., 71
 William 29,47,48,113,124,
  126,156
Fields
 C. S., 168
 Charles, 51,90,133,136
 Elizabeth A., 16
 Geo., 131
 Lillian, 27,35,37,76,164,165
 Margaret, 16
 Rebecca, 27
Fields Bros., 114,116
Fierstein
 Wm. J., 113
Fink
 Elsie, 24
Finley
 H. J. Mrs., 21,39,120,162
 Henry J. Mrs., 72,161
Finneyfrock
 Joseph, 150
 S. J. Mrs., 119
First Nat. Bank of Gaithersburg
 1913, 4
 1914, 51,91
 1916, 134
First National Bank of Sandy
 Spring
 1914, 91
 1916, 134
Fise
 Charles A., 118
Fish
 Joseph, 80
Fishbaugh
 Ernest Clyde, 70
Fisher
 Catherine, 24
 Charles, 142
 Fisher cont'd. next column.

Fisher cont'd.
 Glenna E., 65,69,154
 Helen, 126
 Irma, 165
 James Spencer, 173
 Karl, 2
 Leland Lawrence, 88
 Leland, Mrs., 119
 Madison, 34
 Mary E., 137
 Millard, 56,104,107,140
 Sarah Agnes, 134
 Willard C., 10
 William J., 34
 Zelda, 24
Fisk
 Howard W., 107
Flack
 E. Bruce, 158
 G. Raymond, 109
 Lawrence, Mrs., 77,164,165
Fleckenstein
 Harvey K., 107
Fleming
 John A., 150
Fletchall
 A. P., 126
 Arthur, 21,62,124
 Clarine, 33,154
 George Walter, 41
Fletcher
 Ethel, 147
Fling
 Eugene, 47
Flint
 A. L., 135
Flore
 Fannie Virginia, 78
Flournoy
 Addison H., 82
 Benjamin C., 82
 Edmund S., 82
 P. P., 162
Fontaine
 Sallie, 23,24

Ford
  Edith, 19,154
Forest Glen postmaster 1915, 109
Forsythe
  James, 34
Fort
  J. E., J. F., 72,114,143
  John E., 161
Fox
  Ashton S., 92
Fraley
  Alfred L., 79
  F. F., 35
Franklin
  Neal D., 153
Frasier
  Richard H., 81
Frazier
  C. A., 169
Frease
  Edward H., 84
Freeman
  Theodore, 72
French
  Walter, 142
Frey
  F. D. Mrs., 33,73
Frizell, Frizzell
  Agnes, 15,16,20,147,154
  Kate, 67,147,154
  Laura, 12,15,17,20,68,131, 147,155
  Louise, 65
Frost
  Allan F., 41
  William W. Mr. & Mrs., 41
Fry, Frye
  Edwin, 101,146
  Geo. C., 50,52,76
  Margaret, 95
  Mary, 24
  Ft. McHenry, 70
Fugitt
  Mollie, 151
Fulks
  Carrie, 147,154,161
  Edgar, 100
  Elizabeth, 80
  I. T., 83, 134
  Ignatius T., 4, 91
  Iva, 15, 20
  Joy, 30
  L., 81
  Mary Elizabeth, 111
  Ruth, 80, 81
  T. I., 21
  Thomas I., 45, 51, 150
  William R., 27
Funk
  Lester B., 58
Fussell
  Mordecai, 72,114
Fyfffe
  Mary, 24
Gaddes
  T. S., 71
Gaither
  Edward C., 84
  Louise Mobley, 20
  Mary Lee, 20
  Oscar, 80,149,164
  Stanley D., 43
  W. F., 168
  W. Frank, 17,31,40,72, 98,105,121,127
Gaithersburg
  Election 1914, 63
  High School 1913, 20,38,39
  High School 1915, 104,107
  High School 1916, 149
  High School class 1913 reunion, 118
Galliher
  J. Clark, 168
Galt
  Norman, Mrs., 129

Gammon
  B. R., 71
Gandy
  Edward, 146
Gangewer
  Ida A., 97
Gardiner – see also Gardner
  Bernadine K., 61
  Edmonia, 76,163,164
  G. L., 151,168
  Geo. L., 128
  Geo. L., Mrs., 154
  Helen, 77, 83
  Henry B., 46,55,84
  John, 32,59,62
  L. G. Mrs., 83
  Lucille, 2
  Mildred, 83
Gardner
  E. Grafton, 175
  E. Otis, 69
  Edmonia, 76,78,163,164
  Essie Lillian, 1
  Helen, 36
  J. W. Mr. & Mrs., 1
  John, 8,121,126,131,
    136,149,168
  L. G. Mrs., 119
  Marie, 36,78
  Mildred, 117
  Rachel A., 175
Garner
  Hezekiah, 151
Garrett
  Alex, 168
  Alexander, 43,108,149,158
  Arthur R., 82
  Charles R., 18
  E. Olin, 110
  George, Geo., 87,88,103,149
  Huber, 146
  J. William, 26,156,
  James E., 140
Garrett cont'd. next column.

Garrett cont'd.
  John A., 47,66
  Lucy, 2
  Porter, Mr. & Mrs., 108
  Robert L., 8,22
  Roland, 30
  Roscoe, 142
  William, Wm., 146,171
Garrett Park 1913, 18
Garstin
  Bertram Neynoe, 83,85,86
Gartner
  Jacob, 69,162
  James E., 133
Gartrell
  Edgar, 8
Gaskins
  Julia A., 22
Gassaway, Alexander A., 71
  Helen, 36,72
  John H. Mrs., 51
Gates
  Charles E., 141
  Geo., 87
  Marbury, 146
  T. D., 105
  Wm., 77,95
Gatley
  Albert S., 56,140
Gayley
  A. F. Miss, 19
Geddes
  T. A., 64
Genon
  J. S. Mrs., 37
Gering
  Florence A., 67
Germantown High School
  1913, 20
  1916, 149
Getty
  George G., Mrs., 34,40
  Graham E., 149
Getzendanner
  F. G., 106

Gibbons
  Priscilla D., 160
Gibbs
  Israel, 104
Gibson
  Charles, Chas., 26,95,103, 134,139,155
  Jos. A., 153
  Marie Viola, 146
  R. Frank, 124,156
Giddings
  Frank, Mrs., 113,114
  James H., Mrs., 72
  Jas. H., 94
  Wm. O., 69
Gill
  James P., 55
  Jessie B., 133
  O. Mrs., 145
  R. H. K., 143
  Russell, 113,153
Gilligham
  Rev., 108
  O. A., 103
Gillis, Gilliss
  Edith E. O., 18
  Henry Magruder, 49
  J. S., 163
  John S., 55,116
  Myrtle, 165
  Olive, 2,118
  Viola, 24,154
Gillott
  R. E. L., 168
Gilpin
  Anna, 157
  C. I., Mrs., 35
  Clarence L., 139
  Elizabeth, 18,157
  Elizabeth P., 18
  Fred, 142
  Harold, 146
  Wm., 35,116

Gingell
  Artemesia, 96
  Helen Zanette, 111
  Henry R., 15
  James M., 96
  Lawrence, 149
  Stanley, 130,161
  T. Stanley, 173
  W. W. Mr. & Mrs., 119
  Wm. E., 170
Gittings
  Jed, 49,135
  Mary, 36
  William F., 15
  William, Mrs., 165
Gladhill
  F. S., 115,155
Gladmon, John, 113,153
Glascott,
  Craig, 146
  Evelyn Wailes, 7
Glaze
  Wm., 163
Glazebrook
  L. W., 6,87
  Larkin W., 53
Gleeson
  Capt., 66
Glen Echo election 1914, 63
Glesner
  Philip, 53
Glorius
  Andrew, 85
Glover
  E. S. R., Miss, 36
  Emily, 37
  Joseph B., 124
Gloyd
  Alma, 147
  Arthur, 150
  Clara Ellen, 131
  Clements, 80,142,146
  Dorsey, 144
  Gloyd cont'd. next page.

Gloyd cont'd.
  E. D., 154,168
  Edmund A., 124
  Frances, 80
  George, 6,156
  Perry A., 93,124,156
  Ruby A., 99
  William C., 149
Golden
  Blanche, 15,81,104,107
Goldsborough
  Heath, 77,117
  L. B., Mrs., 37
  Lila, 77,117,120
  Martha Pearce Laird, 107
  P. L., 60
  Phillips, 18,117
Golin
  Clarence, Mrs., 71
Gooding
  Lizzie M., 120
Gorck
  Nellie, 166
Gormley
  M. P., 35
  P. H., 71
Gorsuch
  G. C., 165
  George, 77
Gosnell
  Herbert, 60
Gott
  Alice, 3
  Benjamin T., 156
  J. Forrest, 127
  James P., 17,31,40,124, 126,127
  Kathleen, 24
  Louise, 13
  Lucille W., 134
  Lula Beall, 7,9
  Mabel, 13,147,155
  Mariel, 149,157
  Gott cont'd next column.

Gott cont'd.
  Richard T., 3
  T. N., 168
  Thomas, 31, 96
  Virginia, 24
Gough
  Thomas Reed, 12
Gowan
  Simeon G., 81
Grabill
  L. R., 63
Graeves
  Lewis B. F., 26
Graeves
  Louis B. G., 150
Graff
  J. W., 75,116,163
  James W., 1
  T. T., 37
  Thomas, 75
Graham
  Alice Virginia, 11
  Emma, 119,
Granger
  Hattie, 117,164,165
  Wm. F., 35
Gravers
  Vera, 120
Graves
  Barak T., 144
  Ethel Douglass, 95
  Raymond B., 46
Gray
  Charles R., 98
  Clayton, 146
  F., 19
  Minnie May, 57
  Richard, 3,151
  Samuel, 46,49
  Sarah, 38
  W. T., 70,150,162,166
Greaves
  Lewis B. F., 156

Green, Greene
  A. J., 150
  Clarence E., 99
  Edward, 2
  L. L., 34,37
  Leonidas L., 82
  Margaret A., 90
  Mary A., 23,25,60,147
  Richard, 66
  Thomas Opie, 7
  Win, 146
Gregor
  O. Y., 71
Griffith
  A. H., 108
  A. Hempstone, 82,83
  Alverda, 127
  Amanda, 155
  Artemus, 78,126
  Blanche, 24
  C. M., 167
  Caroline C., 61
  Charles, 74,82,159,167
  Charles G. Mrs., 63,
  Clarence M., 32
  Clyde, 36,168
  Dade, 157,166
  David, 52
  Elizabeth, 47,154
  Frank R., 78
  G. C., 168
  Harriet, 175
  Harry, 16,63,127
  Henry, 28,35,66,155
  Hester, 131
  Howard, 9,168
  Howard, Mrs., 81
  Isabella, 107
  Julian, 26,55,63,136,157
  Katherine, 67
  Lutie, 108,163
  Mildred, 147
  Millard, 142
  Griffith cont'd. next column.

Griffith cont'd.
  N. Lyde, 110
  Nicholas R., 29,82,83,156
  Philemon, 66
  Rebecca, 24
  Ruth, 123,127
  Samuel, 66
  Sarah, 147,154
  Seth, 42,139
  T. Cranmer, 149,155
  Thomas, 42,44
  W. H., W. T., 103,167,168
  William, Wm., 3,17,32,40
    50,69,71,90,102,133,136,146,
    148,149,156,174,158
  Worthington, 150
Griggsby
  Catharyn, 142
Grimes
  Charles, 55,152
  Frances C., 26
  Marjorie, 15
  Nora, 17,38
  Owen, 5
Grimm
  Fred F., 108
Grock
  Nellie, 103,104,155,166
Groomes
  Thomas C., 102
Groot
  Louis E., 131
Grove Hill, 106
Grubb
  C. M., 15
  C. M. Mrs., 119,163
  Ethel M., 143
  Samuel, 169
Gruber
  Helen, 36,120
Gruver
  Helen, 77,120
  J. S. Mrs., 76,165

Gude
  Alexander, 6
Gue
  Edgar B., 55
  Jacob, 74
  Luther M., 32
Guerry
  Homer, 71,150
Gummell
  Ed, 106
Gurley
  Albert H., 30
  Joseph G., 149
Haddox
  Dorothy, 56
  H. D., 25
  Horace C., 91,150
  Horace, Mrs., 72
  R. B., 21
Hager
  Jacob, 100
  John W., 156
Haines
  Granvillle S., 94
  Ruth M., 122
Hale
  J. H., 164
Hall
  Albert, 8,74
  Catherine, 164
  Clarinda Beecher, 61
  Claudia, 115,155
  Curtis Lee, Dr., 118
  Edith, 120
  Elizabeth S., 131
  Forrest Purdum, 66
  J. G., 163
  J. R. Mrs., 163
  John, 26,32,55,14,168
  Joseph, 66
  L. G., L. Y., 117,164
  L. L., Miss, 76
  Margaret, 115
  Hall cont'd. next column

Hall cont'd.
  Randolph, 136
  Rebecca, 139
  S. R., 36,119
  S. R. Mrs., 37,76,118,119
  T. R. Mrs., 16
  T. R., 63,168
  T. Randolph, Mrs., 25
  Thomas R., 55,140
  Thomas R. Mrs., 33
Haller
  Alice, 24
  Frederick, 154
  Lester, 24
Hallowell
  F. M., 77,115,158
  Frank M., 2,34, 82
  R. M., 21
Halpin
  James, 139
Ham
  W. F., 6,53
Hamill
  Henry P., 161
Hamilton
  George, 146
  Jos., 52
  Murray, 14
  S. M., 2
  Sarah Frances, 126
  W. E., 19,59,145
Hamke
  Bertha, 124
Hammond
  Minnie M., 145
  Sarah R., 151
  Weller, 31,69
  William, 67,151
Hampton
  Thomas E., 47
Hanger
  Albert S., 137
  Hugh H., 137
  McCarthy, 137

Gude
  Alexander, 6
Gue
  Edgar B., 55
  Jacob, 74
  Luther M., 32
Guerry
  Homer, 71,150
Gummell
  Ed, 106
Gurley
  Albert H., 30
  Joseph G., 149
Haddox
  Dorothy, 56
  H. D., 25
  Horace C., 91,150
  Horace, Mrs., 72
  R. B., 21
Hager
  Jacob, 100
  John W., 156
Haines
  Granvillle S., 94
  Ruth M., 122
Hale
  J. H., 164
Hall
  Albert, 8,74
  Catherine, 164
  Clarinda Beecher, 61
  Claudia, 115,155
  Curtis Lee, Dr., 118
  Edith, 120
  Elizabeth S., 131
  Forrest Purdum, 66
  J. G., 163
  J. R. Mrs., 163
  John, 26,32,55,14,168
  Joseph, 66
  L. G., L. Y., 117,164
  L. L., Miss, 76
  Margaret, 115
  Hall cont'd. next column

Hall cont'd.
  Randolph, 136
  Rebecca, 139
  S. R., 36,119
  S. R. Mrs., 37,76,118,119
  T. R. Mrs., 16
  T. R., 63,168
  T. Randolph, Mrs., 25
  Thomas R., 55,140
  Thomas R. Mrs., 33
Haller
  Alice, 24
  Frederick, 154
  Lester, 24
Hallowell
  F. M., 77,115,158
  Frank M., 2,34, 82
  R. M., 21
Halpin
  James, 139
Ham
  W. F., 6,53
Hamill
  Henry P., 161
Hamilton
  George, 146
  Jos., 52
  Murray, 14
  S. M., 2
  Sarah Frances, 126
  W. E., 19,59,145
Hamke
  Bertha, 124
Hammond
  Minnie M., 145
  Sarah R., 151
  Weller, 31,69
  William, 67,151
Hampton
  Thomas E., 47
Hanger
  Albert S., 137
  Hugh H., 137
  McCarthy, 137

Hannan
  P. Flack, Mrs., 163
Hardesty
  Abner H., 156
  Benjamin R., 43
Hardin
  Mary E., 145
  Wm. F., 34
Harding
  Jos., 105
  Josephine, 97,105
  Lawrence E., 29,139,156
  Richard T., 171,173
  Samuel T. Mr. & Mrs., 171
  Samuel T., 6
  William C., 158
  Wm. F., 34
Hardy
  John, 51
Hargett
  Albert, 100
  J. F., 151
  John, 150
  Roy, 100
Harmon
  Thawley T., 176
  Harmon, Wm. A., 94,95
Harper
  J. H., 139,145
  Mrs., 19
  Susan, 59
Harr
  T. R., Mrs., 81
Harrington
  Emerson, 42
Harris, Harriss
  Alice E., 100
  C. C., 168
  Clyde, 5,156,173
  Eugenia, 147
  Harvey J., 124
  Henry N., 96
  John P., 82, 83
  Harris cont'd. next column

Harris, Harriss cont'd.
  Joseph M., 124
  Leroy, 127
  Margaret, 59
  Maria M., 96
  Montgomery, 102
  Raymond, 44
  Richard F., 100
  Thomas D., 96
Harrison
  Clara Lillian, 38
  F. P., 59
  J. M., 19,59,145
  James M., 8
  M., M. V., 19,145
  Margaret, 59
Hartle
  Rexford, 155
Hartshorn, Hartshorne
  Anna, 74
  Charles R., 26,124,156
  C. R. Mr. & Mrs., 19
  E. J. Mrs., E. L. Mrs., 6,93
  Elden, 5,58,61
  Elizabeth L., 121
  Ella L., 167
  Nellie L., 161
  Wm. L., 126
Harvey
  B. F., Mrs., 150
  Hiram W., 43
  James, 113,124
  Wm. T., 153
Haugaard
  Victor, 95
Haughton-Burke
  T. A., 101
  Thomas, 19
Havener
  Mason, 139
Haviland
  M. M., 19,21
Hawke
  Edna, 91,112,147,155

Hawkins
  Anna, 96
  Annie Elizabeth, 97
  Elgie D., 156
  Elizabeth Ann, 40
  J. Ernest, 122,167
  James B., 29
  John T., 96,97,126
  Nellie Louise, 174
  Pearl W., 99
  Richard, 63
  Roger, 152
  Thomas F., 32
Hay, Hays
  F. P., 103
  Frederick P., 3,8,50,90,133
  John, 142
  J. Leonard, 82
  L. I. Mrs., 49
  Leonard of F., 168
  Linwood, 12,17
  Nana, 16,33,108
  R. P., 21
  Reginald, 23,
  Wm. P., 65,95,150
Haycock
  Archer L., 156
Haywood
  Edward, 56
Heagy
  J. M., 77
  John, 1,26,111,156
Hearn
  Willard S., 5
Hebbard
  John Marshall, 28
Heenan
  Miss, 2
  Rosemary, 79
Heffner
  Mary E., 135
  Mary Frances,, 174
Heflin
  J. Thomas, 20

Hege
  Edwin S., 28,32,63,140,143
  Mary L., 7
  S. B. Mrs., 76,164
Heim
  Martin, 55,57,94,
    145,159,164
Heiron
  Mrs., 90
Heisler
  John A., 171
Heitmuller
  J. C., 77
  Wilhelmina, 76
Heley
  Rudolph L., 82
Hellen
  Johnson, 18
Helmsen
  Henry H., 8
Hempstone
  William, 66,93
  Wm. Mrs., 81
Henderson
  Caroline, 72,155
  Clara, 35,83
  F. N., 1,19
  Frederick, 162
  Frederick, Mrs., 52
  G. P., Mrs., 117
  Geo., 1,3,26,50,90,133,139
  Geo. P. Mrs., 36,40,76,120
    164,165
  J. Alby, 92,136,139,168
  Jas. B., 3,41
  John, 19,32,39,65,78,94,95,
    110,154,167
  John, Mrs., 19,93
  Joseph, 67
  Miss, 12,38,81
  Myrtle, 142
  O. W., 19
  Oscar W., 25,72,114,157,161
  Rose, 14,128,162

Hendricks
 Ralph M., 139
Hendry
 Isaac S., 108
Henley
 Thomas, 63
Henry
 Anna, 147
 Edw., 39
 Margaretta, 16, 39
 W. Laird, 147
Henshew
 Charles F., 164
Henson
 Ross Heiskel, 29
Hepburn, Alice E., 154
Hermann
 J. P., 19
 J. Philip, Mrs., 107
 J. Phillip, 5, 65
Hermon Presbyterian Church
 1913, 19
 1914, 59
 1916, 145
Hershey
 D. R., 168
 David R., 32,139,150
Hersperger
 Elmer, 150,172
 Sarah, 82,83
Hess
 M. E., 18
Hewitt
 A. R., 85
 Aaron R., 47,55,62,86,99
 Ailees, 52
 Frank, 30,55,71,113,132,139,
  148,150,153,174
 Joseph T., 113,124
 Julia, 44,102
 Marie Maud, 121
 Hewitt, Preston, 48,85,
  105,113,130
 Richard H., 81,102

Hibbs
 William B., 6,53
Hickerson
 C. L. Mrs., 76
 Clarence, Mrs., 19
 H. C., 158
 Lucy Frances, 54
 R. L., 154
 Robert L., 15,28,42,55,
  140,150,155
 Hickerson Bros., 37,165
Hickey
 Edmund J., 119
 Edward J., 165
 J. Albert, 113
Hickman
 Ida M., 154
 John, Mr. & Mrs., 111
Hicks
 Estelle, 165
 Guy, 49
 O. F., 77
 Otis, 66
 T. P., Mrs., , 120
 T. Paret, 14
 W., 1,158
 W., Mrs., 117
 Washington, 8,21,149
Higdon
 John T., 8,43,44,138
Higgins
 Anna Lee, 149
 Annie Lucille, 20,175
 Charles A. C., 45
 Daisy, 65,104,110,
  115,147,155
 Dorothy, 104,107
 Earle M., 137
 Edgar, 76,117
 Edna, 164
 Elizabeth, 37,76
 Florida, 45
 Frances W., 109
Higgins cont'd. next page

Higgins cont'd.
 Frank, 1,2,19,53,73,101,158,175
 Frank, Mrs., 75
 Harriett E., 65
 Helen L., 65,149
 J. A., J. C., J. J., 77,85
  134,158
 James W. C., 124
 Jennie, 36,76,116,117,129
 Jesse, 2,138
 John J., 17,19,51,60,62,63,105,
  132,133,136,137,139,144
 John J., Mrs., 72
 Jose, 36
 Joseph C., 51, 91
 Joshua T., 4
 Higgins, Josie, 36,76,117,119
  129,164
 Laura, 120,165
 Louise, 170
 Margaret, 2,52,117,119,120
 Melissa J., 20
 Robert, 29,40,42,43,
 Higgins, Roberta, 26,112,129,
 Sophia, Sophie, 19,76
Hight
 C. N., 165
Hildebrand
 Edgar, 22
Hill
 A. F., 19, 59, 144
 A. F. Mrs., 19,59,145
 F. G., 145
 George, 8
 J., John, 19,139
 L., Levi, 59,69,144
 Martha S., 30
 Oscar, Mrs., 59
 Paul, 153
 Sallie, 76
 Sarah, 92
 Waverly, 33
 William F., 150
 Hillcrest, 74,121

Hilleary
 Henry, 66
Hilton
 C. C., 150,168
 Clagett C., 63
 Gladys, 118,147,164
 Jas., 12
 John E., 82
 Mabel Magdeline, 175
 Oscar, 113,153
 R. G., 158
 Robert G., 1,16,19,28,32,
  37,62,63,71,106,121,147,167
Hines
 A. E., 36
 C. F., 164
 Catherine, 118,164
 Charles F., 77,118
 Clagett C., 17
 Emmalee Catherine, 171,172
 Gertrude, 77,118,164
 N. P., 35
 R. P., 35,75,76,116,117
  118,119,163,164,165
 R. P. Mrs., 77
Hinner
 A., Mrs., 145
Hobb, Hobbs
 Claude, 140
 Everett Cartwright, 50
 Jerry N., 130
 Lewis, 168
 Louis F., 43
 Martha J., 11
 William T., 3
Hodge, Hodges
 Hamlin, 142
 Helen E., 149
 Maria, 120,165
 Vernon, 150,156
 W. W., 26,73,156
 Windsor W., 111,125
Hoelman
 Luther A., 106

Hoffman
　Adelaide, 15
Hogan
　Charles F., 156
Hogg
　Edith, 120
　Florence, 73
　Mamie, 19
Holland
　C. S., 164
　Charles C., 69
　Charles, Mrs., 19,112,120,165
　Chas. F., 69
　Doree, 71
　Emily Ann, 175
　Ernest, 31
　George, 150
　H., 15
　James, Jas., 92,123,146,162,
　John, 21,14,112,135,175
　Lois, 155,
　Marian, 58,89,
　Martha A., 166,
　Samuel B., 84,
　Tobias, 78
　William G., 43
Holman
　James D., 71
Holmead
　William, 71
Holmes
　G. H., 71
　Wm. H., 31,71,112
Holt
　Mrs., 107
　Thomas, 153
Hopkins
　Archibald, Mrs., 162
　Charles, 34,124
　Martha, 34,106
Hopper
　George S., 80
　Mary Helen, 80

Horine
　Elizabeth, 24
Horn
　William B., 150
Horner
　D. H., 75,164
　David H., 112
　E. W., 35
　Edward, 14
　Frances, 14,91,154
　Frank, 16,112
Horse vs. automobile, 1914, 53
Hoskinson
　Andrew J. Mr. & Mrs., 130
　B. C., 164
　C. H., 134
　Clarence, 4,51,68,91
　Clarence, Mrs., 117
　Irving, 117
　Irving, Mrs., 117
　M. Gertrude, 79
　Mary, 37
　Robert H., 8
　Thomas, 21
　Thomas, Mr. & Mrs., 152
　Thomas, Mrs., 37,76
　W. C., 124
　Wm., 43,69,162
Houck
　Eleanor H., 149
　Margaret, 65,69
Hough
　Henry H., 15
Houghtalling
　Katherine M., 155
Houghton
　Arthur C., 82
　Chas., Mrs., 107
　Minnie A., 44
Houghton-Burke
　T. A., , 25,27
House for rent 1913, , 48
Houser
　Levi, 44
　Houser cont'd next page

Houser cont'd.
Russell, 24
Wm. F., 122
Howard
  A. T., 170
  Brice W., 4,7
  C. L., 1,19,167
  Clifford L., 149
  D. J., 20,141
  Florodoardo, 159
  George W., 11
  Helen, 149,159
  Henry, 21,64,168,
  Henry, Mrs., 158
  Linwood, 150
  Marian, 20,30
  S. Ren, 72
Howes, Howe
  Charles N. L., 70
  Cliff, 71,113,153
  Elias, 121,136
  Ellen E., 174
  Fenton,, 44,
  George R., 18,95
  Helen B., 121,136
  J. Frank, 110
  James, 8,33,38
  Joseph, Jos., 24,44,87
  Kate, 78
  Lenox, 153,162
  Lloyd, 83
  Mary, 18,62
  N. M., 70,162
  Nicholas M., 8, 33
  Robert, 146
  Susie, 121,136
  Walter M., 162
  William, 113,153
Howser
  Margaret, 36,37,77
  Russell, 49
Hoyle
  Anna, 14,20
  Hoyle cont'd next column

Hoyle cont'd.
  Clayton, 100
  Dorothy, 16,17,38
  Elmer E., 9
  John T., 27
  Jones, Mrs., 22,33,118
  Joseph H. C., Mr. & Mrs., 93
  Leonard, 103
  Lillian, 31,61,149
  T. M., 68,139,149
  W. J., 76
  William, Wm., 35,156
Huffer
  Laura B., 84
Huffman
  Frank E., 73
  John W., 94
  John W. Mr. & Mrs., 73
Hughes
  B. C., 75
  B. C. Mrs., 117
  Benjamin C., 78,174
  Bertha, 75
  C. C., 80
  George E., 140
  John Edward, 175
  Katherine, 2,26,154
  Lucy, 69
  M. E., Mrs., 165
  Mamie K., 171
  Margaret E., 149
  O. J., 156,169
  Sarah Virginia, 132
  Thomas L., 34
  Wm. H., 123
Hulings
  Thomas M., 29
Hull
  A. T., Mrs., 76
  E. C., 75
  Edith, 36,76,117,120,64,165
  Sarah, M., 132
Hunckel
  George P., 34

Hunt
　Harry, 165
　Henry J., 62,77,168
　R. C. D., 119,165
Hunter
　Alexander, 68
　Geo. M., 50,55,90,99,133,158
　Geo. P., Mrs., 117
　Thomas, 169
Huntley
　Amelia H., 20,23
Hurlebaus
　Emma, 131
Hurley
　Anna, 69,76
　H. C., 37,75,163
　H. C. Mrs., 36
　Mary, 35,36,77,152
Husband
　John L., 146
Hutchinson
　B. C., B. E., B. F.,　119,165
　Melvin, 174
Hutchison
　Edwin Barbour, 95
Hutton
　Claire, 142,157
　F. C., 75,77,78
　J. J., 158,168
　Josiah J., 21
　Mary Augusta, 89
　W. R., 89
Hyatt
　Emma F., 20
　Floyd, 16
　G. W., 17,168
　Mary, 53,166
　Pearl I., 20
Hyde
　Thomas, 95
Hickerson
　Lindsay R., Mr. & Mrs., 54
Iddings
　B. E., 28
　Iddings cont'd. next column

Iddings cont'd.
　Deborah A., 18,109,112
　　129,154
　Harriet J., 28
　I. B., 42
Ifert
　Daniel C., 123
Iglehart
　Mildred, 20,100
　Wm. G. Mr. & Mrs., 100
Imirie
　John, 150
Ingleside, 106
Inscoe
　Ethel, 147
Isherwood
　I. L. Mrs., 37
　Ida L., 69,155
　Irene, 37
　Isabella Ann, 25
　Robert D., 124
　C. R., 167
Jackson
　Alphonso, 9
　Arthur, 160
　B. Lowndes, Jr., 34
　Bertha M., 160
　Eleanor, 34
　Eliza Canby, 41
　Florence M, 171
　Nellie, 160
　Norman E., 32
　T. L., 92,134
　Thomas E., 29,156
　W. B., 14
　William,　Wm., 14,149
Jacobs
　Judson Wriley, 128
Jacobson
　Jacob, 66
James
　O. F., 17,138
Jamieson
　Archibald M., 13
　Jamieson cont'd. next page

Jamieson cont'd.
　Alexander F., 132
　Annie E., 132
Janin
　Violet Blair, 15
Janney
　Edward, 21
　Joseph, Jos., 25,39,75,76
　　112,124,150,162
　Mary R., 118,122
　Richard, 142
Jarboe
　Eugene, Mrs., 27
　Ida C., 154
　Samuel R., 8
Javins
　Charles, 73
　Francis, 51,60
　John, 73
Javins Bros., 34,78,106,161,163
Jeffries
　Elsie V., 129
　Wm., 153
Johns
　Lane, 115
Johnson
　Addie B., 141
　Agnes I., 110
　Albert, Mrs., 75
　Arch, 113,153
　C. T., 35
　C. C. Mrs., C. T. Mrs., 36,
　　76,77,164
　Carrie V., 121
　Charles, 8,20,21,43,55,62,
　　75,174
　E. G., 119
　E. Miss, 73
　Ella E., 53
　Emma, 76
　Enoch G., 77,135
　Frederick, 9
　G. Cleveland, 110
　Johnson cont'd. next column

Johnson cont'd.
　George H., 8,33,91
　Helen Louise, 81
　J. William, 28,155,172
　John J., 87,134
　Joseph, 125
　Lillian Olivia, 20
　Luther F., 58
　Mary L., 134
　Miriam, 77,117,119
　Oliver, 150
　Oscar L., 14
　Rosie May, 167
　Thomas, 123
　W. G., 168
　Walter A., 125
　William, Wm., 32,111,125
　Wilson G., 26,150,156
Jones
　A. L., 85
　Abraham, 121
　Anna Lee, 147,149
　Arthur L., 17,44,63
　Bessie, 20
　Bettie Williams, 22
　Blanche D., 89
　Calvin, 24
　Charles, 20,28,73
　Chas., Mrs., 112
　Creighton, 31
　Dorsey, 1,113,153
　E. B., 1
　E. Wilkerson, 106
　Edmund, 16
　Elizabeth, 24,142,144,149,171
　Eugene, 4,5,31,33,37,40,42,56,
　　64,65,91,140,151,168
　George H., 26,156
　George, Mrs., 118
　Isabel B., 147,154
　J. A., J. W., 106,133,158
　J. Brooke, 169
　J. Hampton, 106,110,167
　Jones cont'd. next page

Jones cont'd.
  J. W., 34, 60
  James H., Mrs., 31,93,112
  Jas B., 153
  John, Mrs., 16,21, 33, 118
  John, 22,66 30,96, 139,
    143,150,168,168
  John Paul, Admiral, 4
  Josiah W., 2,50,91,94,
    134,136
  Josiah, Mrs., 60,107
  Kirtley, 154
  Lavinia, 35,120
  Lena B., 128
  Lloyd, 31,168
  Margaret, 128
  Marie, 31
  Martha Marie, 90
  Medora, 33,108,118
  Nannie D., 22
  Nena, 37
  Nida, 171,
  Reuben P. Jr., 77
  Somerset O., 61
  Spencer C., 1,3,14,16,29,
    20,50,90,101
  W. K; W. P., 77,133,168,
  William., Wm., 29,51,90,136
Jordan
  W. W., 30,120
Joubenal
  Wilhelmina C., 85
Joyce
  Miss, 97
Joyner
  Huston B., 107
Jurors
  March 1913, 8,9
  March 1914, 55
  March 1914, 56
  March 1915, 94
  March 1915, 95
  Jurors cont'd. next column

Jurors cont'd.
  March 1916, 139
  March 1916, 141
  November 1913, 42
  November 1913, 44
  November 1914, 82,83
  November 1915, 124
  November 1915, 126
  November 1916, 172
Kahlert & Ray, 163
Kalfbus
  John, 164
Kanode
  R. E., 17,32
Karn
  Frank H., 124,126
  Margaret, 69,79
  Mary M., 65
Keating
  Michael F., 89
Keen
  H. M., 161
Kefauver
  Gladys, 165
Keiser
  Cyrus, 55,99,139
  Lewis, 26,156,161,
Kelchner
  George, 29,87,95,106,153,156
  J. F., 1,19
  John H. Mrs., 151
Kelley, Kelly
  A., 169
  Benjamin H., 55,66
  John, 70,72,95,174
  Margaret, 122,
  Mary, 18,118
  W. J., 5
Kemp
  Ida, 38,39, 81,149
  J. E., , 33
  James, 72,150
  Mildred A., 65
  Nellie C., 167

Kendrick
  J. A., 103
Kengla
  Charles, 162
  Harry, 94,95,162
  Lewis Christopher, 154
  Louis C., 172
Kennedy
  Henry, 168
Kenney
  Herman, 58
Kensington
  Chamber of commerce 1914, 65
  Election 1914, 63
Keochling
  Lillian, 14
Kephart
  George M., 69,149
Keplinger
  F., Mrs., 37
  Fred, Mrs., 69,119,163
Kerr
  F. A., 119,165
Keys
  E. C., 169
  Elizabeth, 76,
  Enos C., 8,9,62,171
  Enos, Mrs., 71
  John W. Mr. & Mrs., 142
  John William, 160
  Marion H., 148
  Martha, 19,27
  Mary, 128
  Reuben, 23
  Thomas C., 32,106,114,149,168
Kiefer
  Clarence M., 162
Kilgour
  Alexander, 80,104,108, 122,148
  Alexander, Mrs., 120,162
  Cecelia, 67,86
  Francis S., 16,21,112,150
  Sallie, 86

Kilpatrick
  Derelle, 69
  James, 33,39
  W. B., 135
Kimler
  Irene, 110
King
  Albert, 11
  Charles E. Mr. & Mrs., 176
  Clarence P., 6,53
  Crittenden, 43
  Delaney, 155
  E. C., E. D., 149,159,167
  Elias, 32
  Emma, 15,16
  Erma, Irma, 38,80,176
  Fannie Thelma, 149
  Forrest, 163
  Harry J., 150
  Hiram G., 156
  J. D., 168
  James, 43,82,83,117,154
  James D., Mrs., 154
  John O., 3
  Linda V., 142
  Mabel, 15,20,147,155
  Mary E., 104,107
  Rufus K., 82,83,144
  T. D., 150
  Thurston, 130,140
  William E., 28
Kingdon
  A. G., Mrs., 117
  Carey, 55,63,148
  Carey, Mrs., 119
  Isabel, 25,71,72,92,161
Kingsbury
  Ambrose C., 39
  C. T., 91,124,167
  Elsie M., 93
  Harold S., 108
  M. I., 91
  W. A., 71

Kingsley
　E. D., 156
　Eldridge, 29
　Harold, 29,156
Kinney
　A. Mrs., 19
　Alice, 59
　Dorothy, 3,79
　John, 4
　Lester, 145
　Nathan, 99
Kinsey
　Maude E., 129
Kirk
　C. F., 133,158
　Charles F., 2,32,43,50,51,60,
　　74,90,91,111,134,136
　Donald, Don., 34,73
　Francis, 142
　Wm. K., 90
Kirkpatrick
　Jas., 69
Kisner
　Mary Ellen, 141
　Sarah E., 66
Klingaman, W. K., 91,155
Knapp
　Lewis, 65
Knight
　Elizabeth O., 18,57
　Julia, 142
　M. Donaldson, 59
　Merrill, 104,107
　Owen, 103
Knill
　Simon P., 45
Knott
　Wm., 149
Koehler
　H. S., 48
Kohlhoss
　Charles, 24,61
　Marguerite, 109,149

Koiner
　Garrnett, 64
Koonts
　R. G., 103
Kreig
　Ella V., 14
Kroll
　William, Wm., 55,146
Kruhm
　F. W., 34,73,139,150
Kumler
　Benjamin W., 140
Lackoff
　Oscar, 113
Ladson
　Edna H., 29
LaFetra
　E. E., 63
Lafferty
　Charles H., Rev., 11
Laird
　D., 68,127,136,147,148
　Lamar P. D., 109
Laird
　Philip
　Edith, 49,126
　G. H., 1
Lamar
　G.H. Mrs., 75, 2,21,36,117,149
　George H., 1,9,12,19,92,158
　George H. Mr. & Mrs., 2
　Harmong, 53
　L. Q. C., 113
　Lucile, 2,49,83,134,160
　Rebecca, 2,151,157,164
　Stonestreet, 77,117,164
　W. H., 16,25,89
Lamb
　R. I., Mr. & Mrs., 112
Lambert
　Harry J., 145
Lamphear
　George A., 47

Leith
 Elden Henry, 108
Leizear, Leishear, Leisear
 Charles H., 61
 E. D., 168
 Eli, 49
 Elizabeth, 147
 Frank D., 139
 Louis M., 162
 Martha M., 65
 Samuel, 8
 Samuel, Mrs., 76
 Wm. G. W., 94
Lenowitz
 Ben, 168,
Lethbridge
 John, 164
Letterner, Latterner
 Henry, 111, 125,172
Lewis
 David, 27,60
 Edward D., 93,111,125,149,
 F. C. Mrs., 19,
 Frank, 90
 Geo. E., 19,28,158
 George E., Mrs., 19
 H. Latane, 37,114,135,
   156,172
 J. F., 16
 John, 17,20,25,30,32,37,39,40,
   42,44,47,62,74,91,128,162,
   168
 Julia S., 126
 May B., 98
 Mildred, 87
 R. Frank, 26
 Rosa May, 159
 W. Motzer, Mr. & Mrs., 126
 William, Mrs., 19,20,25
 Wm, 25,64,65,98,139,146,
   153
Liebig, Lieburg
 Thos. M., 106

Ligon
 Percy G., 121
Lillard
 Joseph R., 130
 Lula McQuiddy, 49
Lilly
 R. D., 77
Lindig
 Edith, 115,155
 Ethel, 147
 Henry M., 44
Lindner
 L. W., 153
 Leonard W., 113
Lindsay, Lindsey
 Eliza Earley, 65
 Margaret, 154
 Olivia C., 38
Linkins
 James A., 176
 Raymond B., 137
 Wm., 48,113
Links
 Wm. G., 153
Linthicum
 Cassidy, 149
 Dr., 55
 Earl, 169
 Ella, 19
 Ethel, 169
 George, 100,157
 John W., 123
 Joseph H., 18
 Lloyd G., 128
 Miel, 48,132,168
 O. M., 1,19,57,145,158,161
 O. M. Mrs., 2,37,94,117,
   119,120
 Roberta, 18
 Smith, 74
 William A., 36,83,107
Lippert
 Anna, 144

Lipscomb
　Claire, Clare, 132,137,139
Lochte
　Leroy, 29,51,156
　Maurice A., 147
Lodge
　J. Edwin, 155
Loeffler
　John W., 96
Logan
　Edgar Harbaugh, 65
Long
　Nellie, 117
Loughborough
　James, Mrs., 93,153
　Mrs., 90
Louthan
　Frances Alma, 20
Love
　Gorman, 142
　Philip, 72
Lowe
　C. Edward, 65
　Daisy, 3
　Edward, 67
Lucas
　John W., 55,56,172
Luckett
　Cooke, 33,44
　Mary E., 96
Luhn
　Arthur P., 87
　Edward W., 43
　Esther, 142
　Randolph, 3,27,48,94,140
　Thomas E., 88
Lumsden
　James, 171
Lusby
　Geo. L., 94
　William, 113,153,156
Lydard
　John C., 133

Lyddane
　Charles, 55,74,113,136
　James F., 31
　Mary H., 86
　Robert Clifford, 157
　Robert W. Mrs., 72
　Stephen B., 86
　W. R. Mrs., 77,117,119
　William R., 82
Lynch
　Francis, 36
　John, 48,74,83,162,175
　Joshua, Mrs., 59
　M. V., 144
　Maria C., 48
　O., 19,144
　Odie, 59
　Susie, 145
　Wm., 10,56
Lynn
　Newman E., 41
Lyons
　Katherine M., 85
M. E. Church South of
　Poolesville, 141
Mace
　Arthur M., 55,71,74,87
　Charles R., 71
　Franklin, 71,167
　Samuel, 71
MacGregor
　M. E. Mrs., 120
Mackall
　Upton B., 15,150,156
Mackintosh
　Grace Amelia, 153
MacLane
　Gordon Whiting, 56,66
Maddox
　C. J., 1,32,108
　John, 83,168
Magaha
　Lillian A., 15
　Thomas, Mr. & Mrs.,15

Magee
  John K., 113,153
Magruder
  Allen, 142
  Bradley, 87
  C. C. Jr., 27
  Caleb, 42
  Daisy, 77
  Dorothy, 164
  E. F. Miss, 29
  Effie Virginia, 84
  Eleanor, 15,21
  Elva Ellsworth, 131
  Frances Merle, 122
  H. S. Mrs., 120
  Hampton, 71
  James L., 8
  Jesse, 168
  John, 87
  Laura, 87
  Margaret O., 100,102
  Mary, 35,87,157
  Maurice W., 131
  Russell Scott, 27
  S. W., 34,41,66
  Spencer, 114,115
  Thomas Levin, 69
  W., W. S., W.V., 13,107, 158,168
  Walter, 11,55,161
  Warren V., 26,136
  William, 11,69,82
  Winfield S., 15,102,105, 121,127,145
  Zadoc, 8,132
Mainhart
  Frances Catherine, 152
  Lottie, 24
Mall
  John A., 168
Maloney
  Thaddeus J., 68

Manakee
  Frank H., 48
  Manion, Marion F., 6
  Mary A., 128
Mannar
  Braxton, 142
  C. H., 1,19,57,62,91
  Claiborne, 24,26
  Dr., 55
Mansfield
  Wm. S., 83
Margerum
  Cecelia F., 87
  E. P. B., 55,140
  Edmund P. E., 148
Markley
  Klara, 52
Marlow, Marlowe
  A. T., 80,168
  Charles, Chas., 69,162
  Elias P., 159
  Emma C., 159
  Evaline Hopkins, 27
  Howard, 6, 82,87,150
  Julius, 27
  Pearl, 6
Marsden
  H. H., 88,162
Marth
  Roy I., 57
Martin
  H. M., 168
  Harry, 71
  James, 153
  John T., 156
  Marie Kinney, 3
  Reuben F., 29,156
  Maryland Agric. College., 81
  Maryland National Guard, Co. K., 153,172
Mason
  Randolph, 28
  Shirley Carter, 61
  Mason cont'd. next page.

Mason cont'd.
  Theodore S., 28
  William P. Mr. & Mrs., 54
Massey
  Emily, 15
  James H., Mrs., 107
Mathis
  William M. Mrs., 11
Matlack
  Agnes, 21
Matthews, Mathews
  J. B., 77
  James M., 151
  William, 34,71,73,124
Maughlin
  J. B., 167
  James, 82,149
Maught
  Conrad, 55,56
Maul
  Adele, 35,36,76,164,165
Maus
  I. Mervin, 120,138
  M. P., 33, 49
  Mary Bertha, 68, 79
  Oliver Stonestreet, 104
Maxon
  Louis W., 157
Maxwell
  Celestine, 41
  Emma V., 79
  Wesley, 67,114
McAbee
  Clara M., 104
McAtee
  Eugene A., 17,32,83
  Evelyn, 115,155
  George, 51
  Theodore, 42
  Virginia, 158
  William, 158
McBain
  Lula, 81

McCabe
  Harry, 12, 16
McCammon
  Ormsby, 32, 71,111,125
  Ormsby, Mrs., 71
McCathran
  Irving L., 28
McCauley
  Alice Jane, 158
McCeney
  Anna S., 171
  G. B., 168
  Henry, 171
  John, 140
  Louise, 149
  Wm. H., 150
McClure
  Emma Ivy, 53
McCrossin
  Aubrey, 5
  Bernard W., 141
  William, 44,93,140
McCullough
  Anna M., 16
  Anne M., 20
McDonald
  Jackie, Miss, 86
  John, 1,152,174
  Wilson, 152
McFadden
  Arthur M., 118
McFarland
  A. B., 126,129
  A. Miss, 75, 76
  Addie, 117
  Arlene, 36
  Arthur B., 47
  J. W., 158
McGaha
  John T., 140
  T. C. Mrs., 36,165
  Wm. S., 49
McGregor
  M. Mrs., 36,37,77
  Wm. B., 3

McGrew
  G. H. Mrs., 14,39,162
  George W., 71
McKay
  Benjamin, Mr. & Mrs., 170
  Neal, 170
  Oscar, 71,113
McKeever
  A. F., 23
McKenney
  James H., 41
  Charles, 71
McLachlan, McLachlin
  Eugene H., 156
  E. H., 156
McLean
  Donald, Mrs., 150
McLeod
  Francis S., 29
McMillan
  Alexander L., 57
McNair
  Laura, 164
McNeilly
  J. F., 165
Meads, Meeds
  George W., 111
  Hollyday, 144,145
Means
  Bernadine, 39, 72
  Samuel, 28
Meany
  John T., 23
Meem
  A. F., 4,51,63,91,134
  Cloe E., 79,125
  George W., 81
  Guy, 16, 38
  Mary J., 125
  Nora Sellman, 90
Merritt
  M. A., 35
Merson
  George, 141,149

Metzgar, Metzger
  Amanda E., 125
  N. Hazel, 121,127,128
  Nathan H., 95
  Wm. W., 125
  H. N., 168
Meyer
  Chas., 50
Milburn
  Mary E., 112
Miles
  Henry, 84
  Henson T., 130
  James A., 18
  Nettie, 166
  Richard H., 63
  Samuel P., 149
  Sarah T., 114
  Thomas, 109
Milford
  S. B., 151
Millea
  William L., 163
Miller
  Anna Offutt, 163
  Annie, 18, 33, 34
  Benjamin H. Mrs., 25
  Charles F., 170
  Eliza, 19
  F. Mason, 173
  Francis, 110,134,156
  Gertie, 39, 79
  H. H. Mrs., 112
  Hattie, 70
  Henry H., 10
  Henry H. Mrs., 31
  Jos. D., 139
  Julian Hite, 55
  Katherine, 27
  Lillian C., 56, 66
  Marianna M., 150
  Mary, 19,147
  Mason, 16
  Nellie Josephine, 68
  Miller cont'd. next page.

Miller cont'd.
 Robert, 34,73,150,174
 W. Hite, Miss, 36
 Wilheimer Hite, 37
 Wm. T., 23
Mills
 Ada W., 98
 Beverly, 168
 Charles, 11,135
 E. T., 103
 George, 65,77,94,135
 Havilan, 19
 John H., 55
 Mary, 138
 Nathan T., 153
 Pete, 45
 W. A., 98
 Welby H., 143
 William W., 98
 Willie, Miss, 7
Milstead
 Dorothy, 142
 Ella J., 5
Milton [place], 153
Minneck
 Millard F., 152
Minnis
 Wm. T., 128
Mitchell
 Richard T., 96
Mobley
 Anna, 24
 Frank, 97
 Geo. W., 82
 Henry T., 94
 Mahlon F., 82
 W. W., 168
 Wm. B., 3
 Wm. B., 50,90,99,133
 Wm. Mrs., 25,39,162
Molesworth
 Samuel R., 94,96
Monard
 Lewis, 31

Monday
 Bernard, 3,99
 E. E., E. W, 35,77,117
 E. W. Mrs., 37,76
 Edward, 165
 Edwin W. Mrs., 36,76
 Edwin, 119
 Ella F., 1
 Hughes, 49,163
 Katherine, 83
 Mary O., 99
 Monocacy Cemetery 1915,
  103,108
Monred
 Iantha, 16,157
 R., 38
 Ravenel, 15,81,104
Montg. Co. Agric. Soc.
 1913, 2
 1914, 60
Montg. Co. High School, 1913, 1
Montgomery
 Hattie J., 155
 M. B., 35
 Richard, Gen., 159,
Montgomery Co. Agric. Society
 1914, 50, 90
 1916, 133
Montgomery County Foxhunters
 Association 1915, 126
Moore
 E. W. Mrs., 19,93
 Edgar W., 63
 Hadassah, J., 67
 Ira V., 25
 James T., 112
 Jessie M., 138
 Joseph, Jos., 3,15,50,83,88,92
 Katherine, 18,92,115,155
 L. M. Mrs., 150
 L. W., 19,59,145
 Mary G., 83,85
 R. B., 4,51,91101,105
Moore cont'd. next page.

Moore cont'd.
  Russell, 12
  Samuel, 138
  Virginia, 80
  William W., Jr., 73
  Willis L., 14,35,86,116,164
  Woodville W., 172
Moran
  M. E., 119,163
  M. F. Miss, 76
Morand
  Alice Gertrude, 157
Moreland
  Paul H., 23
Morgan
  Daniel P., 69
  Hezekiah, 57
  John Pierpont, 12
  Lillian, 2,14,112,155
  Wm. E., 146
Morman
  Jas. B., 11
Morris, Morrriss
  Charles R., 119
  Hilmer, 164
  James T., 69
Morrison
  Charles V., 108
  James, 61,168
  L. B., L. V., 36,117,120,165
  Lelia, 75
  Lillian, 77
  Michael, 35
  Mildred, 36,77,117,118,164
  Wm., 77
Mortimer
  Frank L., 172
  L. Curtis, 171
Moss
  Jack F., 71
Mossburg
  Charles, 84
  Edwin Earl, 50
  Mossburg cont'd. next column.

Mossburg cont'd.
  Genevieve, 24
  Mary Alice, 82
  Phillip F., 124,126
  Thos. G., 43
Motter
  John C., 107
Moulden
  Helen, 117,147
  J. S., 77
  Joseph Albert, 26
Mount
  Edward, 164,
  James M., 32,43,111,
Moxley
  H. B., 97
  James, 72
  W. B., 150
  William P., 98
  Willie B., 124
Moyer
  George D., 150
Muench
  Elsa, 112,
Mullen
  George, 8,71,130,135,
Mullican
  John, 34
  Rachel, 34,78
Mullinix
  Calvin, 167
  Claude G., 43
  Clyta, 89
  Edwina, 12
  Emory E. Mrs., 12
  Emory E. Mr. & Mrs., 57
  Emory R., 12
  Joseph, 3,47
  Madge Lucile, 45
  Maude, 12
  Sebastian M., 94
  Virginia, 104,107

Muncaster
  Anna, 36
  Caroline, 147
  Hannah S., 4
  Helen, 35
  J. E. Jr., J. F., Jr., 35, 77
  J. E. Mrs., 35
  John, 7,75,82,116,117,
    118,163,164
  L. M., 35, 75
  O. Z., 51
  Otho M., 143
  Stewart B., 62
  W. E., 4,19,35
Murphy
  Anice C., 154
  Charles B., 8,33,55
  Eugene S., 79
  George W., 100
  Michael, 67
  R. M., 55
  Robert, 78,148
  Violette, 115,155
  William Joseph, 152
Murray
  Frank, 113,153
Musgrove
  Anna Brewer, 20
  Francis B., 29
  Henry Z., 171
  Luther E., 102
  Nathan, 66
  Pearl, 142,169
  Stevens J., 87
  Harry Z., 172
Musser
  Porter, 168
  Sarah M., 160
Myerly
  Malvin, 21,22
Myers
  A., Mrs., 19,145
  Arthur, 82,140
  Myers cont'd. next column.

Myers cont'd.
  Arthur, Mrs., 59
  B. F., 72
  C. G., 154
  Charles, 91,126,147,170
  Elizabeth, 6
  Frank B., 72
  Garrison, 29
  George W., 6
  Harrison, 156
  Harry, Mrs., 86
  Helen S., 148,152
  Hugh G., 65
  W. B., 19,59,145
  Wm. L., 44
Nally
  F. M., 120
Neel
  Guy, 12,16,39,65
  Helen, 91,155
  J. T., 154
  J. T. Mrs., 154
  Walter, 149,21,22
Neff
  Charlotte F., 154
Neitzey
  Eleanor, 6
Nelson
  Jas. Dr., 19
Nesbit
  George F. Jr., 149
  Helen T., 104
Newcomb
  H. T., 21,34
  Harry T., 79
  Lucy, 73
Newman
  Mildred, 50
Nicholls, Nichols, Nicol
  C. B. Mrs., 37
  E. H. Mrs., 37
  Harry B., 97
  Jacob E., 123
Nicholls &c. cont'd. next page.

Nicholls &c. cont'd.
  James W., 174
  Jas. W., Mr. & Mrs., 175
  John H., 82,83
  M. B., 165
  Mary E., 136
  Roger D., 51
  W. D., 56,140
Nicholson
  Arthur P., 53
  Basil W., 139,141
  Blanche, 52,147
  C. T., 77,78
  Caroline, 109
  Carolyn, 133
  Carson Edward, 171
  Charles T., 34,83.116
  Claude, 114
  Clifton R., 150
  Dorsey W., 9
  Elizabeth B., 20,91
  Elsie May, 4
  F. B., 121
  Geo. W., 32,75,78,162
  Harry L., 167
  Jesse, 26,168
  L. I. Mrs., 21,36,119,165
  Leonard L. Mr. & Mrs., 38, 119,147
  Mary Elizabeth, 40
  William, 64,74
Noland
  Agnes, 106
Norment
  Clarence E., 6,53
Norris
  Adelia E., 44
  Charles, 112
  Clifton, 1,2,79,
  Lydia, 58,
  Nathan, 24,
Norwood
  Geo. W., 69

Nourse
  Charles H., 21,91,150
  Rebecca, 13
  U. D., Mrs., 72
  Upton D., 91
Noyes
  Edmund, 95
  Edward, 146
Noyes
  Elizabeth T., 15
  Mary Edna, 81
O'Brien
  George, 34,113
  J. F., 114
  John William, 34
  Matthew, 55
O'Donnell
  H. F., 71,169
  Hugh, 48,73,113
O'Neale
  John H., 8
Oak Grove, 172
Oberlin
  L. D., 141
Offutt
  A. L., 36
  Adelaide S., 133
  Alexander, 146
  Anna, 36,149
  Clarence, 31
  Clements, 54
  Edward Winsor, 41
  Elizabeth H., 83,85
  Ellen P., 65
  Emma, 67
  Gertrude Estelle, 149
  H. W., 124,139,168
  Harry G., 79
  Hilleary, 38,39,82
  James, 43,44
  Jane, 37,117,165
  John, 31,90,133
  Offutt cont'd. next page.

Offutt cont'd.
  Lee, 2,3,14,21,34,50,51,63,
    90,106,233,145
  Lee, Mrs., 19,52
  Lemuel Clements, 57
  M. W., 29,36,74,119
  Mary Emma, 160
  Nicholas, Jr., 60,62
  Pearl E., 28
  R. J., 114
  Rafael, 49
  Raphael T. Mr. & Mrs., 31,
    160
  Richard, 9,168
  Scott, 35
  T. L., 35
  Thomas H., 82
  W. Ernest, 17,32,37,40,42,
    44,111,127,130
  W. J., W. W, 36,168
  W. Lyle, 29,168
  Wilson, Jr., 163
  Winfield, 144
Ogle
  Ada Marie, 169
Oland
  David F., 43
  Leona F., 136
  Marie, 94
  Susie V., 53
Oldfield
  Fannie, 77,117,164
  Lewis P., 139
Olds
  Edson, 71
  Katherine Sergeant, 15
  Marian, 95
Oliphant
  M. Campbell, 144,145
  Mary E., 154
Orme
  Archibald, 132
  Charles C., 69,162
Orndorf
  Wm. O., 109
Osborne
  Albert, Mrs., 20
  Sarah A., 28
Osmond
  A. H., 58
Otwell
  J. C., 164
Owen, Owens
  Clarence E., 110
  Claude W. 32,57,65
  Nannie, 117,120
  Ruth, 37
  Susie, 37
  Thomas J., 30,72,114,161
  Wm. T., 94
Owings
  Alice D., 65
  Alverda, 45
  H. W., 34
  Katherine, 101,107
  Stanley D., 104
  Thomas, 42
Oxley
  Charles W., 134,173
  Charles, Mr. & Mrs., 95
  Edgar F., 128
  Katherine Emily, 95
Pace
  Anna C., 155
  Annie C., 109
Packard
  Thomas J., 7
  J. A., 150
  Thomas Edgar, 165
  Thomas, 120
Page
  D. M., 163
  Frederick W., 32,43,106
  Junius, 128
  Louisa, 13
  Mary M., 172
  Page cont'd. next page.

Page cont'd.
Nathan, 172
Roland, 57
Parker
  Charles H., 114
  George, 42
Parks
  Charles, Mr. & Mrs., 123
  Charles R., 113,153
Parsley
  Bertie, Mrs., 4
  Grace, 172
  Isabel, 93,97,99
  J. H., J. R, 4,39,
    90,133,168
  John H. Mr. & Mrs., 97
  Mary Louise, 70
  Roger, 43
  Wilbur O., 43
Parsons
  H., Mrs., 97,107,150
Pate
  Ethel, 106,110
Patterson
  Calhoun, 106,
  Elizabeth H., 6
  J. C. Mrs., 120
  James, 71
  Perry, 71
Payne
  Lewis, 85
Peake
  Geneva E., 143
  M. E. 130,140,168
Pearce
  Harry F., 15
  Leonard G., 74
Pearre
  Frank, 67
  George C., 149
  James G., 97
Peddicord
  Herbert, 146
  Peddicord cont'd. next column.

Peddicord cont'd.
  Margaret Louise, 91
  Mary E., 20,149
Peele
  Arabella C., 114
  Stanton J., 98,147
Penn
  Ignatius, 112
  M. S., 24
  Mary, 112
  Sadie, 36
Pennefill, Pennifill
  S. R. Mrs., 59,145
Pennifield, Pennyfield
  Charles, Chas., 69,162
  George W., 70
Perkins
  Robert, 158
Perrel
  Samuel Philip, 38
Perry
  Benjamin, 8
  H. Clay, 102
  Margaret, 81
  N. M., 168
  Ninian, 150
  Walter E., 24
Pessou
  Molly Z., 64
Peter, Peters
  Allen, 123
  Amy C., 41
  Arthur, 4,16,63,71
  Dorsey L., 37,96
  E. C., EdwardC., 1,14,16,19,
    20,27,63,66,71,83,112,
    113,158
  E. H., 116
  Edward, Mrs., 37,52
  Elizabeth, 67
  Fountain, 168
  George, 5,23,61,65,123
  George, Mr. & Mrs., 144
  Peter, Peters cont'd. next page.

Peter, Peters cont'd.
  Harry Theron, 67
  John, 18,137
  Michael, 22
  Norman, 23,144
  R. B., 1,28,32,55,57,66,
    105,133,168
  Rosa Virginia, 86,
  William Thomas, 67
Petty
  Alma Virginia, 84
Phair
  Geo. F., 94
  Wm. H., 14
Pheobus
  Maurice, 33
Phillips
  Fannie, 164
  Ivy Alice, 82
  M. A. E., Miss, 6
  Samuel L., 16,63
Phoebus
  Ernest, 20
  J. C., 63
  Maurice, 8,33
  Nettie, 15
  Sylvester, 146
Pierce
  Edward, 171
  Elwood K., 175
  Harold Clifford, 171
  Lillyan, 171
  T. F. Mrs., 165
Pine Groves Poultry Farm, 77
Pitcher
  Mary, 120
Plant
  Walter, 72
Plaskett
  J. M., 163
Pleasant Fields Farm, 73
Plummer
  Arthur, 53
  Plummer cont'd. next column.

Plummer cont'd.
  Clay, 100
  Ella, 120
  Ewell R., 8
  George Pope, 41,45
  Hattie, 51
  Hazel, 118
  M. S., 116,117
  Marjorie, 16,38,39
  Mary Gertrude, 8
  S. R., 4,51,82,83,91,
    124,134,149
  Walter, 149,169
Plyer
  Mabel M., 97
Polio epidemic 1916, 167
Pollock
  Findley, 80
  George F., 149
  John Emory, 153
Poole
  Catherine, 37,165
  Eugene A., 1
  J. Edward, 130
  J. Sprigg, 79
  Katherine, 76,117
  Lewis W., 32,37
  Lucretia, 22
  M. S., Miss, 77
  Martha, 36,165
  Melvin M., 140
  Nannie, 81,130
  Oscar, 12,131
  Reginald D., 99,150
  Sarah A., 83
  Thomas, Dr., 3
  W. W., 103,124,126
  William, 39,96,124
Poolesville
  Election 1914, 63
  High School 1913, 24
  High School 1916, 149
Pope
  Ruth, 131,155
  Thomas H., 124

Popkins
  Edward, 146
Porter
  Charles Gassaway, 27
  E. C., 31
Posey
  Wm. A., Mrs., 117
Poss
  Bernard, Mrs., 75,164
  Clyde, 129
  H. G. Mrs., 35
  Harry G., 1
  J., 63,75,79,116,154
  M. S., 153
  Wm. S., 113
Post
  Ruman S., 44
Powell
  A. T., 115,116,163,164
  Mildred, 104,149,164
  Rose May, 110
Power
  John, 7,54,94
Prather
  Helen, 142
Pratt
  W. T., 84,130,145,168
  Walter S., 103
  William, 69,86,91,150
  Wm. T. Dr. & Mrs., 86
Presbyterian Meeting House, 169
Prescott
  A. F., 161
  Alexander F., 23,54,61
  Billy, 83
  E. L., E. S., 21,65
Ricketts
  Wallace, 1,72,73
  Wallace E., Mrs., 76
  Wm. W., 10
  Zadoc, 82
Riddleberger
  Mrs., 35

Ridgeway
  Roscoe E., 156
  William T., 55
Ridgley
  Bessie Louise, 84
  Melvin L., 164
  Thomas A., 93,98
  W. T., 116
Riffet
  J. F., 165
Riggs
  Artemus, 67
  B., 35
  Brownell, 2,75,174
  Douglas H., 94
  Graham, 53
  Harry, 46,84,87,130
  Helen, 75
  I. E., 95
  J. Edward, 44
  Jane Adele, 92
  John A., 27
  Joshua L., 83
  L. E., 167,174
  Laura, 30
  Laureson B., 26,45,139,148
  Ledoux E., 28,55,113,155
  Leta, 20, 112,155,161
  Margaret Howard, 20,48,49
  Marguerite duMeste, 93,98
  Mary N., 108
  Remus, 143
  Reuben, 83
  Samuel, 31,43,129,135,167,172
  Sarah J., 143
  T., 141
  William, 52,87,113
  Wm. G., Mrs., 11
Riley
  Charles E., 173
  Frederick A., 53
  James D., 63
  Riley cont'd. next page.

Riley cont'd.
  Lloyd, 61
  Myrtle Irene, 173
  W. E., Mrs., 117
Riordan
  Edward F., 42
Rippey
  C. W., 119,165
Roach
  Anna H., 150
  Roscoe M., 55
  Wm. H., 17,63,136,138
Roberts
  O. W., 126,168
  Willie, 24
Robertson
  Amy, 2,18,35,118
  Benjamin F., 55
  C. H., 168,176
  Claudia, 116
  Clifford H., 22,29,40,63
    146,156
  Elliott, 176
  Ennis, 142
  Harry, 154
  J. Hillis, 8
  Lillian, 116,164
  Lona, 36
  Nelson H., 139
  Ruby A., 147
  Ruby, 2,67,91,112,155,157
  Thomas E., 19,21,29,156
  Valeria, 18,106
  Wm. E., Wm. V, 46,139
Robey
  Edward C., 69,162
  Grace E., 132
  Odorion, 16,17,32,37,40,
    42,44,47
  Thomas J., 150
  Vivian, 2,18
Robinson
  Charles O., 156
  Robinson cont'd. next column.

Robinson cont'd.
  Claudia, 165
  Helen E., 19
Robison
  J. Hills, 111
  Philip, Mrs., 89
Rock Hall, 172
Rockville & Potomac Percheron
  Co., 116
Rockville Academy
  1913, 24
  1914, 66
  1916, 152
Rockville election
  1914, 63
  1916, 145
Rockville Fox Hunt club, 113
Rockville High School
  1913, 18
  1914, 65
  1915, 104, 107
  1916, 149
Rockville
  Auto speed law 1913, 13
  Confederate monument, 16
  Public library 1915, 94
  Sanitary conditions report
    1914, 57
  Sewer system 1914, 56, 108
  Volunteer fire department, 175
Rogers
  H. E., 43,132,139,159
  Ruth W., 115
Roller
  Mary, 24
Rollison
  Annie M., 7
Rome
  John, 55
Ronsaville
  Edwin, 146
  W. H., 65
Rosemont Farm, 34,78,116
Rosenburg Bros., 131

Rosensteel
  C. O., 71
Rosier
  Charles B., 48
Ross
  Samuel, 87
Rover
  Theo., 72
Rowdybush
  Charles R., 65
  Harold Quinby, 39
Royer
  H. E., 17
  W. J., 149
Ruel
  Jacob, 56
Rumer
  Henry, 95,99
Russell
  M. T., 14
  Wm. W., 114
Rutherford
  Allan, Mrs., 154
Ryan
  Grace L., 157
Sabin
  Arthur, 113,153
Sage
  Charles W., 139
  Lillian, 22,25,112,147,155
Sale
  Leonard D., 157
Sampson
  Thomas, 85
Sands
  H. E., 68
  Rosa V., 111
Sandy Spring High School
  1913, 18
  1915, 104
  1916, 149
Sauder
  Delma E., 69

Sauerwein
  Howard C., 149
Saul
  B. F., 34,37,75,77
  Wm. B. Mrs., 27
Saunders
  Addie Lee, 101
  Charlotte, 6
  Nathan W., 7
  Richard L., 102
  Robert L., 33,48,97,138
  Robert, Mrs., 86
Savage
  Frank, 153
  Harry R. Mr. & Mrs., 38
  Harry Raymond, 38
  Joseph, 113,153,
Savings Institution of Sandy
  Spring, 136
Sawyer
  J. L. H., 71
  John H. L., 140
Saxon
  John W., 63,153
Sayer
  Clarence V., 156
Schaeffer, Schafer, Schaifer
  Bertha Adele, 159,160
  Edward F., 113
  Elizabeth, 94
  Emma Marie, 57
  Frank, Mrs., 154
  Jacob, 150
  Katie L., 68
  William L., 8,137
Schaub
  D. W., Mrs., 37
Scheirer
  Alexander C., 175
Scherer see also Scherrer
  Kate, 120
Scherrer
  Mary, 30,64
  Scherrer cont'd. next page.

Scherrer cont'd.
  Philip, 30
  Rebecca, 76,
Schirer
  A. C. Mrs., 76
Schley
  W., 59,145
Scholl
  Louis B., 94,150
Schrider
  James E., 9,33
Schuerman
  Nancy C., 129,130
Schultz
  Grace Eugenia, 48
Schwartz
  Cleveland, 3
  Edward P. Mrs., 60
  Hannah, 147
  Helen, 14,65,112,155
  Imogene, 164
  Joseph B., 94
  Marian, 142
Scott
  Esther, 104,109,112,
    147,154
Screen
  Margaret, 112
Seek
  Adam, 162
Selby
  Brice P., 107
  Eden, 176
  George A., 58
  Joseph V., 47
  Martha Ann, 176
  Olive, 16,17,38,157
  Wm., 56,161
Selby Bros., 114
Sellman
  A. H., 141
  Charles B., 94
  Sellman cont'd. next column.

Sellman cont'd.
  Edward, 50
  F. May, 16,21,49,135
  Hunton, 14,16,20
  John P., 135
  May, 21
  Maynard, 24
  R. J., 34
Selvage
  C. J., 114
Service
  R. J. Mrs., 20
Servis
  Thomas D., 149
Severance
  F. B., 134
  Frank, 4,21,22,51,55,56,91,103
Sewell
  Richard, 101
Sexton
  Maddie, 77
Shafer, Shaifer
  Carl, 153
  Chas. S., 55
Shalcross
  Jacob T. S., 114
Shaub
  D. W. 37,75
Shaw
  George, 25,35,75,117,164
  J. Lacey, 172
  Katie, 36
  Laura V., 117,120,128,130
  Mabel, 36,37,117
  Ollie, 140
  Roger, Mrs., 37,76,1120,164
  Thomas E., 8,33
  Walter, 3,80
Sheckells, Sheckels
  Nathan E., 8
  Ruth A., 15
Sheets
  W. S., 72
  W. S. Mrs., 34,73

Shield
  James M., 118,122
Shine
  Margaret A., 170
Shipley
  C. Gassaway, 98
  John W., 135
  Mary Katherine, 98
Shoemaker
  A. E. Mrs., 21
  Albert E., 39,72
  Charles, 113,149,153
  H. R., 18,141
  J. Janney, 29,55,139,149
  Leon P., 113,153
  Louis E., 133
  Maurice Eugene, 126
  Ruth, 155
  William, 147
Shorb
  D. W., 116,154
Shorts
  A. M., 36
  Anna, 118
  Annie, 77,117,164
  Arthur, 164
  J. H., 77,119,165
  Lily, 163,164
  M. B. Mrs., 119
  M. E., 117
  Maggie, 36
  Margaret B., 77
  Marian, 165
  Marion B., 36,75,76
  Mary G., 7
  Nettie, 117,164
  Thomas, 7,35
Shreve
  A. B., 31
  Benjamin F., 55
  Bradley, 31
  Carroll A., 82
  Charles W., 86
  Shreve cont'd. next column.

Shreve cont'd.
  D. T., 150
  Daniel, 29,135
  Effie, 147,154
  Wm. A., 98
Shults
  Annie M., 36
Shumaker
  Mary, 24
Sibley
  Irene, 155,
  Russell, 147
Sieman
  Paul, 111
Silver Spring fire dept. 1915, 120
Silver Spring Water Co., 30
Simmonds, Simmons
  A. W., 73
  Hazel, 120
  Jas., 153
  Samuel T., 160
  Savilla, 160
Simons
  Harry, 14
Simpers
  Helen M., 20
Simpson
  Lucy, 25,162
  Mary, 13,83,107
  Sallie W., 110
Sisson
  Aubrey, 142
Skillman
  Wm., 69,162
Skinner
  W. W., 151
Slaymaker
  E. S., 76
  F. S. Mrs., 77
  S. F. Mrs., 117
Sleman
  Paul, 125
Slicer
  Harry, 131

Slifer
  Louise Waters, 127
  Thomas, 127
Small
  Ada Virginia, 138
  Annie Briggs, 54,93
  Archibald, Mrs., 19,25,39
  Euphemia, 132
  James, Jas., 82,150
  Thomas, 3,140
  Wm. H., 153
  Walter, 13
Smith
  Alva, 35,36
  Anna M., 141
  Beverly, 135
  D. P., 77,119,165
  Dorothy Putman, 6
  Duncan, 28
  E. C. Taylor, Mrs., 163,165
  Edwin, Mrs., 120
  Elgar, 2
  Estelle, 165
  Frank P., 135
  Gilbert T., 129
  Harry E., 28
  J. Bond, 71,169
  James B., 69
  Jesse B., 150
  John W., 70
  Joseph, 134,143
  Leroy, 29
  Lucy M., 119
  Margaret, 134
  Mary, 117
  Oliver, 175
  Phillip, 147
  R. E. L., 15, 33,39,149,158
  R. E. L. Mrs., 2,25,72,161
  Rufus, 160
  Wightman, 65,103,142
Smoot
  Charles, 31,47
  Smoot cont'd. next column.

Smoot, cont'd.
  Henry, 44
  L. R., 141
  William S., 144
Snouffer
  John, 149
  Mary M., 82
  Ruth Adelaide, 49
Snowden
  Francis, 26,31,37,40,42,44,96
  Frank, 163
  Marjorie, 106
Snyder
  Donald, 12,15,16,38,
    39,61,103,105
  F. A., 163
  Florence, 119,163
  Jacob C., 139
  John H. L., 55
  Loretta, 80
  Preston L., 29,55,114,
    150,156
  Preston L. Mrs., 71
Somerville
  Thomas, 152
Sonnenburg
  A. Mr. & Mrs.., 170
Soper
  Carey, 67
  Edna, 24
  Eliza Matilda, 148
  Elsie M., 22,112,154
  Isaac, 148
  Laura V., 102
  Leona White, 149
  Lingan, 24
  R. P., 150
  Robert P., 124
  Robert, Mr. & Mrs., 119
  Wm. G., 129
Souder
  A. W., 168
  Archie W., 29,32,94
  Souder cont'd. next page.

Souder cont'd.
　Delma E., 127
　Lora A., 99
　Phillip B., 21
Spark, Sparks
　Harry, 153
　Henry, 113
Sparrough, Sparrow
　Benjamin F., 63
　Clarence, 162
Spates
　Alice, 2,18,109,115,155
　C. A. Mrs., 76
　Ethel L., 152
　Maria, 154
　R. Marie, 109,115
　Richard, 13,43,55,87
　Roger, 87,101
　Ruth Marie, 158,160
　W. O., 87,113
　Webster, 30
Speare
　A. R. Mrs., 36,76,165
Spencer
　Frank A., Mrs., 162
　Mabel Anderson, 92
　Mary J., 72
Spinney
　Lillian, 97
Sponseller
　J. D., 48
　Myrtle M., 78
Sprigg
　Richard, 90
Springarth, Springirth
　Carl B., 113,153
　Reimy, 69
Spurrier
　H. W., 168
　Howard, 63,72,114,143,161
Srother
　Milton W., 41
St. Barnabas Church, 51

St. John's Catholic Church,
　Forest Glen, 1913, 33
St. John's Episcopal Church,
　Bethesda, 65
St. Mary's Catholic Church,
　Barnesville 1913, 31
Stabler
　Albert, 73,164
　Anna McF., 134
　Arthur, 134
　Asa, 25,39,91,134,150,162,
　Asa M. Mr. & Mrs., 142
　Caroline, 157
　Charles, 25
　Elgar, 73
　Elizabeth T., 88
　Emma, 35,75,76,116,117,119
　F., 164
　Frederick, 116,156
　Hanna, 76,117
　Isabelle, 77
　Joseph, 89
　Lillie, 117
　Mary, 36,75,76,117,164,165
　Maurice J., 8,159
　Mortimer O., 32,43
　Newton, 8,69,150,162
　Philip T., 143,159
　Roland, 164
　Sarah E., 25
　Tarlton, 92,134,156,166
　Wilson, 142
Staley
　Dora, 137
Stallsmith
　Dorothy, 117
　Wm. P., 43,80
Stang
　Bertha, 13
　Josephine, 13
　Peter, 13,126,
Stankey
　Warren, 9

Stanley
 R. H., 168
 Richard, 26,82,136,156
Stansbury
 Mrs. 19
 P. R. Mrs., 7
 R. P. Mrs., 40
Star Spangled Banner, 70
Starkey
 J. H. Mrs., 165
Stauffer
 Courtney, 119
Stearman
 H., 169
 Mark, 71
Stearn
 Charles, 150
 E. Mrs., 19
 Earl, 111,145
 Emma, 59
 J. H. Mrs., 145
 Joseph J., 95
 M. Victoria, 115
Stein
 Benjamin C., 139
Steinbraker
 Charles H., 173
Stephens
 Edgar R., 1
Stevens
 E. E., 21
 Eugene, 14,20,25,33, 107,113,162
 John, 153
 R. Hugh, 106,108
Steward
 Arthur P., 127
 Eleanor M., 127
Stewart
 Bertie, 22
 Donald H., 23
 Earl M., 6
 J. W., Mrs., 39
Stewart cont'd. next column.

Stewart cont'd.
 James, 142
 Milton, 142
 Samuel Elsworth, 74
Stillwell
 E. J., 80
Stockberger
 W. W., 25
Stokes
 H., 1
 R. H., 41,55,99
 Richard, 1,3,50,57,90,133
Stone
 Charles, 29,128,139,156
 Dunbar, 145
 Ella M., 143
 F. P. Mrs., 19,27,59,86,90,93
 F. P., 19,59,145
 J. P. Mrs., 19
 John G., 60,139,168
 John G. Mrs., 86
 R. W. Mrs., 19,145
 Robert P., 131
Stonestreet
 A. W., 34
 Arthur W., 8,35,116
 Gertrude W., 12
 O. T., 34,78,164
 Virginia, 109
Storey
 Thomas, 57,62,
Story
 Edward, 139
Stout
 John, 156,168
 R. W., 24,154
Stover
 J. B., 134
 John A., 91
Stratmeyer
 Everett, 105
 H. E., Mrs., 35,116, 119
 S. T., Mrs., 35

Strong
  Gordon, 141
Stubbs
  E. C., 169
  F. D, 56
  Frank, 11,29,140, 156
Stup
  Maurice F., 54
Suddath
  Robert S., 167,170
Sullivan
  A., 119
  Artemus, 47,60,105,113, 130,165
  Artemus, Mrs., 36,164
  Emma, 76,117
  George, 118
  J. Mahlon, 163
  J. P., 150
  Ralph E., 13
  Susie Frances, 38
Summers
  Dorothy, 45
Sunny Slope Farm, 3
Surratt
  John Harrison, 145
Sutherland
  Katherine, 119
Sutton
  James, Mr. & Mrs., 142
Swain
  John, 40
  Mary V., 162
Swindells
  Lucian G., 173
Taff
  H. F., 63
Tait
  Galen L., 32,41,74,111,125
Takoma Park
  Election 1914, 63
  Election 1913, 17

Talbott
  Bertha, 76,120
  H. M., 4,51,91,134,136
  H. W. Mrs., 21,37
  Laura V., 61
  Marie, 19,27,37,76,93,120
  Miriam, 49
  Nathan, 66
  W., 103,145,158,168
  Randolph, 28,160
  W. H. Mrs., 16,19,21
  Wm. H., 35,77,158
Taney
  Ann Louise, 46
Tatum
  Lydia H., 18
  Wm. R., 47
Taylor
  James, 20,172
  Walter G., 107
Teacher assignments 1916, 154
Templars, Damascus, 1913, 12
Ternant
  Effie,70,115,154
Terrell
  Samuel, 31
  Wm. M., 65
Thall
  Arthur, 72
Thom
  Lucy, 142
Thomas
  A. G., A. M., 14,86,162,174
  Alban G., 25,91,134
  Allen Bowie, 53
  Amanda G., 44
  Anna, 23
  Ashley, Mr. & Mrs., 1
  Bentley, 21
  Bruce, Dr., 11
  Ellen, 154
  Ethel F., 6
Thomas cont'd. next page.

Thomas cont'd.
 Francis, 18,19,116,134
 Frederick L., 72,91,134
 J. Roy, 176
 John, 170
 Margaret Inez, 1
 Mary E., 6,19,88
 R. B., 35
 R. B. Mrs., 36
 R. Bentley, 6,32,37,73,116,161
 Samuel, 29,51,71,88
 Stella, 65,115,147,155
 Thos., 135
 William D. Mrs., 38
Thompson
 A. B., 69,162
 A. R., Mrs., 37,120
 Ada, 76
 Andrew J., Mr. & Mrs., 176
 Edgar, 7,101,112,122,161,175
 Edna May, 58
 Elijah, 96
 Elizabeth H., 97
 Ernest, 174
 H. G., 168
 Helen, 19
 Horton, 82,169
 Hugh O., 113,153
 J. Lawn, 108
 J. T., 80
 Jas., 150,172
 Jesse R. Mrs., 30,149
 Jesse, 3
 John, 70,78,162
 Keefer L., 166
 M. L., 165
 Madeline, 51
 Magnus S., 28
 Margaret A., 138
 Mary, 154
 Maud, 142
 Samuel, 164
 Sidney, 122
 Thompson cont'd. next column.

Thompson cont'd.
 Susan B., 135
 Susie, 80
 Thomas P., 25
 W. S., 164
 W. S. Mrs., 163
 Walter, 29, 113,124,153
 Wm., 131,163
Thoms
 W. H., 49
Thrift
 C. M., 168
 Charles H., 82
Thurston
 P. K., 25
Tibbott
 O. H. Mrs., 19,39,72,162
Tippett
 P. F., 164
Titus
 Thornton B., 8
Tolson
 Alfred C., 105,112,121,127
 Annie E., 146
 Catherine, 133
 Nan, 49
 Robert, 139,155
 W. Z., 82,168
Tombly
 Paul, 103
Torpin
 Richard, 75
Touhey
 Dennis, 67
Towers
 Irving Lewis, 23
Townsend
 Catherine, 104
 Charles L., 33
 Grace, 154
 Hugh C., 82,99
 J. Mrs., 107
 James, 8,45
 Townsend cont'd. next page.

Townsend cont'd.
  Katherine H., 149
  Sylvia, 115
  Wilson L., 111,134
Tracey
  Mary F., 6,155
Trail
  Annie E., 109
  H. Mrs., 165
  Morgan Lee, 157
  Walter, 175
  William, 48,130,160
Train – airplane race 1913, 31
Trammel
  Geo., 131
Travers
  Mary, 120
  Vera, 165
Travilah Gun Club 1913, 5
Trip
  Charles S., 110
Tromby
  Paul, 65
Troth
  J. Ezra, 68
Trout
  Charles H., 162
Trowbridge
  H. O., 23,56,65,140
Troxall
  Thomas W., 91,105,155
  William, 142
True
  Marian, Marion, 155
Truesdale
  George, 6,53
Truman
  L. C., 36
Trundle
  A. D., 77
  A. Dawson, 126
  Alice, 15,105
  Trundle cont'd. next column.

Trundle cont'd.
  Americus Dawson, 11
  Annie, 16,80,104,107
  Barbara J., 149
  Courtland, 164
  Dawson, 60
  James, 118,139
  Otho, 107
  W. B., Mrs., 37,165
  William B.,51,60,61,90,
    133,136
  Wm. B., Mrs., 76,120
Trundle Bros., 35,77
Truxton
  Jane, 33
  Wm., 33
Tschiffely
  Betty, 59
  Cecil Eunice, 41
  Dolly, 170
  Dorothy, 36,117,120
  Edgar, 21
  Elgar L, 16,21,112
  Elgar L. Mr. & Mrs., 174
  F. A., F. S, 14,16
  Frederick Adolphus, 20
  Mabel, 49
  Wilson B., 3,50,69
Tucker
  Eli, 13
  Mary Lucretia, 13
Tull
  S. Webster, 152
Turner
  Elsie Charlotte, 84
  James F., 141
Tutow
  Rogers P., 113
Tyler
  Wm. S., 60,113,153
Tyner
  Esther, 2
Typhoid epidemic 1914, 52,54

Umstead
  Edward, 87
  Eleanor, 119
  Ellen, 12
  Jacob, 92,126
  Jacob, Mrs., 119
  Joe, 114
  John J., 156
  Kate, 77
  W. J., W. T., 43,161,167,169
Valdenar
  Francis E., 162
Valentine
  Margaret, 14
VanFossen
  Lester G., 84
VanHoesen, VanHosen
  F. J., 151
  Fred, 163
VanHorn
  Ernest, 113,153
  Geo., 113,153
  Nettie E., 53
VanNess
  Frank, 70
VanVleck
  Cynthia N., 159
  Florence Noyes, 152
Vaughan
  J. P., 19,59
Veirs
  Charles, 37,50,60,75,90,116,
    123,133,136,163,169
  Clifton C., 127
  Eugene A., 146
  Florence, 44,46
  Frances S., 105,148
  Gertrude, 36,77
  Jas. P., 163
  S. Clark, 68
  Sarah, 68
  Turner, 39
  Veirs cont'd. next column

Veirs cont'd.
  W. V., 168
  William C., 43
Veitch
  Annie Howard, 140
  Jesse Herbert, 86
  John W., 140
  Robert L., 50
Viett
  Henry, 1
  William, 47,145
Vincent
  Brooke, 161
  Charles H., 148
  W. Brooke, 114
  Wm. B., 55
Vinson
  E. A., 168
  R. W., 1,62,158
  Thomas, 1,19,26,40,0,55,63,
    99,133,136,148,158
Vogt
  Henry, 31
Voters, by count 1913, 42
Wachter
  Wm. H., 8,46
Waddill
  Claude, 153
Wade
  Marcellus E., 43,44
  W. E., W.H., 150,168
  William H., 26,32,74,121,148,
Waesche
  Catherine A., 173
  Eleze, 109
  Mary, 16,39,104,107
Wagner
  I., Miss, 75
  Irving, 116
  Lavinia, 36,165
  Mary, 117
  Minnie, 75
  R. L., Miss, 158,
  Wagner cont'd. next page.

Wagner cont'd.
  Rose, 36,75,76,117,119,
    163,164,165
  S. Peter, 119,163
  Urban, 29,35,82,116,
    117,156,164
Walker
  Blanche M., 91,155
  Crittenden H., 17,37,40,42
    44,47,143
  E. W., 71,73,111,161,162
  Elizabeth, 38
  Eugene W., 172
  Evelyn, 15,20
  Forest, 100,139,168
  G. W., 20,103
  J. W., 134
  John W., 4,16,51,63,91,159
  Laura, 27
  M. M., 100
  Marshall, 101
  Mary Elizabeth, 42
  McKendree, 139,151
  Mrs., 86
  Nathan J., 17
  Parepa Wesley, 20
  R. H., 23
  S. H., 23
  Samuel H., 161
  Virginia, 41,45
  Walter, 116
  Wilson, 114
  Wm. F., 107
Wall
  W. E. Mrs., 27
Wallace
  Mary C., 144,145
Wallach
  Alice Douglas, 3
Walling
  B. W., 63
  Katherine V., 122
Walsh
  E. J. Mr. & Mrs., 33

Walstrum
  Anthony, 147
Walter
  D., 119
  Donald, 118
  Frances, 89
  George B. F., 158
  Myrtle E., 39
Walters
  Ann America, 95
  Eloise, 93
  Frank, 111
  Geneva, 66,69,155
  George, 118
  J. F., 67
  J. F. Mrs., 117
  Julian B., 94,112,113,160,166
  Lucien T., 55
  Richard H., 95
Ward
  A. H. Mrs., 76
  Barry Ella, 149
  Carson, 63
  Darby, 146
  Dora, 165
  Edward G., 53,103,161
  Emma B., 159
  George P., 62
  Gertrude, 24
  Harrison G., 111,125
  Ianthe, 38
  Ignatius, 174
  J. H. Mrs., J. M. Mrs., 36,
    76,164
  J. Howard, 140
  John. 16,144
  Joseph H., 124
  Laura, 15,17,72,87
  Lottye Belle, 1
  M. S., 2
  Mabel, 75,76,119,165
  Margaretta Edna, 46
  Marie, 74,75
Ward cont'd. next page.

Ward cont'd.
　Mary, 39,81
　Milburn, 83,118
　N. H.,　N. J., 90,133,136
　Nettie G., 90
　Otho C., 55
　Porter G., 55,170
　Richard T., 4
　Silas, 31
　Thomas H., 42
　W. E., 72
　W. E. Mrs., 36,117,119
　W. S., 76,117,
　W. S. Mrs., 2
　Wilson S., 147,154,161,175
　Wilson S. Mr. & Mrs., 2
　Wilson, 19
　Wm. E., 114
Warfeld
　John W., 77
Warfield
　Ada, 6,75,77,117,119,164
　Albert, 111
　Basil T., 94,95
　Bessie, 60
　Bradbury B., 102
　C. G., 2,
　Charles L., 1
　Clarence O., 94
　D. H., 133
　D. H. Mrs., 49
　David H., 51,90,136
　Dorsey, 10
　E. D., 56,140
　E. Ray, 69
　Edwin, 60
　Elisha, 49
　Eliza Ellen, 66
　Ethel, 49
　G. C.,　G. P., 1, 2
　Gaither, 2,18,24,118
　George, Mr. & Mrs., 15
Warfield cont'd next column

Warfield cont'd.
　Henry, 35,164
　Israel, 72,150
　J. C., 12
　John F., 118
　Lee C., 97, 99
　Margaret, 18,21,23
　Mehrle, 12
　R. C., 1,2,61,102,158
　R. C. Mrs., 2
　Raymond L, 45
　Robert, 2,7,18,23,58,65,
　　103,156,166
　Robert C. Mrs., 20
　S. Lavinia, 83
　Seth, 35,75,116,117,163,164
　Seth, Mrs., 75,117
　Thurman, 12
　W. T., 167
　William, 17,31,134,149,161
　Zaccheus, 124
Warner
　B. H., 48,56,71,74,140,
　Brainard, ,22,65,72,83,
　　85,111,148
　L. V., 10
　Southard P., 63
Warrington
　Everett F., 128
Warthan　see also Warthen
　A. C., 30,64
　A. C. Mrs., 36,76,77,
　　117,164
　Carroll A., 38
　Gerald, 71
Warthen
　Albert E., 5,114,126,
　　155,156,161,174
　Ethel, 58
　Gerald H., 29,113
　J. P., Mrs., 120
　Jason P., 94,95
　Jesta, 154,165

Wash. Elec. R.R. Co., 1913, 6
Washington & Rockville Electric
  RR. Co., 53
Washington Suburban Sanitary
  Comm. 1914, 54
Washington, Woodside, Forest
  Glen R.R. Co, 53
Washington
  Emma, 112,155
Waters
  Alice H., 18,93
  Artis H., 141
  B. F., 167
  Bowie F., 9,129,158
  Bowie F. Mrs., 93,120,165
  C. C., 134,167
  C. C. Mrs., 71
  Carroll, 147
  Charles C., 42,44,49,60,73
  Clinton, 165
  E. M., 174
  Edwin, Mrs., 47
  Ella Virginia, 138
  Ellen, 120
  Ethel, 152
  Eugene, 17,31,37,40,
    42,44,69,72
  Geo. T., 102
  H. A., H. D., 90,186
  Harold, 99,110,115,145
  Hattan, 1,19,44,133
  Horace D., 16,63,74,139,141
  Ignatius, 66
  John B., 124
  Lillian, 104,107
  Margaret, 13,57,58
  Marguerite, 109
  Marjorie, 12,15,17,39,61,
    81,86,109
  Martha Elizabeth, 93
  Mary, 20,60,149
  McCubbin, 127
Waters cont'd. next column.

Waters cont'd.
  P. E., 133,16
  Paul Y., 45,121,127
  Perrie E., 3,21,50,51,90,100,
    133,136,138,150,167,174,175
  Perrie E. Mr. & Mrs., 93
  R. K., R. L., 154
  R. L. Mrs., 93,154
  Richard, 39,62,66,68,73,79
  Richard L. Mr. & Mrs., 93
  Richard L. Mrs., 93
  S. W., 72
  Samuel D., 10
  T. W. Mrs., 36
  Thomas, 57,116,135
  Thomas, Mrs., 35,77
  Waters, Virginia, 112,132,
    147,154
  Washington D., 137
  William, 82,83,94,108
  Z. M., 12,26,56,87,95,140,
    149,155,159
Watkins
  Alburn H., 39,43,123
  Bell, Belle, 15,155
  Bradley, 43,122
  C. W. Mrs., 35
  Charles, 131,139,167
  Christopher E., 100
  Clayton K., 132,168
  Darius, 69,162
  Edna Estelle, 74
  Edward K., 4,5
  Eleanor J., 5
  Frank W., 155
  G. W., 149
  Grace, 69
  Guy, 116
  Isabel P., 20
  Jane D., 157
  John O. T., , 149,
  Joseph G., , 122,
Watkins cont'd. next page.

Watkins cont'd.
  L. D., 149
  Lorenzo, 157
  Margaret, 154
  Noah, 10,31,56,95,140
  Oliver, 5,62
  R. L., 126
  Raymond, 31,39
  Sallie Blanche, 171
  Susan, 131
  Tobias, 72,149
  Vernon D., 12,39,43,123
  Vernon, Mrs., 12
  Vivian Myrtle, 130
  W. E., 150
  Wilbur, 147
  William E., 82
Watson
  D. M. Mrs., 36
  Ella, 173
  Josephine, 24,66,117
  L. R., 119,165
  Lewis R., 21,33,64,66,77,
    101,116,135,152
  Louis, 19,83,145
  Nancy, 83
Watts
  Linda, Lina, 24,154
Waverly Literary Soc.
  1913, 15,16,1738,39
  1914, 61,80,81
Wear
  L. Jr., 168
Weaver
  Harrison, 84
  John L., 4,21
  Robert D., 87
Weber
  C. S. Mrs., 165
Webster
  F. M., 56,86
  Helen, 73
Wedderburn
  Chas. F., 105

Weeds
  C. T., 143
Weer
  Jos. F., 10
  Leonard, 10,55,56,134,140,151
Weiner
  Frank A., 2,68
Weissner
  H. F., 161
Welch
  John, 67
Weller
  C. Parker, 32,43
  Gene D., 96
  Parker L., 56,94,140
Welliver
  Allan, 147
  Edward, 147
  J. C., 158
  J. C. Mrs., 21
  Judson, 25,109,130
Wells
  Chester, 27
  H. L. Mrs., 35,162
  Harry L. Mrs., 25
  Lester, 142
  Margaret, 144
  Robert, 71
Welsh
  Amy, 35
  Anna, 75,120
  Asa H., 83
  Catherine Victoria, 27
  Edward E. Mr. & Mrs., 111
  F. Barnard, 53
  Francis Eugene, 135
  Frank, 43,135
  Harry A., 153
  Ietta E., 148
  J. B., J. L., 164,168,
  Welsh, John, 147
  Lucile, 2,120,141
Welsh, cont'd. next page.

Welsh, cont'd.
  Lucy, 16
  Margaret, 35,77,111,164
  Mary, 6,83,116,117,120,165
  Miss, 16,38
  Rhoda, 164
  Samuel S., 149
  Virgie, 135
  W. W. Mrs., 19,116
  W. W., 1,19,55,57,158
  Wallace W. Mrs., 72
  Wellington W., 47
  Wm. H. Mrs., 40
  Wm. W., 16,63,82
Welti
  Margaret, 81
  Marguerite, 15,38,39
Wenche
  Miss, 1
Wenner
  Max, 73
West
  Clarence, Mrs., 31
  Erasmus, 159
  H. C., 168
  Harry, 32,50,55,150
  Homer R., 159
  John E., 42,45,87,105,
    121,127,128
  McKinley, 160
  Mrs., 107
Wetherald
  Samuel B., 55,56,62
Whalen
  B. P., 168
  B. Peyton, 17, 96
  Benjamin P., 31, 37,40,42,44
  Harry T., 102
  J. F., 56,140
  Joseph, 10,94,159
  Peyton, 71,113
  Sheriff, 100

Wheatley
  George E., 78
Wheeler
  Gladys W., 167
  Harry S., 34
  W. T., 168
  William R., 150
Whipp
  Amos, 95
Whispell
  Edna L., 137
Whitacre
  Ira C., 71
White
  Alice M., 54,56
  Amy, 17,20
  Benjamin Rush, 6
  Byron, 2
  E. V., Col., 28
  Edith Blanche, 149
  Elizabeth, 16
  Elsie Lee, 99,33
  Faith, 126
  George E., 156
  H. W., 115
  Harry, 48,49
  Harvey J., 124,126
  Henry Whitmore, 23
  J. Furr, 8,311,37,40,42,44,
    122,123,124,168
  Jas. W., 147,155
  Jos. M., 91
  Jos. M. Mrs., 25
  Joseph T., 21
  L. A., 103
  Laura A., 67
  Lula,   Lulu, 20,147,154
  Mansfield, 42,44
  Mary, 17,18,38,39,69,109,
    131,154
  Nathan S., 18,118
  Oliver Belt, 7,9
  White cont'd next page.

White cont'd.
  Richard, 47, 68,162,164
  Roger C., 125
  Samuel R., 54
  Thomas Earl, 173
  Walter H., 94
  William R., 38,42
Whiteford
  Roger, 2,81
Whitehead
  Richard, 121
Whites Ferry Company, 137
Whiteside
  John W., 87, 88
Whiting
  Frances, 36
  Julian W., 28
Whitmore
  Jos., 14
Wick
  Frank W., 153
Wiggins
  Ernest, 68
Wilburn
  Geo. A., 153
Wilkins
  Frank, 30
Willard
  C. F. Mr. & Mrs., 7
  C. Frank, 130
  Charles V., 26,155
  Chas. Mrs., 166
  D. J., 24
  Dewalt L., 139
  Ellie, 166
  George, Mrs., 81
  H. L., 63
  Harry L., 55
  Lauretta, 7
  Louis H., 118
  Mary M., 55
  Nannie, 130
  Stephen D., 42

Williams
  A. Dawson, 65
  Anna, 39,61,81,149
  Arthur, 16,23,64,82,98
  Bernard H., 174
  C. M., 77
  Carolyn, 24
  Carrie W., 170,172
  Charles M., 116
  Dawson, 71
  Downey, 139
  E. M. Mrs., 36
  George M., 111
  Georgia A., 137
  Gladys, 142
  H. C., H. N., 168
  Harry C., 82,83,121,150,
     159,174
  Henry Ralph, 25
  J. D., 168
  J. Dawson, 5, 17, 23, 31, 33,
     40, 63, 64, 148
  J. T., 129
  J. T. Mrs., 81
  James E., 3, 50, 90, 133
  Jane, 154
  John, 26,63
  Jonathan, 137
  Lewis W., 96
  Loraine, 38,39
  Margaret, 24,154
  May M., 22
  O. B., 34,37,75,139
  O. B. Mrs., 31
  Roland C., 113
  Rose F., 145
  Stephen W., 63
  Sweetie, 142
  Thompson, 86
  W. W., Mr. & Mrs., 110
  Walter A., 1
  William, 27,55,59,82,139
Williamson
  Mr., 108

Willsey
  Mary G., 10
Wilson, Willson
  A., 85
  Alexander, 58
  Alfred, 30,31,55,98,140,168
  Amanda, 71
  Anne, 19
  B. P. Mrs., 163
  Betty, 49, 83
  Charles G., 73,114
  Clara R., 90
  Elizabeth, 50,57, 60,147,157
  Ellen T., 20
  Frank, 8,156
  Frank, Mrs., 93
  George A., 44
  I. Thomas, 148
  J. F. Mrs., 25, 27,72, 93,162
  J. Frank, 49, 55
  Karl Miller, 106
  Laura C., 129
  Lea Gilpin, 23
  Lottie, 147
  Mae, 118
  Michael, 50
  President, 129
  Ray, Miss, 73
  Robert, 66,124
  Ruth, 120
  Sarah Ray, 68,79
  Selina D., 92
  Selma, 67
  V., 119
  Virginia, 93
  W. P.,   W. V., 71,77,174
Wilt
  W. E, 77,116
Wimsatt
  Robert, 72
  S. C., Mrs., 164,165
  W. A., ,30
  William, Mrs., 71

Winchell
  William H., 170
Windham
  Camden, 140
  Ethel Virginia, 152
  George T., 11,114,129
  Margaret K., 13
  R. C., 169
  Spencer, 34,73
  George, 94,150
Windsor, Winsor
  Anna, 124
  J. S., 134
  James S., 4,21,91,150
  Mary S., 28
  Randolph, 55,149
  Robert S., 155
  William, 21,124
  Zachariah L., 96
Winebrenner
  D. C., 98
Wineth farm, 112
Winslow
  E., 76
  M. A., Miss, 165
  M. A. Mrs., 120
  M. O. Mrs., 120
  W. E. Miss, 166
Wise
  Edward S., 47
  Grace, 24
Wissner
  B. M. Mrs., 165
Witherow
  L. S., 68
  Lester, 101
Witter
  H. B., 75, 77
Wolfe
  F. M., 169
  George M., 148
  Jesse P., 140
  Josephine, 87
  M. M., 47

Wood
  Charles J., 31
  E. B., 168
  Earle B., 50
  Leta R., 31
  Marie, 79
  Octavia B., 47,128
  Prof., 16
Woodfield
  Bradley, 104,107
  John R., 111,125
  Leslie W., 89
Woodlands, 89
Woodward
  Bennie O., 139
  Bessie, 64,71, 155
  Miss, 111
  Nannie O., 80
  Rosell, 140
Woolford
  Harry, 142
Wootton
  Edward Chiswell, 22
  Ella, 38
  Norman, 30,102,168
  Richard Sprigg, 66
  Roland, 1,17,19,28,63
Work
  James, 24
  Malvin, 24
Worthington
  A. S., 18
Wright
  Charles, 43,44,71
  Clarence H., 93
  Dr., 71
  Elmer, Mrs., 14
  Herbert, 56,140,
  Lewis A., 141
  Lucy Eleanor, 114
  Marcia Katherine, 141
  Ray, 71
Wright cont'd. next column.

Wright cont'd.
  Roy L., 69,162
  Wm., 84
Yancy
  Lorenzo H., 160
Yeabower
  John, 142
Yearly
  Anna, 76
  Jane, 37
Yellott
  Mary Virginia, 61
  R. E., 32,71
Yingling
  Nicie Tabitha, 157
Young
  Amos S., 90
  Crawford W., 100
  Della, 81
  H. Delma, 88
  Horace, 74
  James D., 17,21,32,10,150
  John, 166
  L. H., 116
  Luther H., 121
  Marion B., 96
  Maude, 24
  Orlando, 103
  Robert A., 43,168
  Samuel C., 96
  Sarah Elizabeth, 42
  Thomas C., 132
  William O., 146,149
Zeitler
  C. M., C. N., 97, 149
Zihlman
  Frederick, 146
Zimmerman
  Henry T., 9
Zither
  Mildred, 142
      End

www.ingramcontent.com/pod-product-compliance
Lightning Source LLC
Chambersburg PA
CBHW050137170426
43197CB00011B/1864